WHAT'S NEXT
IN
MASS COMMUNICATION

Readings on Media and Culture

WHAT'S NEXT
IN
MASS COMMUNICATION

Readings on Media and Culture

Christopher Harper

Ithaca College

St Martin's Press
New York

Sponsoring editor: Suzanne Phelps Weir
Associate development editor: Michael Gillespie
Managing editor: Erica T. Appel
Project editor: Harold Chester
Production supervisor: Joe Ford
Art director: Lucy Krikorian
Cover art and design: Kay Petronio

Library of Congress Catalog Card Number: 97-65639

Manufactured in the United States of America.

3 2 1 0 9 8
f e d c b a

For information, write:
St. Martin's Press, Inc.
175 Fifth Avenue
New York, NY 10010

ISBN: 0-312-16743-1

Acknowledgments
Acknowledgments and copyrights are continued at the back of the book on pages 213–214, which constitute an extension of the copyright page.

ABOUT THE AUTHOR

Christopher Harper has worked as a journalist for the Associated Press, *Newsweek*, *ABC News*, and ABC's *20/20*. During his career of more than two decades in the media, he has traveled to more than sixty countries and forty states, where he has reported on Pope John Paul II, terrorism, wars, and even a few fun topics such as the history of Motown music and rebuilding Florida's coral reefs.

A professor at Ithaca College, Harper has written extensively about the media, in particular about online journalism, for *American Journalism Review* and *Editor & Publisher Interactive*. He lives in Ossining, New York, with his wife, Elizabeth, and daughter, Cecylia.

CONTENTS

Contents

printers, laptops and a variety of paraphernalia. There's a new pitch, too, for pornography on the Internet."

PREFACE

What's Next in Mass Communication examines how communications are changing and how niche communications are becoming more pervasive as we look
toward the next century. What effects will emerging technologies such as the
Internet and the World Wide Web have on individuals within society, on our
ability to communicate, and on traditional media? This text can be used in a
variety of core and special-topics courses in communication and journalism departments as well as in courses in rhetorical composition.

If you look at human history as a twenty-four-hour day, the information
age is just a fraction of that time. The invention of speech, which occurred
more than 100,000 years ago, took place at about 9:30 P.M. Language happened
about eight minutes before midnight. The telegraph, telephone, radio, and
television arrived about eleven seconds before midnight. The digital computer
made it just under the wire, at two seconds before midnight in our human-
history day.[1]

Those last eleven seconds cover roughly the past 150 years, which can be
described as the era of communication. During that time the telephone moved
from the laboratory into nearly every home in the United States, as did radio.
Then television arrived. Today, nearly 99 percent of all American households
have at least one television set.

During the past fifty years, these forms of mass communication have
brought the United States—and sometimes the world—together. Much of the
nation listened to the 1938 heavyweight championship between Joe Louis and
Max Schmeling on the radio. Louis knocked out his German opponent in the
first round in what many people saw as a battle between American democracy

---

[1] *W. Russell Neuman,* The Future of The Mass Audience *(New York: Cambridge University Press,
1995), p. 7.*

and Nazi dictatorship. On December 7, 1941, the nation shared the common shock of the Japanese attack on Pearl Harbor. On November 22, 1963, the nation suffered together through the assassination of John F. Kennedy. On July 20, 1969, hundreds of millions of people throughout the world watched on their televisions as astronaut Neil Armstrong walked on the moon. Most Americans watched on August 9, 1974, when Richard M. Nixon became the first president to resign. Many also watched the events of the Persian Gulf war, sharing in the triumph of the Allies' victory.

For the most part, however, few people today talk about what *60 Minutes* aired on Sunday as they did only a decade ago. Some talk about *Seinfeld*. Fewer still talk about what they read in newspapers or find on America Online. Occasionally, mass communication reaches a massive audience, such as the verdict in the first O. J. Simpson trial or the Oklahoma City bombing. The shared experience of mass communication is changing. In a digital age, someone in a small town in Indiana can find someone in Australia with similar interests. Those interests may be as diverse as the poet Emily Dickinson, antique jewelry, or parrots.

What's Next in Mass Communication focuses on today's issues and looks forward to the next millennium. In some instances, specific case studies focus on issues affecting an individual medium. At the end of each reading, questions provide the basis for additional discussion. The text contains seven areas for discussion and debate: the innate need for humans to communicate effectively; the development of new technologies; the media of sound and image such as radio, television, music, and film; traditional media such as books, newspapers, and magazines; the persuasive media of advertising and public relations; the culture of the news, including government, the law, and ethics; and the uncertain future into the next millennium. A brief description of each area follows.

The Need to Communicate. The first section centers on how human beings communicate and the need to make our beliefs known to others. The means of communication are primarily oral and textual in interpersonal communication, either through speech or writing.

The Brave New World. We need to understand how new technologies may affect communication. In this emerging era of communication, it is necessary to describe what is out there—to analyze it, interpret the data, and evaluate the information. Throughout the book there are sections on how new media may affect existing methods of communication.

The Sound and the Image. The third section focuses on popular culture and communication. The readings include a variety of selections about controversial issues from talk radio, the decline of television news, rap music, and a film about publisher Larry Flynt.

Traditional Media. This section analyzes the future of books, newspapers, and magazines, and specifically how these media may be affected by new technologies.

Advertising and Public Relations. These readings focus on communicating a message through advertising and public relations in the age of the World Wide Web.

The Culture of News, the Law, and Ethics. These chapters analyze the current state of the news, including a case study of the Communications Decency Act and the role of obscenity on the Internet.

The Future. Several writers in this section analyze what the media face in the years ahead and what future media users and providers should know as we move into the twenty-first century.

Each section attempts to pose questions and potential answers about the past, present, and future of communication. To that end, discussion questions and exercises follow each chapter. These questions are critical to anyone who uses the mass media for news and information, and for those in the fields of reporting, advertising, and public relations.

It is important to keep in mind during your discussions that an opinion or point of view should include a rational or reasonable explanation of why you believe your view to be relevant and correct. It is essential that individuals proceed carefully and logically in explaining why they think the way they do. Diverse points of view should be tolerated because they are the essence of democratic life. That doesn't mean you have to accept someone else's belief; you simply have to respect the manner in which a person presents an argument. That's the only way to evaluate an argument's validity.

This book is first and foremost dedicated to my wife, Elizabeth, who has seen me through the long days and nights of working in the media, and to my daughter, Cecylia, who already is part of the digital generation. It is also dedicated to my late father, Ray, who wanted me to become a lawyer but decided that journalism was a decent craft, and to my late friends and colleagues, Frank Maier, Don Schanche, and Edwin Diamond.

I want to thank Jim Neal, Jim Patten, Roderick Gander, and Stan Opotowsky for their faith in my abilities as a journalist. I also thank Suzanne Phelps Weir and the people at St. Martin's Press for their confidence in me to publish this book.

Christopher Harper

CHAPTER 1

COMMUNICATION

Mike Rose, *Reading My Way Out of South L.A.*
Malcolm X, *A Homemade Education*
W. Russell Neuman, *The Media Habit*

An individual must find a way to communicate—a means by which one's words, actions, or expressions can be interpreted by another person.

Finding a way to communicate is the focus of this chapter. In the first reading, Mike Rose writes about his adolescence in South Los Angeles in the 1950s, then an area of Italian immigrants. His teachers determined that he should study "vocational education." For Rose school was a place of boredom, until he got a chemistry set. The chemicals and the mixtures he made excited Rose and made him interested in learning more about science and the world. As an adult Rose became a poet and writer, and eventually a professor of education at UCLA.

The second reading, by Malcolm X, examines how in the early part of his life he could barely read or write. When he was imprisoned in 1946 in the Norfolk Prison Colony in Massachusetts, Malcolm started reading a dictionary. He worked methodically from A to B and all the way to Z, trying to understand the words. He wrote the words over and over again to improve his writing skills. After he was released from prison in 1952, Malcolm became one of the most important advocates for African Americans.

In the third reading, Professor W. Russell Neuman, one of the foremost media analysts, looks at how the media try to communicate with us and determines there may be a good deal of information we receive from them and little we retain.

As the media move on to the Internet, computer-mediated communication poses a significant problem in using language. Electronic mail users have found a new way to communicate in a written form with "emoticons." Here are a few examples:

:-) or :)	a smiling face
;-) or ;)	a winking, smiling face
:-(or :(	unhappy face, or "unsmiley"
:-P	someone sticking out his tongue
>:-O	someone screaming in fright
:-&	someone whose lips are sealed
!#!^*&:-)	a schizophrenic

As evidenced by these symbols, humankind has an incredible ability to find a means to communicate.

Reading My Way Out of South L.A.

Mike Rose

∎

Some people who manage to write their way out of the working class describe the classroom as an oasis of possibility. It became their intellectual playground, their competitive arena. Given the richness of my memories of this time, it's funny how scant are my recollections of school. I remember the red brick building of St. Regina's itself, and the topography of the playground: the swings and basketball courts and peeling benches. There are images of a few students: Erwin Petschaur, a muscular German boy with a strong accent; Dave Sanchez, who was good in math; and Sheila Wilkes, everyone's curly-haired heartthrob. And there are two nuns: Sister Monica, the third-grade teacher with beautiful hands for whom I carried a candle and who, to my dismay, had wedded herself to Christ; and Sister Beatrice, a woman truly crazed, who would sweep into class, eyes wide, to tell us about the Apocalypse.

All the hours in class tend to blend into one long, vague stretch of time. What I remember best, strangely enough, are the two things I couldn't understand and over the years grew to hate: grammar lessons and mathematics. I would sit there watching a teacher draw her long horizontal line and her short, oblique lines and break up sentences and put adjectives here and adverbs there and just not get it, couldn't see the reason for it, turned off to it. I would hide by slumping down in my seat and page through my reader, carried along by the flow of sentences in a story. She would test us, and I would dread that, for I always got Cs and Ds. Mathematics was a bit different. For whatever reasons, I didn't learn early math very well, so when it came time for more complicated operations, I couldn't keep up and started daydreaming to avoid my inadequacy. This was a strategy I would rely on as I grew older. I fell further and further behind. A memory: The teacher is faceless and seems very far away. The voice is faint and is discussing an equation written on the board.

It is raining, and I am watching the streams of water form patterns on the windows.

I realize now how consistently I defended myself against the lessons I couldn't understand and the people and events of South L.A. that were too strange to view head-on. I got very good at watching a blackboard with minimum awareness. And I drifted more and more into a variety of protective fantasies. I was lucky in that although my parents didn't read or write very much and had no more than a few books around the house, they never debunked my pursuits. And when they could, they bought me what I needed to spin my web.

One early Christmas they got me a small chemistry set. My father brought home an old card table from the secondhand store, and on that table I spread out my test tubes, my beaker, my Erlenmeyer flask, and my gas-generating apparatus. The set came equipped with chemicals, minerals, and various treated papers—all in little square bottles. You could send away to someplace in Maryland for more, and I did, saving pennies and nickels to get the substances that were too exotic for my set, the Junior Chemcraft: Congo red paper, azurite, glycerine, chrome alum, cochineal—this from female insects!—tartaric acid, chameleon paper, logwood. I would sit before my laboratory and play for hours. My father rested on the purple couch in front of me watching wrestling or *Gunsmoke* while I measured powders or heated crystals or blew into solutions that my breath would turn red or pink. I was taken by the blends of names and by the colors that swirled through the beaker. My equations were visual and phonetic. I would hold a flask up to the hall light, imagining the veils of a million atoms dancing. Sulfur and alcohol hung in the air. I wanted to shake down the house.

One day my mother came home from Coffee Dan's with an awful story. The teenage brother of one of her waitress friends was in the hospital. He had been fooling around with explosives in his garage "where his mother couldn't see him," and something happened, and "he blew away part of his throat. For God's sake, be careful," my mother said. "Remember poor Ada's brother." Wow! I thought. How neat! Why couldn't my experiments be that dangerous? I really lost heart when I realized that you could probably eat the chemicals spread across my table.

I knew what I had to do. I saved my money for a week and then walked with firm resolve past Walt's Malts, past the brake shop, across Ninetieth Street, and into Palazolla's market. I bought a little bottle of Alka-Seltzer and ran home. I chipped up the wafers and mixed them into a jar of white crystals. When my mother came home, dog tired, and sat down on the edge of the couch to tell me and Dad about her day, I gravely poured my concoction into a beaker of water, cried something about the unexpected, and ran out from behind my table. The beaker foamed ominously. My father swore in Italian. The second time I tried it, I got something milder—in English. And by my third near-miss with death, my parents were calling my behavior cute. Cute! Who wanted cute? I wanted to toy with the disaster that befell Ada Pendleton's brother. I wanted all those wonderful colors to collide in ways that could blow your voice box right off.

But I was limited by the real. The best I could do was create a toxic antacid. I loved my chemistry set—its glassware and its intriguing labels—but it wouldn't allow me to do the things I wanted to do. St. Regina's had an all-purpose room, one wall of which was lined with old books—and one of those shelves held a row of plastic-covered space novels. The sheen of their covers was gone, and their futuristic portraits were dotted with erasures and grease spots like a meteor shower of the everyday. I remember the rockets best. Long cylinders outfitted at the base with three slick fins, tapering at the other end to a perfect conical point, ready to pierce out of the stratosphere and into my imagination: X-15s and Mach 1, the dark side of the moon, the Red Planet, Jupiter's Great Red Spot, Saturn's rings—and beyond the solar system to swirling wisps of galaxies, to stardust.

I would check out my books two at a time and take them home to curl up with a blanket on my chaise lounge, reading, sometimes, through the weekend, my back aching, my thoughts lost between galaxies. I became the hero of a thousand adventures, all with intricate plots and the triumph of good over evil, all many dimensions removed from the dim walls of the living room. We were given time to draw in school, so, before long, all this worked itself onto paper. The stories I was reading were reshaping themselves into pictures. My father got me some butcher paper from Palazzolla's, and I continued to draw at home. My collected works rendered the Horsehead Nebula, goofy space cruisers, robots, and Saturn. Each had its crayon, a particular waxy pencil with mood and meaning: rust and burnt sienna for Mars, yellow for the Sun, lime and rose for Saturn's rings, and bright red for the Jovian spot. I had a little sharpener to keep the points just right. I didn't write any stories; I just read and drew. I wouldn't care much about writing until late in high school.

The summer before the sixth grade, I got a couple of jobs. The first was at a pet store a block or so away from my house. Since I was still small, I could maneuver around in breeder cages, scraping the heaps of parakeet crap from the tin floor, cleaning the water troughs and seed trays. It was pretty awful. I would go home after work and fill the tub and soak until all the fleas and bird mites came floating to the surface, little Xs in their multiple eyes. When I heard about a job selling strawberries door-to-door, I jumped at it. I went to work for a white-haired Chicano named Frank. He would carry four or five kids and dozens of crates of strawberries in his ramshackle truck up and down the avenues of the better neighborhoods: houses with mowed lawns and petunia beds. We'd work all day for seventy-five cents, Frank dropping pairs of us off with two crates each, then picking us up at preassigned corners. We spent lots of time together, bouncing around on the truck bed redolent with strawberries or sitting on a corner, cold, listening for the sputter of Frank's muffler. I started telling the other kids about my books, and soon it was my job to fill up that time with stories.

Reading opened up the world. There I was, a skinny bookworm drawing the attention of street kids who, in any other circumstances, would have had me for breakfast. Like an epic tale-teller, I developed the stories as I went along, relying on a flexible plot line and a repository of heroic events. I had a great time. I sketched out trajectories with my finger on Frank's dusty truck bed. And I stretched out each story's climax, creating cliff-hangers like the ones I saw in the Saturday serials. These stories created for me a temporary community.

It was around this time that fiction started leading me circuitously to a child's version of science. In addition to the space novels, St. Regina's library also had half a dozen books on astronomy—*The Golden Book of the Planets* and stuff like that—so I checked out a few of them. I liked what I read and wheedled enough change out of my father to enable me to take the bus to the public library. I discovered star maps, maps of lunar seas, charts upon charts of the solar system and the planetary moons: Rhea, Europa, Callisto, Miranda, Io. I didn't know that most of these moons were named for women—I didn't know classical mythology—but I would say their names to myself as though they had a woman's power to protect: Europa, Miranda, Io. . . . The distances between stars fascinated me, as did the sizes of the big telescopes. I sent away for catalogs. Then prices fascinated me, too. I wanted to drape my arm over a thousand-dollar scope and hear its motor drive whirr. I conjured a twelve-year-old's life of the astronomer: sitting up all night with potato chips and the stars, tracking the sky for supernovas, humming "Earth Angel" with the Penguins. What was my mother to do but save her tips and buy me a telescope?!

It was a little reflecting job, and I solemnly used to carry it out to the front of the house on warm summer nights, to find Venus or Alpha Centauri or trace the stars in Orion or lock onto the moon. I would lay out my star maps on the concrete, more for their magic than anything else, for I had trouble figuring them out. I was no geometer of the constellations; I was their balladeer. Those nights were very peaceful. I was far enough away from the front door and up enough from the sidewalk to make it seem as if I rested on a mound of dark silence, a mountain in Arizona, perhaps, watching the sky alive with points of light. Poor Freddie, toothless Lester whispering promises about making me feel good, the flat days, the gang fights—all this receded, for it was now me, the star child, lost in an eyepiece focused on a reflecting mirror that cradled, in its center, a shimmering moon.

DISCUSSION QUESTIONS
1. What course or teacher had an impact on you?
2. How does communication enable an individual to succeed or fail?
3. What role should tracking—placing students in college preparatory courses or vocational training according to academic ability—play in secondary education?

A HOMEMADE EDUCATION

Malcolm X

■

I t was because of my letters that I happened to stumble upon starting to acquire some kind of a homemade education.

I became increasingly frustrated at not being able to express what I
wanted to convey in letters that I wrote, especially those to Mr. Elijah Muhammad.[1] In the street, I had been the most articulate hustler out there—I had
commanded attention when I said something. But now, trying to write simple
English, I not only wasn't articulate, I wasn't even functional. How would I
sound writing in slang, the way I would *say* it, something such as, "Look,
daddy, let me pull your coat about a cat, Elijah Muhammad—."

Many who today hear me somewhere in person, or on television, or
those who read something I've said, will think I went to school far beyond the
eighth grade. This impression is due entirely to my prison studies.

It had really begun back in the Charlestown Prison, when Bimbi first
made me feel envy of his stock of knowledge. Bimbi had always taken charge
of any conversation he was in, and I had tried to emulate him. But every book
I picked up had few sentences which didn't contain anywhere from one to
nearly all of the words that might as well have been in Chinese. When I just
skipped those words, of course, I really ended up with little idea of what the
book said. So I had come to the Norfolk Prison Colony still going through
only book-reading motions. Pretty soon, I would have quit even these motions,
unless I had received the motivation that I did.

---

[1] Mr. Elijah Muhammad (1897–1975): Leader of the Nation of Islam, a militant Muslim organization committed to the idea of black nationalism.—Ed.

I saw that the best thing I could do was get hold of a dictionary—to study, to learn some words. I was lucky enough to reason also that I should try to improve my penmanship. It was sad. I couldn't even write in a straight line. It was both ideas together that moved me to request a dictionary along with some tablets and pencils from the Norfolk Prison Colony school.

I spent two days just riffling uncertainly through the dictionary's pages. I'd never realized so many words existed! I didn't know *which* words I needed to learn. Finally, just to start some kind of action, I began copying.

In my slow, painstaking, ragged handwriting, I copied into my tablet everything printed on that first page, down to the punctuation marks.

I believe it took me a day. Then, aloud, I read back, to myself, everything I'd written on the tablet. Over and over, aloud, to myself, I read my own hand-writing.

I woke up the next morning, thinking about those words—immensely proud to realize that not only had I written so much at one time, but I'd written words that I never knew were in the world. Moreover, with a little effort, I also could remember what many of these words meant. I reviewed the words whose meanings I didn't remember. Funny thing, from the dictionary first page right now, that "aardvark" springs to my mind. The dictionary had a picture of it, a long-tailed, long-eared, burrowing African mammal, which lives off termites caught by sticking out its tongue as an anteater does for ants.

I was so fascinated that I went on—I copied the dictionary's next page. And the same experience came when I studied that. With every succeeding page, I also learned of people and places and events from history. Actually the dictionary is like a miniature encyclopedia. Finally the dictionary's A section had filled a whole tablet—and I went on into the B's. That was the way I started copying what eventually became the entire dictionary. It went a lot faster after so much practice helped me to pick up handwriting speed. Between what I wrote in my tablet, and writing letters, during the rest of my time in prison I would guess I wrote a million words.

I suppose it was inevitable that as my word-base broadened, I could for the first time pick up a book and read and now begin to understand what the book was saying. Anyone who has read a great deal can imagine the new world that opened. Let me tell you something: From then until I left that prison, in every free moment I had, if I was not reading in the library, I was reading on my bunk. You couldn't have gotten me out of books with a wedge. Between Mr. Muhammad's teachings, my correspondence, my visitors—usually Ella and Reginald—and my reading of books, months passed without my even thinking about being imprisoned. In fact, up to then, I never had been so truly free in my life.

The Norfolk Prison Colony's library was in the school building. A variety of classes was taught there by instructors who came from such places as Harvard and Boston universities. The weekly debates between inmate teams were also held in the school building. You would be astonished to know how worked up convict debaters and audiences would get over subjects like "Should Babies Be Fed Milk?"

Available on the prison library's shelves were books on just about every general subject. Much of the big private collection that Parkhurst[2] had willed to the prison was still in crates and boxes in the back of the library—thousands of old books. Some of them looked ancient: covers faded, old-time parchment-looking binding. Parkhurst, I've mentioned, seemed to have been principally interested in history and religion. He had the money and the special interest to have a lot of books that you wouldn't have in general circulation. Any college library would have been lucky to get that collection.

As you can imagine, especially in a prison where there was heavy emphasis on rehabilitation, an inmate was smiled upon if he demonstrated an unusually intense interest in books. There was a sizable number of well-read inmates, especially the popular debaters. Some were said by many to be practically walking encyclopedias. They were almost celebrities. No university would ask any student to devour literature as I did when this new world opened to me, of being able to read and *understand.*

I read more in my room than in the library itself. An inmate who was known to read a lot could check out more than the permitted maximum number of books. I preferred reading in the total isolation of my own room.

When I had progressed to really serious reading, every night at about 10:00 P.M. I would be outraged with the "lights out." It always seemed to catch me right in the middle of something engrossing.

Fortunately, right outside my door was a corridor light that cast a glow into my room. The glow was enough to read by, once my eyes adjusted to it. So when "lights out" came, I would sit on the floor where I could continue reading in that glow.

At one-hour intervals the night guards paced past every room. Each time I heard the approaching footsteps, I jumped into bed and feigned sleep. And as soon as the guard passed, I got back out of bed onto the floor area of that light-glow, where I would read for another fifty-eight minutes—until the guard approached again. That went on until three or four every morning. Three or four hours of sleep a night was enough for me. Often in the years in the streets I had slept less than that.

The teachings of Mr. Muhammad stressed how history had been "whitened"—when white men had written history books, the black man simply had been left out. Mr. Muhammad couldn't have said anything that would have struck me much harder. I had never forgotten how when my class, me and all of those whites, had studied seventh-grade United States history back in Mason, the

---

[2]Charles Henry Parkhurst (1842–1933): American reformer and president of the Society for the Prevention of Crime.—Ed.

history of the Negro had been covered in one paragraph, and the teacher had gotten a big laugh with his joke, "Negroes' feet are so big that when they walk, they leave a hole in the ground."

This is one reason why Mr. Muhammad's teachings spread so swiftly all over the United States, among *all* Negroes, whether or not they became followers of Mr. Muhammad. The teachings ring true—to every Negro. You can hardly show me a black adult in America—or a white one, for that matter—who knows from the history books anything like the truth about the black man's role. In my own case, once I heard of the "glorious history of the black man," I took special pains to hunt in the library for books that would inform me on details about black history.

I can remember accurately the very first set of books that really impressed me. I have since bought that set of books and have it at home for my children to read as they grow up. It's called *Wonders of the World*. It's full of pictures of archaeological finds, statues that depict, usually, non-European people.

I found books like Will Durant's *Story of Civilization*. I read H. G. Wells's *Outline of History*. *Souls of Black Folk* by W. E. B. Du Bois gave me a glimpse into the black people's history before they came to this country. Carter G. Woodson's *Negro History* opened my eyes about black empires before the black slave was brought to the United States, and the early Negro struggles for freedom.[3]

J. A. Rogers's three volumes of *Sex and Race*[4] told about race-mixing before Christ's time; about Aesop being a black man who told fables; about Egypt's Pharaohs; about the great Coptic Christian Empires; about Ethiopia, the earth's oldest continuous black civilization, as China is the oldest continuous civilization.

Mr. Muhammad's teaching about how the white man had been created led me to *Findings in Genetics* by Gregor Mendel.[5] (The dictionary's G section was where I had learned what "genetics" meant.) I really studied this book by the Austrian monk. Reading it over and over, especially certain sections, helped me to understand that if you started with a black man, a white man could be produced; but starting with a white man, you never could produce a black man—because the white chromosome is recessive. And since no one disputes that there was but one Original Man, the conclusion is clear.

---

[3]Will Durant (1885–1981): A popular historian whose eleven-volume *Story of Civilization* (1935–1975), coauthored with his wife Ariel, has been described as a "biography of manki G. Wells (1866–1946): British author of *Outline of History: Being a Plain History of Life and Mankind* (1920); W. E. B. Du Bois (1868–1963): Pioneering black historian and activist, whose *Souls of Black Folk* (1903) ranks as one of the most influential works on racism in America; Carter G. Woodson (1875–1950): Author of *The Negro in Our History* (1922), Woodson is considered the father of black history.—Ed.
[4]Joel Augustus Rogers (1883–1965): His three-volume *Sex and Race* (1940) was subtitled "Negro-Caucasian Mixing in All Ages and All Lands."—Ed.
[5]Gregor Mendel (1822–1884): Pioneering Austrian botanist and geneticist. He published his theories of dominant and recessive genes in a scientific journal in the 1860s, but his work remained unknown until the twentieth century.—Ed.

During the last year or so, in the *New York Times*, Arnold Toynbee[6] used the word "bleached" in describing the white man. (His words were: "White (i.e., bleached) human beings of North European origin. . . .") Toynbee also referred to the European geographic area as only a peninsula of Asia. He said there is no such thing as Europe. And if you look at the globe, you will see for yourself that America is only an extension of Asia. (But at the same time Toynbee is among those who have helped to bleach history. He has written that Africa was the only continent that produced no history. He won't write that again. Every day now, the truth is coming to light.)

I never will forget how shocked I was when I began reading about slavery's total horror. It made such an impact upon me that it later became one of my favorite subjects when I became a minister of Mr. Muhammad's. The world's most monstrous crime, the sin and the blood on the white man's hands, are almost impossible to believe. Books like the one by Frederick Olmstead[7] opened my eyes to the horrors suffered when the slave was landed in the United States. The European woman, Fannie Kimball,[8] who had married a Southern white slaveowner, described how human beings were degraded. Of course I read *Uncle Tom's Cabin*.[9] In fact, I believe that's the only novel I have ever read since I started serious reading.

Parkhurst's collection also contained some bound pamphlets of the Abolitionist Anti-Slavery Society of New England. I read descriptions of atrocities, saw those illustrations of black slave women tied up and flogged with whips; of black mothers watching their babies being dragged off, never to be seen by their mothers again; of dogs after slaves, and of the fugitive slave catchers, evil white men with whips and clubs and chains and guns. I read about the slave preacher Nat Turner,[10] who put the fear of God into the white slavemaster. Nat Turner wasn't going around preaching pie-in-the-sky and "nonviolent" freedom for the black man. There in Virginia one night in 1831, Nat and seven other slaves started out at his master's home and through the night they went from one plantation "big house" to the next, killing, until by the next morning fifty-seven white people were dead and Nat had about seventy slaves fol-

---

[6]Arnold Toynbee (1889–1975): English historian, author of the twelve-volume *A Study of History* (1934–1961), which described history in terms of the cyclical development and decline of civilizations.—Ed.

[7]Frederick Olmstead (*sic*) (1822–1903): Frederick Law Olmsted, a founder of landscape architecture in the United States, was also a social critic and reformer. His criticisms of slavery were published as *The Cotton Kingdom* (1861).—Ed.

[8]Fannie Kimball (*sic*): Frances (Fanny) Kemble (1809–1893) was a noted British actress and abolitionist who recounted her experiences in the South in *Journal of a Residence on a Georgia Plantation* (1863).—Ed.

[9]*Uncle Tom's Cabin* (1852): An antislavery novel by Harriet Beecher Stowe (1811–1896), often cited as one of the causes of the Civil War.—Ed.

[10]Nat Turner (1800–1831): Led the bloodiest slave revolt in U.S. history. His four-day revolt in August 1831 left fifty-seven whites dead and led to the retaliatory killings of many innocent slaves.—Ed.

lowing him. White people, terrified for their lives, fled from their homes, locked themselves up in public buildings, hid in the woods, and some even left the state. A small army of soldiers took two months to catch and hang Nat Turner. Somewhere I have read where Nat Turner's example is said to have inspired John Brown[11] to invade Virginia and attack Harpers Ferry nearly thirty years later, with thirteen white men and five Negroes.

I read Herodotus, "the father of History,"[12] or, rather, I read about him. And I read the histories of various nations, which opened my eyes gradually, then wider and wider, to how the whole world's white men had indeed acted like devils, pillaging and raping and bleeding and draining the whole world's nonwhite people. I remember, for instance, books such as Will Durant's story of Oriental civilization, and Mahatma Gandhi's[13] accounts of the struggle to drive the British out of India.

Book after book showed me how the white man had brought upon the world's black, brown, red, and yellow peoples every variety of the sufferings of exploitation. I saw how since the sixteenth century, the so-called "Christian trader" white man began to ply the seas in his lust for Asian and African empires, and plunder, and power. I read, I saw how the white man never has gone among the nonwhite peoples bearing the Cross in the true manner and spirit of Christ's teachings—meek, humble, and Christ-like.

I perceived, as I read, how the collective white man had been actually nothing but a piratical opportunist who used Faustian machinations to make his own Christianity his initial wedge in criminal conquests. First, always "religiously," he branded "heathen" and "pagan" labels upon ancient nonwhite cultures and civilizations. The stage thus set, he then turned upon his nonwhite victims his weapons of war.

I read how, entering India—half a *billion* deeply religious brown people—the British white man, by 1759, through promises, trickery, and manipulations, controlled much of India through Great Britain's East India Company.[14] The parasitical British administration kept tentacling out to half of the subcontinent. In 1857, some of the desperate people of India finally mutinied—and, excepting the African slave trade, nowhere has history recorded any more unnecessary bestial and ruthless human carnage than the British suppression of the nonwhite Indian people.

Over 115 million African blacks—close to the 1930s population of the United States—were murdered or enslaved during the slave trade. And I read

[11]John Brown (1800–1859): In 1859 Brown and his followers attacked the arsenal at Harpers Ferry, intending to arm the slaves and encourage them to rise up in rebellion against their masters.—Ed.

[12]Herodotus (484?–425? B.C.): Greek historian whose account of the Persian Wars was the first narrative history in the Western world.—Ed.

[13]Mahatma Gandhi: Mohandas K. Gandhi (1869–1948), dubbed "Mahatma" or "Great-Souled," advocated nonviolence in the fight for Indian independence from British rule.—Ed.

[14]The British East India Company: Chartered by Elizabeth I in 1600, this association of merchants was given rights to develop the colonies of the British Empire on the Indian subcontinent.—Ed.

how when the slave market was glutted, the cannibalistic white powers of Europe next carved up, as their colonies, the richest areas of the black continent. And Europe's chancelleries for the next century played a chess game of naked exploitation and power from Cape Horn to Cairo.

Ten guards and the warden couldn't have torn me out of those books. Not even Elijah Muhammad could have been more eloquent than those books were in providing indisputable proof that the collective white man had acted like a devil in virtually every contact he had with the world's collective non-white man. . . .

Mr. Muhammad, to whom I was writing daily, had no idea of what a new world had opened up to me through my efforts to document his teachings in books.

When I discovered philosophy, I tried to touch all the landmarks of philosophical development. Gradually, I read most of the old philosophers, Occidental and Oriental. The Oriental philosophers were the ones I came to prefer; finally, my impression was that most Occidental philosophy had largely been borrowed from the Oriental thinkers. Socrates, for instance, traveled in Egypt. Some sources even say that Socrates was initiated into some of the Egyptian mysteries. Obviously Socrates got some of his wisdom among the East's wise men.

I have often reflected upon the new vistas that reading opened to me. I knew right there in prison that reading had changed forever the course of my life. As I see it today, the ability to read awoke inside me some long dormant craving to be mentally alive. I certainly wasn't seeking any degree, the way a college confers a status symbol upon its students. My homemade education gave me, with every additional book that I read, a little bit more sensitivity to the deafness, dumbness, and blindness that was afflicting the black race in America. Not long ago, an English writer telephoned me from London, asking questions. One was, "What's your alma mater?" I told him, "Books."

Discussion Questions

1. What is your impression of the importance of Malcolm X in American culture?
2. Is there a difference between the education of whites and that of minorities in American education?
3. Should the individual or the educational system be responsible for success or failure in learning?

The Media Habit
W. Russell Neuman
■

Abundant Media Exposure

If we are to understand how the new media will be used, it would certainly seem appropriate to take a long, hard look at how the current media technologies are used in day-to-day life. How much time does a typical American citizen spend with the mass media on an average day? How attentive are people to the messages the media carry? How much do they remember? How often do they learn or change their opinions in response to what they hear and see from the media? Does the weight of the evidence point toward addiction or active selectivity?

One thing is clear: There is a lot of exposure. The media are heavily used by virtually every segment of the population. Television is the dominant medium in terms of time use, representing about 50% of media exposure per day for the average citizen (Neuman and Pool 1986). A. C. Nielsen estimates that the average household television set is on for an average of a little over 7 hours per day, with the average adult watching for about 4.5 hours (Nielsen 1990). At the peak of "prime time" (about nine o'clock in the evening), some 60% to 70% of American households are viewing. There is some variation among different demographic groups, but even those in the lowest viewing category (teenage girls, who may have a number of other things on their minds) watch 3.5 hours per day. Radio is next, with well over 2 hours of exposure per day. A fair amount of that exposure takes place in cars (97% of cars sold in the United States have radios); the peak exposure times for radio are in the mornings and evenings as commuters commute and many others listen as they attend to personal tasks and prepare meals.

Estimates of newspaper reading per day, depending on research methodology, vary from 18 to 49 minutes. Estimates of magazine reading vary from

6 to 30 minutes per day per person (Hornik and Schlenger 1981). Those substantial variations in estimates are due to the difficulty people have in recalling their behavior over the past 24 hours. The broadcast data are in large part derived from electronic viewership meters and thus are a bit more reliable. Book reading is estimated at about 18 minutes per day, and that includes pleasure reading as well as work- and school-related reading for appropriate segments of the population (Newman and Pool 1986). Taking the rather conservative estimates, all that still adds up to a rather impressive 6 hours and 43 minutes of media exposure per day.

INFORMATION OVERLOAD

The television set presents 3,600 images per minute per channel. Radio, on average, generates just under 100 words per minute, totalling between 3,000 and 5,000 words broadcast by radio each minute of each day in the typical urban area. The average daily newspaper contains 150,000 words and several thousand graphic images. Magazines and books add to the flow on a similar scale. Are we beginning to press up against the psychological limits of human ability to process information? Are there unanticipated effects of media abundance? Indeed, some analysts conclude that overload may result in intrapsychic trauma and conflict, withdrawal, confusion and frustration (G. A. Miller 1956; J. G. Miller 1960; Deutsch 1963; Milgram 1970; Lipowski 1971; Klapp 1978; Malik 1986).

Miller (1956), for example, has demonstrated through experimental tests that the human mind has a limit of about seven factors that it can process simultaneously. The increased complexity and speed of decision making would seem to threaten this physiological barrier. Studies of battlefield commanders, business executives, and air traffic controllers have provided further evidence of significant psychological pathologies (Raymond 1962; Van Gigh 1976; Toffler 1980).

It appears, however, that media audiences have developed considerable skill in organizing, filtering, and skimming information through coping strategies of partial attentiveness. Most people do not feel bombarded or overloaded by an expanded array of available mass media. On the contrary, for the most part they seek out more media and respond enthusiastically to expanded choices. Media behavior is voluntary behavior. People choose to be exposed.

On reexamination of the overload literature, we find that the bulk of the studies have reviewed the work setting rather than the home. Indeed, executives, battlefield commanders, and air traffic controllers are in positions of high-salience decision making under extreme time pressures, precisely the opposite of the casual, entertainment-oriented mass media consumer. Although there may be social pressure to be informed or to keep up with bestsellers and popular television shows, the parallel with the work setting is decidedly weak.

The fact of the matter is that the human capacity for selective attention is indeed well developed. The average individual is bombarded with 1,600 advertisements per day, but responds (not necessarily positively) to only 12 (Draper 1986, 16). The mind, medical authorities remind us, has a remarkable capacity to filter signals. The brain responds consciously to only one sensory stimulus among each million stimuli being sent (Blumler 1980, 231). Although new cable systems provide a cornucopia of available channels, it has been found that tripling the number of channels available leads typically to regular viewing of only two or three additional channels (Lemieux 1983). The concern about information overload, at least in the context of mass communications would seem to be overdrawn.

THE CASUAL USE OF MULTIPLE MEDIA

There is an inherent contradiction in the media use statistics. The media exposure studies indicate a total usage of 6 hours and 43 minutes per day. But other, independent studies of time use indicate that only 5 hours and 43 minutes per day are available for all leisure activities, many of which, of course, do not involve media at all. It appears that a considerable portion of leisure time is devoted to media use and that media use will overlap with other household activities or the use of other media, typically reading the newspaper while the television is on. This overlapping use of media is an important clue to understanding the nature of the media habit. It indicates that use of the media is active and selective, but casual, habitual, and only semiattentive, a picture rather different from Orwell's portrayal of the attentive and transfixed audience for Big Brother's orations.

MODEST RECALL OF MEDIA CONTENT

Given the massive flow of media messages and the casual attentiveness of the typical audience member, we might expect that a rather small proportion of the communications flow will be remembered. That is indeed the case. In the middle of election campaigns, for example, only rarely are as many as half of the adult population able to name any of the candidates in their congressional districts or any of the candidates in the senatorial races. This is true despite the fact that frequently one of the candidates is an incumbent and has been receiving extensive press coverage as a prominent political official. Such commonly used terms as "tariff," "private enterprise," and "NATO" can be defined by less than half of the population. The Bill of Rights, a fundamental concept of American government frequently cited by journalists and public officials, can be correctly identified by only one in five citizens (Neuman 1986).

In a study of recall of network news programming on television (Neman 1976), subjects were called at random in the evening and asked if they had watched the news that evening, and if so what they could recall of what they had just seen. On average, respondents could recall only one news story out of 20 without additional prompting. When they were read a list of headlines from the news programs they had watched, they could recall four additional stories and provide details about those stories. They claimed to recall another four stories, but could not remember any of the details. So as a rough rule of thumb, 5% of the stories are recalled unaided, and another 45% with prompting, only half of which are substantiated with supporting details. These general parameters have been supported by subsequent research (Katz, Adoni, and Parness 1977; Gantz 1978; Gunter 1981; Robinson and Levy 1986). Robinson and Levy, for example, focused on only the most prominent stories and found that the accumulative impact of all media over the course of a week led to recall and comprehension of roughly one-third of the stories examined (Robinson and Levy 1986, 92).

The extensive research on recall of commercial messages reveals similar conclusions. Jacoby and Hoyer (1982) found that only 17% of their sample who were watching television commercials within the especially attentive circumstances of an experimental setting could correctly answer six "relatively simple" questions about a commercial they had just seen. Only 4% got all 12 answers right for the two commercials they saw. Burke Marketing Research has been conducting telephone-based and more naturalistic "Day After Recall" research for some years, providing advertisers with information on how well their commercials are remembered. On average, only one in four commercials seen can be recalled the next day, even with prompting from the interviewer. What is more revealing is the range of recall rates. Some commercials are recalled by as few as 2% of the people who saw them whereas others are recalled by 77% of the viewing audience (Burke Marketing Research 1974). A great deal depends on the character and quality of the commercial. The relationship between the audience member and the television set is complex. Recalled impressions vary greatly as a result of selective attention and selective memory. There is a media habit, but not a pattern of helpless addiction. Far from a pattern of information overload, we find that for the most part the audience handles the flow of communications casually, successfully, and enjoyably.

MEDIA AND BEHAVIOR: EVEN MORE MODEST EFFECTS

The limited ability of typical media consumers to recall much of the information flow hints that they may not be heavily conditioned and manipulated by the flow of messages. Is there evidence that the media can induce the public to buy products they do not want, change their fundamental beliefs, or vote for highly advertised political candidates? Although most people assume otherwise, the answer, based on the accumulated results from systematic research over several decades, is no.

This is indeed ironic, given the massive investment of some $50 billion per year in advertising in the United States. McGuire (1986), for example, suggests that hardheaded American business people would be expected to keep their eyes on the bottom line and to have good evidence that advertisements pay off, that, at the margin, a dollar invested in advertising will generate at least that much in additional sales. His conclusion, however, based on an extensive review of the behavioral literature, is that there is no evidence of persistent or substantial advertising effects. Other recent analyses have come to the same conclusion (Comstock et al. 1978; Schudson, 1984; Lodish 1986). Schudson concludes, for example, that "most firms resort to rules of thumb . . . and rely on 'essentially illogical' approaches to determine their advertising budgets" (1984, 17). Schmalensee's carefully conducted econometric analysis (1972) would seem to support such a conclusion. He found that advertising budgets were more closely correlated with sales in the preceding quarter than with current sales or sales in the following quarter. This would suggest that advertisers are spending the available funds on advertising, but are not boosting sales. In other words, the causal arrow may point in the opposite direction: successful sales leading to expanded advertising, not the reverse. What an irony.

There have been widely cited examples of particular advertisements or advertising campaigns that have seemed to capture the public's fancy and dramatically boosted product awareness. A million-dollar television campaign during the 1972 summer Olympic Games telecasts, for example, reportedly raised the Northwestern Mutual Life Insurance Company from 34th to 3rd place in public recognition of insurance company names (Comstock et al. 1978, 363). But, ironically, those advertisements that are most successful in attracting public attention, such as the series of popular ads for Alka-Seltzer, often are found not to be particularly successful in boosting sales of the product.

One of the most detailed experimental field studies yet published (Naples 1979) reveals that, at most, a 2% increase in sales will be associated with multiple exposures to an advertising campaign under ideal conditions. Lodish (1986) reports that more recent and more refined studies of the advertising–behavior link are even more sobering in revealing how seldom and how unpredictably measurable increases in sales can be attributed to advertising exposure. Study after study reveals no effects, highly conditional effects, or very small effects of advertising (McGuire, 1986). But because of the vested interests of advertising executives connected with the media, the agencies, and the manufacturers themselves, and because of the persisting fears and suspicions of the critics of advertising, the myth of pervasive advertising effectiveness perseveres.

THE NATURE OF
INFORMATION-SEEKING
BEHAVIOR

There have been many theories put forward in an attempt to make sense of how individuals seek out, filter, and store information about the world around them. Most such theories characterize an active, rational, purposive media user. Atkin (1973), for example, describes media behavior in terms of an instrumental utility theory: "To the extent that an individual perceives that environmental objects may personally affect him, he will want to achieve a criterion level of awareness and understanding of them. . . . Basically the individual desires to formulate precise cognitive orientations toward those stimuli that potentially or currently impinge on his well-being" (1973, 208). Such a formulation, however, is fundamentally misleading.

Although typical television viewers and newspaper readers are not passive, dumbfounded, and effortlessly persuaded by each and every message, neither are they, for the most part, attentive and alert information seekers. The day-to-day accumulation of information and ideas from the media is a casual, semiattentive process. People do not approach a television set, a radio, or a magazine with a clearly articulated game plan for what they want to learn and how they are going to learn it. Although research in the tradition of uses and gratifications attempts to make a great deal of the distinction, people do not separate the information and entertainment components of their habitual newspaper reading and broadcast use. It is true that people will answer questions about their relative interest in news and entertainment in polite response to a survey, but their responses probably reflect more their sense of what they perceive as socially acceptable than real distinctions associated with differences in behavior.

Perhaps the classic caricature of media behavior is Paul Klein's Least Objectionable Program model of television viewing (1975). He describes the viewer as seldom deciding on a particular program. Rather, the process for the great bulk of viewing is stepwise: First, the decision is made to watch television. One flips on the set and spins the dial to find out what is on. Whatever is least objectionable is watched. Occasionally, nothing whatever attracts the viewer's attention, and the set is turned off, but that is rare. His speculations turn out to be supported by a great deal of research and apparently are characteristic of other media as well (Comstock et al. 1978; Goodhardt, Ehrenberg, and Collins 1980; Barwise, Ehrenberg, and Goodhardt 1982; Television Audience Assessment 1984; Bower 1985; Levy and Windahl 1985).

Another clue to understanding the media habit is to examine the amounts of other household activities that take place simultaneously with media exposure. Much of the work in this area has focused on television, but the pattern is true for radio and print media as well. Researchers in England

and the United States have put cameras on top of television sets to record attentiveness and physical behavior during viewing (Bechtel, Achenpohl, and Akers 1972; Anderson and Lorch 1983), and what has become clear is that media use is part of the fabric of daily life around the household. At least a third of the time, television viewing is a secondary activity while individuals talk, read, answer the telephone, eat, or take care of household chores (Robinson 1972; Comstock et al. 1978). These researchers have found that the eyes of viewers frequently stray from the television set to other objects and activities in the room. Radio use takes place so frequently as a background activity that individuals dramatically underestimate their recent exposure when recounting their activities over the past 24 hours, in effect forgetting that they had the radio on (Robinson 1977).

The notion of individuals staking out a daily set of specific information needs is not supported by research on actual behavior. Only 5% of the population, for example, report consulting an encyclopedia or dictionary in the preceding six months. The estimate is that the average individual spends only 35 seconds per day consulting non-news information resources. The list of information resources consulted is also rather mundane in character. The telephone book is the most often consulted (21% of the population, on average, per day), followed by cookbooks (18%) and product catalogs (9%) (Sharon 1972).

Some people claim that they hardly ever watch television, and then only news and sports, but diaries of viewing behavior for such individuals usually reveal otherwise. The great majority of these self-proclaimed selective viewers watch as many action adventures and comedies as everyone else, or only fractionally fewer (Bower 1973). Often these are lawyers, accountants, and professors who claim to have little time for media use, and because of their work schedules, they may indeed watch television less often, but when they watch, they follow the same entertainment-oriented pattern that characterizes everybody else (Wilensky 1964). Those who call for more public-affairs programming on television do not tend to watch it when it is made available (Bower 1973). Those who claim to attend to the media for purposes of acquiring information do score slightly higher on tests of learning and recall, but the differences are surprisingly small (Garramone 1983; Neuman et al. 1997).

Perhaps it is appropriate to draw on the insights of such classic analysts as Herbert Simon (1976) and Anthony Downs (1957), who emphasize the psychological costs of obtaining and processing information. Even though one might wish to explore all the variables before selecting one product from among many, often people "satisfice" rather than maximize their information. They get enough information to make a reasonable decision, rather than the most information to make a maximally rational choice. They act that way with media, too. It is not so much information seeking as doing some filtering on the flow of information and entertainment that comes one's way. It has been said about television, in particular, that "people don't get what they want from TV, they get what they get."

THE SOCIAL CONTEXT
OF MEDIA USE

Another important point about the media habit is that the accumulation of information and ideas from the media takes place in a social context. The choice of medium, the definition of appropriate use, and the interpretation of information are all very much influenced by the cultural and social milieu of the media user. The thrust of mass society theory, for example, posits that media use substitutes for social interaction, but the accumulated research reveals that the relationship between social isolation and media use is weak, and in many cases social integration increases media uses of various types (Johnstone 1974; Levy 1979). There is ample evidence of extensive discussion of news and public-affairs items (Katz and Lazarsfeld 1955; Robinson 1972; Rogers 1973); the fact is that people rely heavily on others to help make media choices and to interpret content. The image of a helpless, isolated individual might be appropriate for framing a good novel, but it is a naive and inappropriate basis for a serious scientific investigation of political communications and media technology.

A THEORY OF LOW-SALIENCE
LEARNING

A more appropriate model for proceeding should be based on accumulative learning from the mass media under conditions of limited attention and interest (Neuman 1986). Such a model will help to put the research on habitual media use in perspective and guide our analysis of the impact of new media. The basic dynamic of the model is that media exposure is substantial, but its impact is not. This fundamental fact of media use today is likely to be even more central to the new media environment. There are many hours of use, but the psychological salience of any one element in this massive flow of information is correspondingly low. We tend to value things that are expensive and rare. The media are neither. They are taken for granted. They become comfortable household companions. They share the attention of the individual with numerous other activities in the household. Attentiveness is casual, not like in the workplace or classroom. The media user is not passive, but is somewhere in the middle on a scale from passive to active. The user's behavior is voluntary, and individuals actively scan, select, and interpret the flow of information that comes their way.

DISCUSSION QUESTIONS
1. Throughout one day, write down precisely what you read and what you watch. Compare your list to those of others in your class. What are the similarities or differences among your lists?
2. How do you use media?
3. What do you find that is positive or negative in the media you use?

CHAPTER 2

NEW MEDIA

Christopher Harper, *Digital Journalism: Doing It All*

LynNell Hancock, *Computer Gap: The Haves and the Have-Nots*

Amy Harmon, *Bigots on the Net*

The word *Internet* is often used improperly. The Internet includes electronic mail, the graphic-oriented World Wide Web, and Usenet for discussion groups. The computer network started in 1969 as a way for scientists working with the U.S. Department of Defense to communicate with one another about research projects. In short order, the scientists adapted the system to send electronic mail to one another, and the first online discussion group began about science fiction, not scientific projects. Today, more than fifty million people in North America use the Internet either at home, at work, or through a library.

The World Wide Web is truly the first new medium in more than fifty years since television was introduced. The readings in this chapter focus on several issues regarding the Internet, such as: How are news and information presented on the Internet? Precisely what *is* an online reporter?

The first reading examines the role of the journalist at the *Chicago Tribune*'s online publication. The research and reporting skills necessary to perform the job remain the same as for other journalists, but online reporters are called upon to do much more.

The second reading asks: Is there a potential information gap in a digital age? Rough profiles of those who use the Internet and those who do not are being drawn. Who will be the "haves"? Who will be the "have-nots"? What are the implications of this disparity?

Because of the openness of the Internet, there are many advantages to further communication and conversation. The third reading assesses how open and unrestricted use of the Internet can be disadvantageous to society. For example, hate groups have turned to the Internet to spread messages of bigotry against blacks, whites, Jews, Catholics, and others.

DIGITAL JOURNALISM:
DOING IT ALL

Christopher Harper

■

Cornelia Grumman presses the sixth-floor button on the elevator at the Henry Horner public housing project. The City of Chicago has planted flowers outside the building, where gangs and drug pushers often run the West Side neighborhood. But the elevator does not work well and reeks of urine. After two tries at the button, Grumman finally reaches the fifth floor and walks up one flight of garbage-laden stairs. Two young boys climb on a safety fence that's supposed to keep them from falling into the garden below, but the fence seems more like a cage to keep them in.

Grumman, a reporter for the *Chicago Tribune*, wants to know what people on welfare think about massive changes in the federal program. She visits 24-year-old Melineice Reed and her three children who live in a well-kept, but tiny, three-room apartment. Reed has lived in the projects all her life. The next day she has an interview for a job as a cleaning woman, and she's a bit nervous. "Do you have anything to wear that's nice?" Grumman asks. "Nice enough," the woman says. Nearby, a group of worshippers gathers at a Baptist church for Sunday services. Grumman finds several people willing to talk about the federal plan that would limit benefits to the poor. One woman, Demitraius Dykes, has spent all of her 26 years on welfare. A recovering drug addict, she has five children. Dykes says she's trying to turn her life around, attending a course in office skills. "I don't want my kids to grow up and think they should sit around and wait each month for their check," she says. Grumman scribbles notes, runs a tape recorder, and takes a picture later. Although she does not like using video cameras, Grumman wishes she had one along for this interview because Dykes is a good talker.

The 33-year-old reporter is one of a new breed of journalists—the digital journalist. Although more than 200 American newspapers offer an online edition, most are simply an electronic version of the printed newspaper—a "shovel-down" version as it's known on the Internet. The *Tribune*, however, is one of the few newspapers in the country that has devoted reporters like Grumman to work exclusively for the Internet edition. The reporters write stories, take pictures, operate video cameras, and even create digital pages. With 20 other staff members, the seven reporters produce one of the most innovative online editions available today.

Internet editor Leah Gentry intends to deliver to users what she thinks they should have and what they want. She proudly calls her team "the hardest working band in the business." Gentry is the band leader, and the 36-year-old former editor for the *Orange County* (California) *Register* has a set of exacting standards that would make any conductor envious. She calls them "Leah's Rules."

1. All the regular rules of journalism apply. Reporting and editing must be solid. Facts must be checked and rechecked.
2. If you're going to use this week's gizmo, it has to help advance the telling of the story in a meaningful way.
3. No instant publishing. Everybody has his or her finger on the press, but nobody is allowed to post a page that hasn't gone through the editing process.
4. Reporters need to think of the medium while reporting. In addition to story information, they must gather or assign information for animated or still graphics, video, and audio. "The main rule: what we're doing is journalism, not stupid technology tricks," she says.

The *Tribune* Internet edition, which started in March 1996, contains most of the information from the print version—news, sports, job listings, real estate and automobile advertisements, weather, stocks, and television listings. For its readers, the Internet edition offers in-depth stories, special technology reports, games, discussion groups, and everything someone would ever want to know about the Chicago Bears and the Chicago Bulls. The Internet edition also provides audio interviews and information from the company's radio station, and video from the *Tribune*'s 24-hour-a-day news service, Chicagoland Television.

The Internet band includes 44-year-old Tom Cekay, a former financial editor of the *Tribune*. He is the editorial controller—the gatekeeper of what makes it online and what does not. "The traditional role of the editor stays the same. Do the readers need to see this? Is it intelligently done? Is it sophisticated reporting? Is it what the *Chicago Tribune* wants?" observes Cekay, a longtime *Tribune* editor who also has worked for newspapers in Ohio and Oregon.

"The differences are the demands on the editor are much higher because the editor has to know a lot more stuff than on the paper. The editor has to know about the audio that goes into these packages. The editor has to know about the video that goes into these packages." And he admits, "I have to edit a whole lot faster" because of the constant deadline pressure of the up-to-the-minute Internet edition.

The rest of the band is young, energetic, serious, and sometimes irreverent. The newspaper editors and reporters at the *Tribune* tend toward blue shirts, khaki pants, and expensive shoes. With few exceptions, this band tends toward T-shirts, blue jeans, and tennis shoes.

Grumman, by far the best-dressed in her business suits, studied public policy at Duke University and the Kennedy School of Government at Harvard. She worked as a freelance reporter in China, including booking rock and roll bands there. Another reporter, Darnell Little, 30, studied computer programming and developed telephone software for Bell Labs before becoming a journalist. Stephen Henderson, 26, wrote editorials for newspapers in Lexington, Kentucky, and Detroit, before joining the *Tribune*'s Internet staff.

During the Democratic convention in Chicago, the Internet edition of the newspaper reached nearly 100,000 users a day—more than most newspapers in the nation—by putting together a mixture of original reporting, audio reports from the *Tribune*'s radio station, video clips from two *Tribune* television stations, and articles from the printed edition. Reporter Little conceived a historical tour of some of the 25 previous political conventions in the city, starting with the one that nominated Abraham Lincoln in 1860. Little, who received both a master's degree in engineering and journalism from Northwestern, went to the Chicago Historical Society to get a visual sense of how to conduct a tour on the World Wide Web.

"The idea was to take people on a tour that was a virtual museum. There were three parallel streams. There was the tour guide—a walk through six conventions. The second was a behind-the-scenes look at what was happening in Chicago at the time. The third part included archives and political cartoons," Little explains. "The reporting is the same as working for a standard newspaper—gathering the information and talking to people. But you put it together and write it differently."

Before writing the story, Little designs a series of storyboards for what each of the main pages will show—a practice used extensively in the film, television, and advertising industries. The storyboard contains an outline of a page's content, graphics, and computer links to other stories.

After Little reports a story, he then follows his original storyboards—with adaptations—to make certain that the reporting, photography, headlines, and navigation make the stories easy for the reader to enjoy.

Little tends toward the storytelling of the *Wall Street Journal* articles on the front page, which he says works well on the Web. The first page uses an anecdotal lead to draw the reader into the story. The second page broadens the story with the "nut graph." The other pages flow from these first two pages to allow the reader to follow a variety of links that expand on each report.

The process is called "layering." Because a computer screen contains less space than the front page of a newspaper, the first layer or page of a digital story contains a headline, a digital photograph, and text that makes the user want to continue to the next layer. The pages are usually less than 500 words with the option for the reader with a click of a computer mouse to follow a highlighted path set out on a guide. But a user may want to follow another path. He or she could read about the 1860 convention and want to learn more about what was happening in Chicago during that period. After searching through the archives of that time, the user can proceed to the next convention or even skip ahead to another convention. The layers provide a logical way to proceed, but the layers can also enable the user to read the digital page in any order.

"I write the story in chapters," Little says. "What works the best is when you have a design on the Web that is the equivalent of the layout of a magazine and your eye and attention are focused on one part, which is easily digestible, and it flows and leads you into other parts."

When he wears his Detroit Tigers baseball cap, reporter Henderson looks like a young Spike Lee. The 26-year-old Henderson studied political science at the University of Michigan and started as an editorial writer at newspapers in Kentucky and Detroit. Within days after his arrival in Chicago, he noticed a story about the 1995 murder rates in the city.

"It wasn't a big deal. It was a story that the paper does every year," he recalls. "I said to myself, 'I bet there's a lot more there.'" Henderson asked the print reporters for all the information about the murders—the time, the neighborhood, the cause of death, and a variety of other statistics. He put together a map of the city and allowed every citizen to look for information about his or her neighborhood—again with a click of the mouse rather than a visit to the records office of the police precinct.

"We got thousands of people interested," he says. "If we use a big database in telling a story, you also have to give the readers a chance to use that database. That's giving people information that's important to them."

. . . At the *Tribune* and elsewhere, digital journalism remains in its infancy, and there are growing pains. The reporters at the Internet Tribune sometimes resemble one-person bands, carrying a variety of technical instruments without the necessary skills to do the job properly. At a printed newspaper, the reporter generally takes a pen, a notebook, and sometimes a tape recorder. At the electronic version, the reporter carries a pen, a notebook, a tape recorder for audio clips, a digital camera for single snapshots, and sometimes a consumer video camera for video clips. Those closest to the electronic product realize the medium must win converts—both readers and fellow journalists—to join Gentry's band. "This medium is in its infancy," Gentry explains. "There are thousands of ways to do things. We just have to figure them out and convince people we're right."

DISCUSSION QUESTIONS

1. Read the print version of a newspaper and then its online version. What are the similarities and the differences between the two?
2. In your opinion, what are the advantages and the disadvantages of the print version and the online version?
3. Do you prefer one version to the other? Why, or why not?

COMPUTER GAP: THE HAVES AND THE HAVE-NOTS

LynNell Hancock

■

Aaron Smith is a teenager on the techno track. In America's breathless race to achieve information nirvana, the senior from Issaqua, a middle-class district east of Seattle, has the hardware and hookups to run the route. Aaron and six hundred of his fellow students at Liberty High School have their own electronic-mail addresses. They can log on to the Internet every day, joining only about 15 percent of America's schoolchildren who can now forage on their own for documents in European libraries or chat with experts around the world. At home, the eighteen-year-old e-mails his teachers, when he is not prowling the World Wide Web to track down snowboarding conditions on his favorite Cascade Mountain passes. "We have the newest, greatest thing," Aaron says.

On the opposite coast, in Boston's South End, Marilee Colon scoots a mouse along a grimy Apple pad, playing a Kid Pix game on an old black-and-white terminal. It's Wednesday at a neighborhood center, Marilee's only chance to poke around on a computer. Her mom, a secretary at the center, can't afford one for their home. Marilee's public-school classroom doesn't have any either. The ten-year-old from Roxbury depends on the United South End Settlement Center and its less than state-of-the-art Macs and IBMs perched on mismatched desks. Marilee has never heard of the Internet. She is thrilled to double-click on the stick of dynamite and watch her teddy-bear creation fly off the screen. "It's fun blowing it up," says the delicate fifth grader, twisting a brown ponytail around her finger.

Certainly Aaron was born with a stack of statistical advantages over Marilee. He is white and middle class and lives with two working parents who both have higher degrees. Economists say the swift pace of high-tech advances will only drive a further wedge between these youngsters. To have an edge in

America's job search, it used to be enough to be well educated. Now, say the experts, it's critical to be digital. Employees who are adept at technology "earn roughly 10 to 15 percent higher pay," according to Alan Krueger, chief economist for the U.S. Labor Department. Some argue that this pay gap has less to do with technology than with industries' efforts to streamline their workforces during the recession. Still, nearly every American business from Wall Street to McDonald's requires some computer knowledge. Taco Bell is modeling its cash registers after Nintendo controls, according to Rosabeth Moss Kanter. The "haves," says the Harvard Business School professor, will be able to communicate around the globe. The "have-nots" will be consigned to the "rural backwater of the information society."

Like it or not, America is a land of inequities. And technology, despite its potential to level the social landscape, is not yet blind to race, wealth, and age. The richer the family, the more likely it is to own and use a computer, according to 1993 census data. White families are three times as likely as blacks or Hispanics to have computers at home. Seventy-four percent of Americans making more than $75,000 own at least one terminal, but not even one third of all Americans own computers. A small fraction—only about 7 percent—of students' families subscribe to online services that transform the plastic terminal into a telecommunications port.

At least in public schools, the computer gap is closing. More than half the students have some kind of computer, even if it's obsolete. But schools with the biggest concentration of poor children have the least equipment, according to Jeanne Hayes of Quality Education Data. Ten years ago schools had one computer for every 125 children, according to Hayes. Today the figure is one for twelve.

Though the gap is slowly closing, technology is advancing so fast, and at such huge costs, that it's nearly impossible for cash-strapped municipalities to catch up. Seattle is taking bids for one company to wire each ZIP code with fiber optics, so everyone—rich or poor—can hook up to video, audio, and other multimedia services. Estimated cost: $500 million. Prosperous Montgomery County, Maryland, has an $81 million plan to put every classroom online. Next door, the District of Columbia public schools have the same ambitious plan but less than $1 million in the budget to accomplish it.

New ideas—and demands—for the schools are announced every week. The Nineties populist slogan is no longer "A chicken in every pot" but "A computer on every desk." Vice President Al Gore has appealed to the telecommunications industry to cut costs and wire all schools, a task Education Secretary Richard Riley estimates will cost $10 billion. House Speaker Newt Gingrich stumbled into the discussion with a suggestion that every poor family get a laptop from Uncle Sam. Representative Ed Markey wants a computer sitting on every school desk within ten years. "The opportunities are enormous," Markey says.

Enormous, yes, but who is going to pay for them? Some successful school projects have relied heavily on the kindness of strangers. In Union City,

New Jersey, school officials renovated the guts of a one hundred-year-old building five years ago, overhauling the curriculum and wiring every classroom in Christopher Columbus Middle School for high tech. Bell Atlantic provided wiring free and agreed to give each student in last year's seventh-grade class a computer to take home. Even parents, most of whom are South American immigrants, can use their children's computers to e-mail the principal in Spanish. He uses translation software and answers them electronically. The results have shown up in test scores. In a school where 80 percent of the children are poor, reading, math, attendance, and writing scores are now the best in the district. "We believe that technology will improve our everyday life," says principal Bob Fazio. "And that other schools will piggyback and learn from us."

Still, for every Christopher Columbus, there are far more schools like Jordan High School in South Central Los Angeles. Only thirty computers in the school's lab, most of them twelve to fifteen years old, are available for Jordan's two thousand students, many of whom live in the nearby Jordan Downs housing project. "I am teaching these kids on a system that will do them no good in the real world when they get out there," says Robert Doornbos, Jordan's computer-science instructor. "The school system has not made these kids' getting on the Information Highway a priority."

DONKEY KONG

Having enough terminals to go around is one problem. But another important question is what the equipment is used for. Not much beyond rote drills and word processing, according to Linda Roberts, a technology consultant for the U.S. Department of Education. A 1992 National Assessment of Education Progress survey found that most fourth-grade math students were using computers to play games, "like Donkey Kong." By the eighth grade, most math students weren't using them at all.

Many school officials think that access to the Internet could become the most effective equalizer in the educational lives of students. With a modem attached, even most ancient terminals can connect children in rural Mississippi to universities in Asia. A Department of Education report released [in February 1995] found that 35 percent of schools have at least one computer with a modem. But only half the schools let students use it. Apparently administrators and teachers are hogging the Info Highway for themselves.

There is another gap to be considered. Not just between rich and poor, but between the young and the used-to-be-young. Of the one hundred million Americans who use computers at home, school, or work, nearly 60 percent are seventeen or younger, according to the census. Children, for the most part, rule cyberspace, leaving the over-forty set to browse through the almanac.

The gap between the generations may be the most important, says MIT guru Nicholas Negroponte, author of the new book *Being Digital*. Adults are the true "digitally homeless, the needy," he says. In other words, adults like

Debbie Needleman, forty-three, an office manager at Wallpaper Warehouse in Natick, Massachusetts, are wary of the digital age. "I really don't mind that the rest of the world passes me by as long as I can still earn a living," she says.

These aging choose-nots become a more serious issue when they are teachers in schools. Even if schools manage to acquire state-of-the-art equipment, there is no guarantee that trained adults will be available to understand them. This is something that tries Aaron Smith's patience. "A lot of my teachers are quite illiterate," says Aaron, the fully equipped Issaqua teenager. "You have to explain it to them real slow to make sure they understand everything." Fast or slow, Marilee Colon, Roxbury's fifth-grade computer lover, would like her chance to understand everything too.

DISCUSSION QUESTIONS

1. Do you think there is a significant gap based on race, age, or income between those with computers and those without?
2. What do you think about the goal to wire all the public schools in the United States by the year 2000?
3. In your opinion, how important will computer skills be in the future with respect to life at home and at work?

BIGOTS ON THE NET

Amy Harmon

■

Alarmed by the growing presence of hate groups in cyberspace, the Simon Wiesenthal Center[1] Tuesday sent a letter to the Prodigy online computer service protesting the "continued use of Prodigy by bigots to promote their agendas of hate."

The Los Angeles–based center said it has tracked increasing activity over the last few months by more than fifty hate groups using online services and the popular Internet global computer network. "More and more of these groups are embracing and utilizing the information superhighway," said Rabbi Abraham Cooper, associate dean of the center. "The slurs are the same but the venue is different."

The center called on commercial online services to keep hate groups out and proposed that the government play a similar policing role on the amorphous Internet. Of particular concern, Cooper said, is that young people could be exposed to white supremacy in an environment unmediated by teachers, parents, or librarians. Much of the activity takes place on open electronic forums accessible to anyone with an Internet account or a subscription to a commercial service.

About twenty million computer users are connected to the Internet, and another five million use commercial online services, including more than two million on Prodigy.

---

[1]Simon Wiesenthal Center: Founded in 1978, the Simon Wiesenthal Center educates today's generation about the Holocaust, and fights the hatred and prejudice that enabled the Holocaust to occur.—Ed.

But civil libertarians—and white supremacists themselves—say that cyberspace, like any other medium of expression, must remain open to free speech. And in an uncharted territory where the rules of engagement are still unformed, the center's offensive is sure to sharpen the ongoing debate over electronic censorship.

"It's a genuinely difficult problem," says Marc Rotenberg, director of the Electronic Privacy Information Center, an online civil liberties organization. "And there are no paradigms to turn to."

It's a problem that is quickly becoming relevant to a lot more people. All sorts of enterprises, from businesses to charity organizations, have been rushing to get hooked up to computer networks, which offer fast, convenient communication at increasingly lower prices.

But for white supremacist groups like the National Alliance and the American Renaissance, cyberspace offers benefits that are proportionately far greater.

Marginalized by traditional media and short on funds, hate groups have been learning to use low-cost online communications to gain recruits and spread propaganda across state and even national boundaries, giving them access to a far wider audience than they have historically been able to reach.

Valerie Fields, for example, a West Los Angeles resident and political junkie, signs on to her Prodigy account a few times a week to read the discussion of local politics. Last month, she clicked her way into the "News" forum to find an anti-Latino diatribe that closed with a plug for a $20 subscription to the newsletter of Louisville, Kentucky–based American Renaissance.

"Around the election the messages about [Proposition] 187[2] got pretty nasty," Fields said. "But then I saw this one that seemed to be from an organized white supremacist group, and that really freaked me out."

The message Fields saw, and several others, including one that referred to *The Diary of Anne Frank* as a "Jewish hoax" prompted the Wiesenthal Center to ask Prodigy to strengthen its guidelines to delete such messages from its boards.

"We're having a discussion with them," Prodigy spokesman Brian Ek said Tuesday afternoon. "Our feeling is we already have a good system in place. But we have more than 1.7 million notes on the board at any given time, and we can't read them all."

Prodigy was the focus of controversy involving antisemitic comments in 1991, and worked with the Anti-Defamation League at the time to craft a policy that forbids "blatant expressions of hatred" on its boards. All messages are also run through a computer that scans for obscenities before they are posted. But Cooper says the service should look more carefully at messages that target groups rather than individuals.

Prodigy is not the only online service to be utilized by hate groups.

---

[2]Proposition 187: A controversial California ballot measure that denied schooling, medical care, and other governmental services to illegal immigrants.—Ed.

Kevin Strom, who produces a weekly radio show for the National Alliance, and has been active online, said he was recently blocked from the "Political" and "Issues" forums on CompuServe.

"Apparently somebody complained that our articles were bashing ethnic minorities," Strom says. "So the system operator decided we didn't deserve freedom of speech."

Strom says the articles he posted on the forums were among those which users transferred most frequently to their home computers. One titled "The Wisdom of Henry Ford," which reviewed the book *The International Jew*, was downloaded 120 times one week, he said.

CompuServe leaves the decision of what to screen out to the individual "sysops" who are hired to moderate the service's discussion forums. Says Georgia Griffith, the Politics sysop: "We don't block users for what they believe or say, but how they say it. The First Amendment allows people to publish what they choose, but we are not obliged to publish it for them."

The legal issue of who is ultimately responsible for what does get "published" online is a thorny one that has yet to be entirely resolved.

A federal judge ruled in 1991 that CompuServe was like a bookstore owner who could not be held accountable for the contents of books on his shelves—a precedent the online services support.

But activists say there are ethical issues at stake, which public opinion can help to enforce—at least in the private sector.

The Internet, a Web of several hundred computer networks not owned by any one enterprise, is a more difficult proposition. Cooper wrote a letter to Federal Communications Chairman Reed E. Hundt last summer suggesting that it "may be time for the FCC to place a cop on the Superhighway of Information."

But such an effort would involve significant technical difficulties, and would also likely encounter vehement opposition from civil liberties groups who want to preserve the Internet as a democratic forum.

Because of its anarchic structure, the Internet has generally been viewed as a "common carrier" much like the telephone company, which cannot be held liable for what passes over its lines.

"That would be a very dangerous path to go down," says EPIC's Rotenberg. "It would lead to an extraordinary amount of censorship and control that would be very inappropriate."

Discussion groups geared toward white supremacist propaganda on the Internet have labels such as "skinheads," "revisionism" and "vigilantes." The Institute for Historical Review recently set up a site on the World Wide Web portion of the Internet, where some of its literature can be obtained for free. A document called "Frequently Asked Questions about National Socialism" is available at several sites.

The computer commands used on the Internet also allow users to access information anonymously, which far-right activists say helps many to overcome the inhibitions they might have about signing up.

The National Alliance rents space on a computer at Netcom Online Communication Services, one of the largest Internet access providers in California, where texts of its radio programs are available. It has also posted flyers on the Internet promoting its radio show, urging readers to send "minority parasites packing to fend for themselves" and condemning community development funding as support for black "breeding colonies."

"We've seen a huge growth in use of the Internet by our people," says Alliance Chairman William Pierce. "The major media in this country are very biased against our political point of view. They present us with ridicule or in a very distorted way. The information superhighway is much more free of censorship. It's possible for a dedicated individual to get his message out to thousands and thousands of people."

DISCUSSION QUESTIONS

1. Should hate groups' use of the media be restricted?
2. Why do you think hate groups use the Internet to spread their message?
3. Should prejudiced propaganda be prohibited from the Internet?

CHAPTER 3

RADIO AND TELEVISION

William B. Falk, *Louder and Louder: A Look at How Talk Radio Has Elbowed Its Way into Media Prominence*
Andrew Heyward, *What We Are Doing Wrong*
Joel Brinkley, *Who Will Build Your Next Television?*

W hen radio first appeared, pundits predicted that newspapers would die. When television appeared, radio and newspapers were predicted to die. When FM radio appeared, AM radio was predicted to die. Technological innovation clearly affects old media, but most news and information outlets adapt. Those that do not adapt—like the afternoon newspaper—usually do die.

Today, AM talk radio permeates the political scene. Rush Limbaugh commands an audience of millions of listeners each day—more listeners than readers of the *New York Times* and more people than those who subscribe each week to *Time* magazine. The first reading in this chapter, by William B. Falk, analyzes the power of talk radio. Falk contends that whether you support or oppose the views of radio talk-show hosts, they command an expanding role in the marketplace of ideas.

In the second reading, CBS President Andrew Heyward tries to determine why people are turning away from network television news. He believes that for the most part, television has not paid attention to its viewers, and more and more of them are turning to the Internet for information and entertainment.

In the third reading, author Joel Brinkley outlines the battle for your eyes between the computer and electronic industry. Are you going to be viewing a computer, a television, or a teleputer? It's a battle worth more than $150 billion for the winner.

LOUDER AND LOUDER: A LOOK AT HOW TALK RADIO HAS ELBOWED ITS WAY INTO MEDIA PROMINENCE

William B. Falk

■

. . . Just 15 years ago, only 82 radio stations waved the all-talk banner, and most of these were in major cities. By 1990, there were 426. Today, there are 1,308, according to the *M Street Journal*, a trade publication. Another 20 stations are converting to talk every month. Talk has become the fastest-growing format in radio, having surpassed all but country music in the number of stations. Half of all American adults, *Talkers Magazine* says, listen to at least one hour of talk radio every week.

Why is the ether so full of yak? Talk burst out of its narrow radio niche in the late 1980s as a result of a confluence of technological, economic and demographic changes.

Halfway through the last decade, it became possible to syndicate talk shows via satellite instead of through cumbersome, telephone-line hookups. The syndicated shows, which small stations could pull off the satellite for free in return for airing the shows' commercials, made it economically feasible for the stations to hire one or two hosts of their own and switch to talk. "Before syndication, talk was a high-budget format," says Randall Bloomquist, news/talk editor of *Radio and Records*, a trade journal. "Suddenly, you could do talk in Tupelo."

Rush Limbaugh rode syndication as if it were a flood tide. When he began offering his show nationally, in 1988, he struck several chords simultaneously, tapping middle-class resentment of Washington, welfare recipients, feminists and environmentalists with humor and bombast that listeners found entertaining. By 1990, he was on 200 stations. Today, he's on 660. "Limbaugh really fueled the renaissance of talk radio," says Tom Taylor, editor of *Inside Radio*, a trade publication. "He showed that a serious talk show can be entertaining."

Simultaneously, a whole new segment of the population was lending its collective ear to radio talk. "Baby boomers got older, and they were less interested in music and more interested in politics and in their community," says Michael Harrison, publisher of *Talkers Magazine*, a trade journal. "At the same time, our society has gotten colder, and people are more isolated. Talk radio is personal. It's emotional. It makes people feel connected."

Talk, in the 1990s, flourished in parts of the country that never before had heard all-day call-in shows. In cities such as New York, which got its first all-talk station in 1964, talk grabbed unprecedented shares of the audience. Take, for example, the morning talk shows, which keep us company in the car and in the kitchen. Every week, Arbitron says, 2.8 million people in the New York metropolitan area tune in to the four most popular morning talk shows—(Howard) Stern on WXRK/92.3 FM (a 7.5 share of the audience in Arbitron's winter ratings), WOR's John Gambling (a 4.0), WFAN's Imus (a 3.6) and WABC's Lionel (a 3.3). Almost one in five radio listeners dial up one of those shows every day.

. . ."Talk radio," Harrison argues, "is the most accurate bellwether of what Americans think. If on any given day you listen to talk radio—not one host, not one station, but a spectrum of talk radio—you will know what Americans are thinking and what they're talking about."

It's a debatable point. Surveys have found that only 2 or 3 percent of all listeners actually call talk shows, and people in the industry say callers are often people who are obsessed with one subject or another. "There is a group of professional callers who call all the time," Lionel says. "You come to recognize them."

Most of the shows have an identifiable political bias, established by the hosts. Industry surveys show that about 70 percent of the talk hosts lean to the right. The reason for talk's conservative character is hotly debated within the industry. Some say it's simply a product of unimaginative station managers trying to duplicate Limbaugh's popularity. "There are literally two hundred guys out there trying to be the local Rush," Bloomquist says.

Others contend there are fewer liberals on the air because they are, by nature, boring. Liberals are for things, conservatives are against them, and it's a lot more fun to be in the opposition, this argument goes. If you don't kick around Hillary Clinton, tree-huggers and feminists, how can you be entertaining? "You have to get people stirred up," Taylor of *Inside Radio* says. "You have to connect with their emotions. Liberals and moderates just don't like to mock people."

While there's probably some truth in both theories, the most compelling explanation for the conservative bent is simply that talk, in the post-TV era, has evolved as an anti-media medium. "People gravitate to talk radio because they're not satisfied with what they see on network TV or from mainstream newspapers," Kurtz says.

Callers to talk shows, he points out, constantly complain that the networks and the media are rotten with liberal bias. They tend to view talk shows as *Radio Free America*, where hosts like (Bob) Grant and (G. Gordon) Liddy—and their callers—can say the unspeakable. "There could never be a liberal who's as supersuccessful as Limbaugh," Kurtz says. "I don't think there is a comparable hunger among liberals for an alternative source of information."

Talk show listeners do, apparently, rely on their favorite hosts for information. A 1993 Times Mirror survey found that an amazing 43 percent of the people polled identified talk radio as their primary source of news. And a 1996 study by the Interep Radio Store, a research organization, found that conservative talk hosts, by and large, preach to a choir of fellow believers: 82 percent of the people who listen to all-talk radio said they tune in to particular hosts because they liked "the opinions or knowledge provided."

In providing opinions and "knowledge," of course, talk show hosts of all political persuasions often toss in a sizable dollop of hyperbole. Even Grant has admitted as much off the air, complaining after his . . . firing that people often laugh off the outrageous remarks of "shock jocks" like Stern and Imus. "Unfortunately, they took me seriously," Grant said.

Does that mean that Grant and Limbaugh and Stern—and the rare liberal such as . . . Lynn Samuels—sometimes act outraged for the sake of ratings?

You betcha.

"The host has to establish a polarity," says Walter Sabo, a former vice president and general manager of the ABC radio networks, who since 1984 has served as an independent consultant to talk stations across the country. "Listeners think the hosts believe every word, but they don't. It's like a bullfight. People come to see the swirl of the cape, the blood, the drama. A good bullfighter doesn't just go in and kill the bull."

DISCUSSION QUESTIONS

1. Listen to a talk radio program. How does the program differ from a radio news program?
2. What impact do you think talk radio has had on contemporary politics?
3. Do you think that talk radio has a positive or negative impact on society? Why?

WHAT WE ARE DOING WRONG

Andrew Heyward

■

P eople are . . . doing other things with their time. The Pew study suggested that rising use of personal computers is partly to blame for the decline in news viewing. And the reason cited most often—especially by young people—for not watching the news: no time, they're too busy.

But I think we contribute to the problem too, every day, in ways we're not even aware of. How? Well funny you should ask, because I happen to have a list here of what I call the Seven Daily Sins.

The First Daily Sin is imitation.

Fred Allen said it: Imitation is the sincerest form of television. But still: How can the network evening news programs be so *similar*? Adam Smith—the real one, not the guy on PBS—must be spinning in his grave, and would certainly be spinning the dial if he were around today. We're in a commercial, highly competitive struggle for viewers, and yet our solution for standing out in the marketplace is—do just what the competition is doing.

Oh I know my colleagues back at CBS will be mad at me for saying this—and of course on any given night any given broadcast might feature reporters and reporting that stand out. Each of the networks takes justifiable pride in the care that goes into the craft.

But think about it from the viewers' perspective. If you could watch only one network for a year, and your neighbor another, how different would the experience be?

And listen to this: Our research shows that half the viewers of any given evening news broadcast—on CBS, NBC or ABC—*half* the viewers—only watch that particular program *one night a week*. The implication is obvious: To these viewers, it doesn't make much of a difference which one they watch—or whether they watch at all.

No one will ever admit it, but on too many nights network news producers judge themselves by how *similar* they are to the competition, as if that were somehow a reassuring sign that our collective news judgment is valid. Imitation is comfy and cozy—it's harder to second guess than originality, I suppose. But in the audience, similarity breeds contempt.

The Second Daily Sin is predictability.

How often are you *surprised* by something you see on the news? We are trapped in our formulas, both for story selection and production. Again, we are afraid to try something new, to move away from what we know how to do. And the result is too often competent but not compelling.

Take the 1:30 news piece—now the universal standard around the world. Think about how much effort goes into slicing and dicing the news we've gathered so we can throw everything into that same recipe . . . and you'll realize why the ingredients have no taste when we're done with them.

No wonder most of the people we interview appear as stick figures or stereotypes: the politician, the expert, the victim, the eyewitness. "It sounded like a freight train." And like a freight train, most of what I see on the news, I can see coming a mile away.

The Third Daily Sin is artificiality.

If we're supposed to reflect and report on reality, why are we so unreal ourselves?

If you stop and really listen to how a typical television reporter tells a story, you'll hear how artificial it sounds. There's an unnatural emphasis, a strange inflection to the words and sentences. Even *words*—"pontiff" comes quickly to mind—that you never hear in real life. Nobody talks that way—except for us.

We also bleach the personality out of our newscasts, especially at the network level. Just for example: How often do your reporters' questions make the final cut? On our hard news broadcasts, almost never. Takes too much time. Yet that's the one chance the reporter has to engage in a normal conversation, as opposed to narration followed by that equally unnatural phenomenon, the soundbite. Somehow there's a fear of reminding the audience that a *real person* is telling the story, as if somehow that would get in the way of so-called objectivity. Baloney.

And I know there's a temptation to put attractive people on television, but I think the audience has to perceive them as authentic. We managers hire the same faces and voices again and again, without paying enough attention to whether they are real reporters who understand and believe what they're saying. Take Edward R. Murrow—thought I'd never get to him, eh? He had to fight to hire William Shirer, the first of the "Murrow boys," because Shirer had a high-pitched voice rather than the authoritative, announcerish voice of a radio host. But Murrow prevailed, and Shirer became one of the great pioneers of broadcast journalism.

And I think the great broadcasters have that quality of authenticity. It's a quality you can't manufacture or fake, but if you find it, treasure it.

The Fourth Daily Sin is laziness. (Come to think of it, that's one of the *deadly* sins too.)

The people I work with put in long hours and are very devoted to their jobs. They're certainly not lazy in the conventional sense. But I think we've all become lazy in our thinking, in our reluctance to dig out original stories and come up with new ways to tell them.

Critics of local news who single out excessive crime and fire coverage often miss the point. They think it's because those stories are sensational. In fact, many crime and fire stories are singularly dull and irrelevant to most viewers' lives. They're just *easy* compared to original reporting.

The same goes for network news. It's a lot easier to round up the usual soundbites and "cover" an incremental development on Capitol Hill or at the White House, than it is to explain how policy made in Washington genuinely affects Americans outside the Beltway.

This is not just a matter of economics, either. Yes, investigative reporting is more expensive than covering an event off the daybook. But *original* reporting is often just a matter of a few more phone calls, of demanding that our producers and reporters go beyond the obvious.

If network news sometimes seems as irrelevant as a fire or murder in somebody else's neighborhood, I think laziness is at least partly to blame.

The Fifth Daily Sin is oversimplification.

That might sound like a strange one. Yes, it's true that our job is to clarify events and issues for our viewers and listeners. And in a one-pass-through medium like broadcast journalism, complexity is particularly scary.

But our audience is smarter and more thoughtful than a lot of us think. The people out there in America know that life is not as simple as what they see on the news: a world of heroes and villains, winners and losers, exploiters and victims. Yet that's what we show them, night after night.

We reduce complicated debates over policy to political slugfests, which we cover as though they were sporting events. We reduce difficult issues to simple dramas—like the current concern over downsizing, which too often shows up on network television as a morality tale pitting evil employers against downtrodden workers. (Harry Smith's recent documentary on this subject was a refreshing exception—please pardon the plug.)

But the world is a complicated place—and the people we're serving know it. There are no easy answers, and we hurt ourselves and drive viewers and listeners away by pretending there are. Most TV sets aren't black and white any more; we're behind the times.

The Sixth Daily Sin is hype.

When I told you before this would be the best Edward R. Murrow address ever, you knew I was kidding. (If you didn't then, you certainly do now.) But think about the ridiculous claims we make all the time—expecting them to be taken seriously. Can you remember the last "story you'll never forget?" How about the one before that? I can't. Barbara Walters refuses to use the word "shocking" in her copy anymore. Good for you, Barbara.

And how about "exclusive?" Soon we'll be pasting the word "exclusive" over Dan, Peter and Tom as they read the news: no one else has HIM, after all.

I don't want to sound naive. I know it's competitive out there, and I know we have to corral and keep viewers. Some of my own fondest memories are of writing teases for the 11 o'clock news.

But curiously, hype has the opposite effect. If everything is momentous, nothing stands out. And if you have to trumpet your wares loudly every day, you need an endless supply of "new" wares to get excited about. That's one reason we do so little follow-up and don't always stick with a good story: It's harder to sell the next day and the next.

Over the years we've exaggerated so much that we've eroded our own ability to convey what's truly significant. I think that's one reason the network news divisions failed to generate much excitement when the Berlin Wall came tumbling down. Here was a perfect television story that also happened to be one of the most significant developments since the Second World War. *Prime Time Live was* live as the wall was "liberated." But to the audience, it was just today's top story . . . just television.

Ironically, despite the hype, the news seems *smaller* since Murrow's day. We've cut and cropped it down to size to fit our little box.

Which brings me to the Seventh Daily Sin. Cynicism.

I think we're cynical about the audience and cynical about our ability to make a difference in people's lives.

All the other daily sins—imitation, predictability, artificiality, laziness, oversimplification and hype—are a reflection of this one.

Yet now more than ever, ours is a business for idealists, for true believers, not cynics. It's become a cliché to say that America is hungry for heroes. Because it's true. Murrow was a hero in his day, not just a star. Journalists today are held in low esteem, but that doesn't have to be. Our viewers and listeners are also hungry for honest information, for help in coping with a bewildering world. We have an enormous opportunity to win our good name back—and ensure our own survival in the bargain.

The transformation of broadcast journalism from a calling and a public service to a profit-making business has been chronicled too many times to warrant repetition here. You all know the story. We all live the story, every day.

. . . So the solution is obvious: Identify a need and become one of the few who can satisfy it. That sounds like a pretty good *business* proposition to me.

DISCUSSION QUESTIONS

1. Watch two television news programs and take notes on them. What stories or aspects of these programs interested you?
2. What do you think television news does well? What does it do poorly?
3. In your opinion, which of these news media has the highest credibility: newspapers, local television, or network television? Why?

WHO WILL BUILD YOUR NEXT TELEVISION?

Joel Brinkley

■

I t's a commercial bonanza with few precedents in American business history: Starting next year, consumers will have to replace every one of their televisions with new digital models—as many as 230 million new sets that could cost $150 billion over the next decade.

Two powerful industries have very different visions of what these new TVs will be. The computer industry wants to muscle its way into the television market and believes the digital capabilities of the new TVs will open the door. Big-screen "PC theater" products, due to go on sale during the next few months, will offer both traditional TV programming and computer functions in the same unit. Starting next year, every PC sold in this country—15 million or more each year—will include a digital television receiver.

The television-manufacturing industry has its own plans to offer digital sets next year that are designed to receive the crystal-clear, high-definition programming and CD-quality sound that TV stations expect to have ready about the same time. Television makers say that by 2002 or 2003 they hope to be selling 1 million digital sets a year, although few are likely to offer Internet access or other computer functions.

Computer executives insist that the game will already be over by then. "By 2003, we'll already have between 20 million and 50 million 'sets' in people's homes," said Robert Stearns, a senior vice president for the Compaq Computer Corp., the world's largest maker of personal computers. "What we're trying to say" to the broadcasters and consumer electronics manufacturers "is that if you don't listen, you're going to be a buggy whip."

But Carl Yankowski, the president of Sony Electronics Inc., an American unit of the Sony Corp., noted that 99 percent of American homes own at least one TV. "And after 15 years," Yankowski said, "the computer industry has

45

achieved penetration into only about 35 percent of American homes. I would call that a failed product launch."

Such are the opening volleys in what promises to be a bruising commercial battle. The computer industry believes that Americans are no longer interested in simply watching television. Instead, computer executives say, most consumers will want to supplement traditional television with browsing the World Wide Web and other forms of interactive entertainment, like e-mail, on-line computer games, and other advanced digital services only being imagined now.

The computer and consumer-electronics industries have each already put a product on the market that tests the public's appetite for interactive television. So far, however, neither has been a rousing success.

A year ago, Gateway 2000 Inc., the personal computer manufacturer, began selling Destination—a big-screen computer-television designed for the family room and aimed at people who already owned a home PC. By most accounts, sales have been lackluster. Stacy Hand, Destination product manager for Gateway, said public expectations were too high, adding, "We spent 1996 educating the market." Last fall, meanwhile, the consumer electronics industry began selling Web TV boxes that allow consumers to browse the Web on conventional televisions. This product is aimed at the estimated 65 percent of households that do not yet have computers.

But retailers have reported that Web TV sales have been disappointing, too. "It has taken a long time to get retailers to a point where they are really demonstrating the product properly," said James Bonan, a vice president for new business development at Sony, one of the manufacturers.

Computer manufacturers say they are not disheartened by their early experiments. Though most are not yet ready to say what their computer-TVs will cost, they say that the merger of the two technologies will be much easier when digital television comes along. At that point everything piped onto the picture tube—whether a movie or a Web page—will be transmitted in a format corresponding to the 1's and 0's of computer code.

"We think it is much easier to have a PC do television than to add personal computing capabilities to TVs," said Rob Siegal, a program manager at Intel, who designed the prototype PC theater that the company is now testing. But for the industry's strategy to work, Siegel added: "The PC has just got to migrate from the home office to the family room."

Television manufacturers have a different vision: They think consumers are most interested in picture quality and cost. They plan to put their new high-definition TV sets on sale in time for Christmas 1998. The first ones are expected to cost at least $2,000.

"At present we are not planning to put any intelligence capabilities in our digital TV," said Richard Kraft, president of the Matsushita Electric Corp. of America, a subsidiary of the Matsushita Electric Industrial Co. in Japan, which makes Panasonic and Quasar televisions.

"We don't believe in this 'convergence' everyone is talking about," Kraft said. "I think people will buy these TVs for entertainment—a great high-definition picture on a big screen."

The television industry contends that computers are too finicky and complex for most Americans, and so few people will want to buy a computer-TV. "One of the reasons we are ubiquitous in American homes is that TVs are simple and easy to use," Yankowski of Sony said. "I think we are more sensitive to that than they are on the computer side."

But computer makers say television manufacturers have fallen behind the times. "What's the biggest innovation of the last 20 years in the TV industry?" asked Steve Goldberg, who manages the digital-television marketing program at Compaq Computer. "The remote control."

Computer executives insist that the new PCs—based in the family room instead of the den—will be easier to use than conventional computers. They also contend that while most people will still use a desk-top machine for pure computing functions, they will use the PC theaters to view movies, sports and prime-time TV fare, and also browse the Web or play interactive games, among other computer-based functions.

An agreement announced yesterday, in fact, could advance that vision. Compaq and the Intel Corp. said that they had reached agreement with the major TV makers to devise common standards for plugging movie players, CD jukeboxes, VCRs, and other devices into PC theaters.

The computer executives are not saying yet whether these sets will be able to offer the full, high-definition programming the broadcasting industry is promising. Still, Goldberg said: "Digital TV will allow us to deliver more than just a passive viewing experience. We know people are also going to want an information-rich, interactive experience."

When people spoke of interactive television a few years ago, the notion was a sort of cable TV on steroids, offering on-line shopping and pay-per-view movies. But that approach proved prohibitively expensive, and, in the end, interactive cable TV never caught on.

These days, though, most of the effort is aimed at linking television to the World Wide Web. The Web, computer executives say, is evolving rapidly and will someday rival television as a source of live-action video. (For now, though, downloading even a short video clip over the Web can take several minutes.)

With that future in mind, Compaq plans to put a big-screen PC theater on the market in the next few months. Company officials say it will combine a conventional TV with a full-feature computer. Later generations of the product will include a digital television.

Compaq also plans to offer a cheaper version sometime in the next year. It will be a device "that looks and acts pretty much like today's TV sets," Stearns said, "and even costs the same, with prices starting at about $500—except that it's digital and interactive."

Compaq officials cite census figures indicating that nearly every American child is being exposed to computers at school, creating what the company assumes will be a market for computer-TVs when they become consumers. And Compaq said that while only about 12 percent of Americans now have regular access to the Internet, that number is growing and people are spending longer periods of time on the World Wide Web. At the same time, Nielsen ratings indicate that people are spending less time watching television. "Most on-line activity in U.S. households is taking place between 7 P.M. and 10 P.M.—right in the middle of prime-time TV programming," Stearns said.

Still, until the Internet is able to compete with television, Compaq and the other computer companies are dependent on broadcasters to provide new types of programming and related digital services. Otherwise, the new hardware may allow little beyond surfing the Web or reading e-mail on a very large screen.

"They are not open to some of the things we are trying to discuss with them," Stearns said of his discussions with the television networks. "In fact they are absolutely resistant. If they don't wake up, five years from now people will get their video content from the Internet, and ABC, CBS, NBC, and Fox will be relegated to obscure Web pages."

Network officials, for their part, say they may offer unspecified, advanced digital services—someday. But for now they say they are concentrating on the very large task of getting digital, high-definition programming on the air.

Some television makers said that they might experiment with offering Internet access or other interactive features. Anything more, in their view, risks raising their costs by including options most consumers will not want.

"I'm not 100 percent convinced that interactivity is going to be the service that drives this product," said Jim Meyer, executive vice president at Thomson Consumer Electronics Inc., maker of the RCA and Proscan brands. His company, the largest television maker in the United States, sells 6 million sets a year, and "we are selling to people in Wichita, Kan., and Gary, Ind. Interactivity may sell in Silicon Valley," he said. "But will it sell in Gary? I don't know."

DISCUSSION QUESTIONS
1. What do you see as the differences between a television set and a computer?
2. What, if any, differences exist between how you use a television and how you use a computer?
3. Do you think it's a good idea or a bad idea to combine the television set and the computer? Why?

CHAPTER 4

MUSIC

John Pareles, *Talkin' 'Bout Two Generations—at Odds*
Phil Patton, *Who Owns the Blues?*
Monica Fountain, *Tucker Battles against Lyrics of Gangsta Rap*

Afew years ago, I played in a rock-and-roll band, who performed what has since become known as garage-band music, made famous by Hootie and the Blowfish. Almost every generation has its own brand of music—a distinctive style for each generation: from Lawrence Welk to Elvis Presley, Perry Como to Jim Morrison, Abba to Tupac Shakur. Accordingly, as a teenager, I realized that there was no way I could make my parents understand the Beatles, the Rolling Stones, and the Doors.

Music has played a significant role in many societies throughout the world. Giuseppe Verdi's opera *Aida* had its world premiere in Cairo, Egypt, on December 24, 1871, to commemorate the opening of the Suez Canal. The canal had been finished two years earlier, but it took Verdi a bit longer to finish the opera. Sometimes the role of music can be taken for granted. For example, Wolfgang Mozart, one of the greatest composers in history, had a small following when he was alive. Some critics considered *The Magic Flute* vulgar because it was intended to reach the mass audiences of the beer halls rather than the social elite of Vienna.

In this chapter, the first reading attempts to analyze the musical gap between the baby boomers and the current generation. The second reading looks at the historic roots of the blues, perhaps the only indigenous American music. Finally, the third reading looks at the role of one individual's fight against gangsta rap.

Talkin' 'Bout Two Generations —At Odds

John Pareles

■

Baby boomers used to be smug about rock music. In our great numbers and concomitant wisdom, we had of course invented youth, rebellion, idealism, sex, recreational drug use and the music that went with all of it. Like pop consumers before us, we found songs that summed up our longings and our resentments. But we were sure that those songs weren't just entertainment; they were the foundation of a new culture, a counterculture. And we decided that the musicians we listened to were exalted creatures. They were no longer mere performers but artists, perhaps even shamans, leading a revolution in consciousness.

But it has been a long time since boomers were in the vanguard. A majority of boomers, who once defined themselves as the youth in youth culture, have found themselves on the other side of a rock generation gap, wondering how kids can listen to that godawful racket and why they have such weird haircuts. They hear singers who bawl constantly, lyricists who use profanities as punctuation, guitarists who spew noise, hip-hop tracks built on sonic irritants. They also hear young musicians recycling things they can't improve, like Oasis trying to be cooler than the Beatles or R. Kelly trying to approach the suavity of Marvin Gaye.

Boomers are smug again this week. Hootie and the Blowfish tops the charts with tunes that hark back to Bob Dylan and the Allman Brothers; folk-rock is thriving as it enters its third decade. See, the boomers insist, younger bands can't top us. But we're just seeing a lull after 20 years of generational battle.

It didn't take long for younger generations to get sick of boomer narcissism. In the late 1970's, punks started sneering at superannuated hippies (although they borrowed the power chords and equipment-smashing of 1960's groups like the Who and the Stooges). Meanwhile, the disk jockeys and rappers of hip-hop ignored boomer precedent and made their own musical break-throughs. Where boomers had trumpeted their artistic freedom, younger listeners often heard pretension, self-indulgence and complacency: music with a paunch. And even now, when boomers prattle about their golden age of rock, the next generation often sees what boomers saw in their parents' musical taste: a pitiable nostalgia.

The hallowed 1960's produced extraordinary music, some of it ground-breaking, but more of it following through on the innovations of 1950's rock-and-roll and rhythm-and-blues. It was a time of fusions: Bob Dylan grafted Rimbaud onto the blues, the Beatles melded Little Richard and English music-hall pop. The most decisive change in the 1960's was that pop musicians seized control of their own repertories from Tin Pan Alley professionals, but they were preceded by performers from Louis Jordan to Buddy Holly. There was no clear break with the past as there was between big-band pop and guitar-driven rock.

The amateurism of 60's rockers sometimes yielded raw genius, sometimes just clumsiness. Younger listeners who investigate the canon of boomer favorites can hear limp rhythm sections, uncertain vocals and weak imitations of blues, gospel and country originals. Only 1960's soul consistently maintained high technical standards and made musical leaps, like the rhythmic revelations of James Brown.

Nowadays, a few younger fans may join the boomers as they turn out one more time to hear the Rolling Stones or Crosby, Stills and Nash crank out the oldies; some are full-fledged aficionados, others curious to see what the legend was about, the way boomers might attend Frank Sinatra shows. Young fans also sustained the Grateful Dead through the 1980's and early 1990's, treating the band's shows as visits to a hedonistic fantasyland, a 1960's theme park. While young listeners don't entirely reject the styles of their elders, the reverse is comparatively rare; far fewer boomers show up to hear the Smashing Pumpkins or the Fugees, if they even know who they are. It takes a Hootie, playing retreads of fondly remembered songs, to bring boomers out in force.

A generation that once prided itself on its adventurousness has been pegged by the music business as people who now want to hear nice, restrained music. Adult Alternative Album radio, playing new releases for boomers, restricts itself to sincere guitar strummers, promoting either familiar names like Sting and Tom Petty or people who work in familiar styles, like Son Volt's country-rock or the Cowboy Junkies' languid folk-rock.

There are virtues worth saving in the older styles: the twang that stays close to blues and country roots; the hands-on, homemade sound; a striving for spontaneity. Although boomer icons like the Beatles thrived on the artifice of the recording studio, most boomers enjoy believing they are hearing real musicians playing in real time, not programmed or disembodied sounds. Boomers may own PCs and VCRs now, but they grew up in an analogue universe. And even if they're still fond of vintage Jimi Hendrix or Led Zeppelin, most boomers don't want to be assaulted by newer music. Wildness, discontinuity and extremes of all sorts are for the young.

Young listeners have advantages as seekers of new sounds: less responsibility, more energy, fewer fixed notions, more time to see shows or to concentrate on a new album and lower expectations about comfort at concerts; boomers aren't thrilled when seeing a band becomes a contact sport. Loud music also goes with mating rituals that are irrelevant to settled boomers. And songs by younger musicians pour out adolescent angsts, lusts and grievances that seem less overwhelmingly important as maturity sets in. As they approach their 50's, boomers who once believed that youth equals truth now have their doubts.

Still, the boomers' demographic advantage lingers. An album that gets boomers' attention, like Eric Clapton's "Unplugged" or Sheryl Crow's "Tuesday Night Music Club," can sell millions. Since younger listeners are endlessly exposed to boomer esthetics, Beatles-style melody and folk-rock guitars never disappear for long; they resurface in Foo Fighters tunes and Hootie and the Blowfish arrangements. Boomer influence also persists in radio formats (notably a boomercentric definition of "classic rock") and in summer-tour rosters laden with bands cruising on old hits; this summer the Eagles, Joe Cocker, Chicago, Steve Miller, Neil Diamond and double bills like Lynyrd Skynyrd with the Doobie Brothers will be on the shed- and arena-circuit.

When younger musicians try to recapture 1960's styles, like the Blues Traveler school of tie-dyed jamming, they often deserve ridicule (although the vintage psychedelic jam was as much about mixing live music and illicit substances as it was about the quality of that music). But boomers never had an exclusive on originality. Rock's headway isn't a matter of destroying the past but of borrowing some of it and ignoring the rest. Even rock's greatest upheavals have been acts of reclamation as well as repudiation.

The boomers' heyday was a lucky time to be a musician and a listener. The Vietnam War catalyzed a separate youth culture that valued music; rock seemed to be honest, unvarnished expression subverting Establishment media. The civil rights movement brought optimistic energy (and, briefly, integrationist ambitions) to black music in places like Detroit and Memphis, and it thrust blues and funk into the foreground of rock. An expanding economy allowed even dropouts to scrape by and provided disposable income for boomers to try the unknown in concerts and albums. And there was room for music on the newly opened FM band, which provided both high fidelity and time for extended, experimental songs.

Since the mid-1970's, musicians have had to contend with a disillusioned public, a stagnant economy and media outlets with narrow formats; the joyous disarray of early FM radio couldn't last when a consistent sound brought more listeners. In response, rock fragmented itself, mirroring a lost sense of a shared youth culture. Boomer musicians also provided useful negative examples for their successors. Their instantly dated cosmic, oh-wow pronouncements showed later rockers that tough-mindedness had more staying power. And after seeing what happened when some 1960's rockers turned into pampered, out-of-touch buffoons, later generations have been ambivalent about show-business success.

Post-boomer scarcity brought out resourcefulness: a do-it-yourself alternative-rock circuit not dependent on commercial radio or major labels, a hip-hop underground that treated the electronic sound scape as a post-modern playground. Hip-hop's radical transformation of sound and structure was as revolutionary as the birth of rock-and-roll and has been just as disturbing to the older generation. Punk, metal and alternative rock, by contrast, are relatively conservative, clinging to guitars and real-time performance. And boomers find them traumatic enough.

Boomers complain that the new music is too artificial. Yet while some musicians have used emerging technology in the most deadening ways (and reaped a windfall with disco), others have exploited it to create music as sensual and psychedelic as anything from the primitive 1960's, in an ever-expanding roster of dance-music and ambient subgenres. And while current rock may have more jolts per minute than its forebears—perhaps as a way to get through to attention spans geared to channel-surfing—some of it also has the unfeigned passion that boomers used to seek out.

The current generational truce arrives as hip-hop and alternative rock take a breather after a run of creativity—as long, actually, as the 1960's golden era from 1963–1970. Alternative rock lost some heart after Kurt Cobain's suicide in 1994; hip-hop's gangsta fad has run its course, though independent-minded rappers like the Fugees are opening up some promising new possibilities.

While musicians on various fringes grope toward something new, some younger musicians are reaching back to boomer esthetics. A songwriter like Joan Osborne taps into the blues even if she sports a nose ring; the folk-rock resurgence signaled by the Counting Crows continues in force; bands like the Goo Goo Dolls have Merseybeat craftsmanship; jam bands like Phish bring virtuosity to their psychedelic rambles.

Looking back is a wise commercial move. Boomer audiences are loyal once reached, while alternative-rock and hip-hop crowds seem to be far more fickle. Yet boomers and later generations both subscribe to American culture's fixation on youth. Older folk-rockers like Jackson Browne haven't followed Hootie and the Blowfish up the charts, and not necessarily because they're played out; some, like John Hiatt, are doing their best work now. Boomers want to hear the styles of their youth played by fresh-faced performers, so they can imagine themselves 25 years younger. And the next generations don't want to party with people who look like their parents.

Some generational gulfs may be impassable. Younger listeners have a different sense of what matters, a different time scale, a different shock threshold, a different tolerance for noise and, increasingly, a different relationship with old-fashioned verse-chorus-verse songs; they can handle the rhapsodic impulses of a Tori Amos or the open-ended vamps of hip-hop.

Someday, boomer esthetics will be about as relevant to pop as the quadrille is now. But in the meantime, boomers can learn from whippersnappers about their gripes and triumphs and yearnings; instead of nostalgic comforts, they can hear the rhythms and textures of the present. That is, if they can stand the excitement.

DISCUSSION QUESTIONS
1. Keep a diary for two days of all the music you listen to and in what settings. Why do you choose these types of music in particular?
2. What do you believe is the importance of music in our society?
3. Do you think that the music of the 1960s and 1970s still dominates American culture?

WHO OWNS THE BLUES?

Phil Patton

■

The big trucks made their way laboriously across the country, hour after hour, day after day, carrying rusty corrugated sheet metal, the skin of the most famous cotton gin house in Clarksdale, Miss., where the young Muddy Waters had once worked as a hand. They also carried soil from the Delta.

A few months later, the gin house had been rebuilt on the Sunset Strip in Los Angeles as the core of the $9 million House of Blues, the club created by Isaac Tigrett, who founded the Hard Rock Cafe chain.

The soil went beneath the stage, where John Lee Hooker, James Brown and Bruce Springsteen performed at the opening before an audience that included Dan Aykroyd, the co-owner of the club, and Steven Spielberg.

The gin house's journey mirrored the move the blues have made in the last few years from juke joint to Hollywood. Beginning perhaps in 1990, when the complete works of Robert Johnson were issued on CD, selling half a million copies and winning a Grammy Award a half century after the blues master died, the blues have been staging the latest of many revivals.

Sales of blues records are up, the number of blues labels has increased, and the number of blues clubs in America has grown by half during this decade, according to the Blues Foundation, a preservationist organization. There are now more than a hundred summer blues festivals. PBS is planning a three-part documentary on the music for next year, and its already published companion volume, "The History of the Blues," by Francis Davis, joins a spate of recent books on the subject. The blues are showing up too in advertising. B. B. King has done spots for McDonald's, and the blues have become music for beer commercials.

In many ways the current revival echoes the revivals of the 60's, when folkies embraced the idealism of the civil rights movement, and of the 30's, when scholars and promoters toured Southern prisons and plantations in search of blues songs and field hollers. But this revival is different, in that it raises questions of authenticity and commercialization that go beyond the blues—questions that arise where the dirt road of pre-commercial folk arts meets the neon-lined strip of modern American media.

Two different visions compete for the soul of the blues. One defines them as a folk art, a collective expression of black American culture and a record of oppression. The other sees the blues as a modernist art of individual genius melding tradition and innovation with technology and commerce, one whose influence pervades all of pop music today.

Nowhere is the conflict more sharply drawn than in the House of Blues. To some, it is the last best chance to keep the form vital; to others, it reduces one of the most profound forms of American music to a Disney cartoon.

Before it became a House of Blues, the cotton gin house from Clarksdale stood close to the crossroads of Highways 61 and 49, in the heart of the Mississippi Delta, in the northwest part of the state. Crossroads figure prominently in songs as places where blues musicians trade their souls to the Devil for the ability to make music.

Today the question is whether the blues have gained popularity by trading their soul to the Devil. Bearded and often dressed in black, Mr. Tigrett could even be mistaken for the Devil. But in his own telling he is an angel, saving the blues, in his words, "for the millennium."

Mr. Tigrett opened his first House of Blues in 1992 near Harvard Square in Cambridge, Mass.; others followed in West Hollywood and New Orleans. Now there are plans for clubs to open next year in New York and Chicago and at Disney World in Florida.

Part nightclub, part restaurant, part gift shop, the House of Blues is a strange warping of cultures: academic, commercial, entertainment and multimedia. It is hard to imagine any other enterprise whose investors include the Harvard Endowment Fund (to the tune of $10 million), Disney, Sir James Goldsmith, Isaac Hayes, Jim Belushi and members of the band Aerosmith.

On its menus and signs, the House of Blues has taken as its trademarked motto the line "We're on a mission from God" from the 1980 film "The Blues Brothers." The club offers Blues Burgers and Elwood sandwiches, named after a character in the film, and each sells guitars, T-shirts, folk art, books and CD's. On Sundays, they serve a "gospel brunch."

Mr. Tigrett himself designs the clubs' interiors. He got the idea for the decor of the original club from a book of photographs called "Juke Joint Interiors," by the noted Mississippi photographer Birney Imes. (The book had been given to Mr. Tigrett by Dr. William Ferris, director of the Center for the Study of Southern Culture at the University of Mississippi.)

Today, the House of Blues is a multimedia conglomerate. Its holdings include a weekly syndicated radio show with Mr. Aykroyd as host, a television show, a record label, a line of clothing and accessories, and a site on the World Wide Web.

"I've seen the House of Blues television show, but they never seem to have any blues on," says Mr. Davis, who is also a music critic and historian. "It's always Public Enemy." Other blues buffs complain how few traditional blues singers actually appear on stage at the clubs.

And to traditionalists of the 60's revival, who saw the blues chiefly as a form of protest music, the idea of a blues chain is disquieting. "It almost becomes a kind of grim joke," says Mr. Davis, "as if after seeing the Holocaust Museum someone created a Holocaust cafe."

Others question why a largely white enterprise would latch on to the blues as its theme. Mayor Ken Reeves of Cambridge early on called the club there "a major commercialization and rip-off of the African American culture."

Mr. Tigrett defends his efforts. "We work hard every day for the right to represent this art," he says. "I feel we are respectfully honoring the music." His goal, he adds, is "to transfer the integrity of the emotion." Indeed, the House of Blues is not a blues club so much as a club whose theme, in Mr. Tigrett's words, "is a tribute to the blues."

"What is the home of the blues?" he asks rhetorically. "Paris. Seventy per cent of blues records are sold in Europe." And it was white college students, he notes, who supported the blues in the 60's, after the music had become an embarrassment to many urbanized blacks. It was then that white producers like Leonard and Phil Chess, founders of the label that bears their name, kept the blues in print.

White rockers, from Eric Clapton to the Allman Brothers, continued to perform the music when the folk-blues revivalists were excluding from their festivals white artists or those who played electric guitar as well as rhythm-and-blues-influenced musicians. "The irony," says Mr. Davis, "was that it left out those artists who still had black audiences."

Decorating each House of Blues are works from Mr. Tigrett's extensive collection of outsider art by painters who share the Southern background of blues singers. "The visual blues" he calls this art.

The artwork and the blues also have something else in common: The legal ownership of both often stands outside modern commercial conventions. Within the last few years, significantly, both Robert Johnson, one of the greatest blues figures, and Bill Traylor, one of the greatest self-taught painters, have become the subjects of tortuous litigation by heirs who sued the owners of their work long after the deaths of the artists themselves. The release of the Johnson CD was delayed for years by legal action involving relatives. In 1992, Traylor's heirs, who had had little use for him before his death in 1947, sued Charles Shannon, the man who discovered Traylor, for a portion of the proceeds from sales of his work; they later settled out of court.

Some early blues songs have survived only in the form of a few copies, or even a single copy, of a 78 record, so collectors, in effect, own entire titles. The rights to Robert Johnson songs and photographs are owned by the researcher Stephen C. LaVere, who zealously guards the rights to reproduce even Johnson's face.

But beyond the legal issues are wider questions of moral right, touching on race and the birth of the blues in oppression. Mr. Tigrett lays claim to the blues tradition by upbringing. "I grew up in those places," he says of the juke joints in Mr. Imes's pictures.

Whether out of purely noble impulse or to soften criticism that he was exploiting black culture, Mr. Tigrett established a House of Blues Foundation, which brings local students to the House of Blues and offers scholarships. He enlisted the W. E. B. DuBois Institute at Harvard and its director, Henry Louis Gates Jr., along with the Center for the Study of Southern Culture, to devise a curriculum. A typical presentation on the blues would suggest links that run from the rap of Snoop Doggy Dogg to the funk of George Clinton to the soul of James Brown before reaching the blues.

This perspective reflects an endorsement of a new blues scholarship that replaces the folklorist emphasis on shared forms and verses. The new approach stresses instead the individuality and professionalism of blues creators. The conflict can become intense. Mr. Davis criticizes folklorists like Alan Lomax, who visited prisons to find traditional songs, while ignoring individual innovators nearby like Charley Patton. "They went into it with the wrong mindset—a noble one but wrong," he says.

In their biography of Patton, Stephen Calt and Gayle Dean Wardlow attack the folklorist view and argue that the greatest blues singers were professional artists, not folk craftsmen. Mr. Calt and Mr. Wardlow maintain that implicit in the folklorists' argument is a suggestion that black culture was incapable of producing powerful individual artists. They contend that such a point of view is at best condescending and at worst racist.

Originality, of course, is a value found more in modern art than in earlier art forms. Even the blues masters never minded borrowing; almost every bluesman took a whack at standards like "Delta Blues," and performers often resorted to a vocabulary of "floating verses" as lyrical boilerplate. Patton cannibalized his own songs, and the Chicago bluesman Elmore James built his entire career on an electrified version of Robert Johnson's acoustic rendition of "Dust My Broom," already an established tune in the Delta by the 30's.

But if there was a different sense of ownership in the blues, it also served record companies to foster it. Stories of exploited blues artists are well known. In the 30's, Patton received about $2 per song for the rights to each. When Elvis Presley recorded Arthur (Big Boy) Crudup's "That's All Right," Crudup received nothing.

In his "History of the Blues," Mr. Davis argues that the music was "shaped as much by the marketplace as by folk tradition." The new school rejects the image of the blues evolving in isolation, maintaining that the marketplace included other forms of music. He notes that Johnson performed the cowboy number "Tumbling Tumbleweed" and that Memphis Minnie played the Woody Woodpecker theme.

Nor, the new school argues, have the blues ever quite fit the folk image of a stable, unchanging art. The movement of the blues from the South to Northern cities changed—literally electrified—the music. But the musical influences since have run both ways. Highway 61 runs not only from Mississippi to Minnesota but in the other direction as well. Bob Dylan's 1965 album "Highway 61 Revisited" was only the first such revisitation.

Along 61 near Duncan, Miss., stands a juke joint called the Purple Rain Lounge, the subject of some of Mr. Imes's best photographs. Its walls are green, like those in a traditional juke joint, but its name comes from the film and album by the artist formerly known as Prince.

This new view of the blues may explain why, despite criticism, many blues enthusiasts seem willing to suffer T-shirts and Blues Burgers for the sake of furthering the music. At the House of Blues, they're willing to see pop acts like Bonnie Raitt and Hootie and the Blowfish get most of the stage time if it gives authentic blues musicians like Koko Taylor and Junior Kimbrough more exposure.

While Dr. Ferris, too, would like to see more blues artists on stage at the clubs, he argues that "the blues have been commercialized at least since the 20's." What the House of Blues is doing, he believes, "is no different from what record companies have done since the music was first recorded."

Increasingly, the culture and audience for the blues is often as strange as the mix of influences found inside a House of Blues. Today, reports Mr. Imes, tour buses full of European and Japanese travelers stop by the juke joints he photographed for his book. They also stop at the grave of Robert Johnson or Stovall Plantation.

All of this is strange, but it is not new. In his autobiography, W. C. Handy, who is commonly credited with first bringing the blues to a national audience, described hearing the music in a train station at Tutwiler, in the Mississippi Delta. But less noticed is a reference a few pages later to another performance, on a nearby plantation, where Handy was struck by "a rain of silver dollars" showered on the performers. "Then," Handy wrote, "I saw the beauty of primitive music."

DISCUSSION QUESTIONS
1. Why are the blues important to American music?
2. How are the blues connected to rock and rap?
3. Does the music you enjoy have a link to the blues?

TUCKER BATTLES AGAINST LYRICS OF GANGSTA RAP

Monica Fountain

■

C. DeLores Tucker is grace under fire. Three subpoenas have just arrived in her office at the Watergate office building, the fruit of lawsuits against her by rap music artists. Even in the midst of conference calls with her lawyers in California, Tucker, co-founder and head of the National Political Congress of Black Women, has time to talk about her crusade and latest battle against gangsta rap.

Tucker, 68, is no stranger to battles. Her office, which overlooks the Potomac River, testifies to the more than 50 years she has fought for civil rights. There's Tucker marching with Rev. Martin Luther King Jr. A large picture of Rosa Parks. Desmond Tutu. President Clinton. Jimmy Carter. Tucker with Colin Powell and Yasser Arafat at Nelson Mandela's inauguration. And a pair of white plastic handcuffs—the latest memento in her collection from an arrest three years ago in front of a D.C. record store. It was the beginning of her stand against what she calls the "gangsta-porno virus that is infecting children all over the world."

Between phone calls, Tucker talks about how children were forbidden to play with her 6-year-old grandniece because she started using profanity found in the lyrics of the hip-hop form of music known as gangsta rap.

"It's destroying our culture and not teaching them to sing the songs of faith. We've always had dark days. We've always had days when racism was strong and worse than what these kids are experiencing. We had to experience hoses, the dogs. We had to live under the law. Yet, we were taught our history and still could sing songs of faith, sing songs of hope."

Days later, when the fires from the latest legal battle have cooled down, Tucker has more time to talk about what has been her passion for the past four years. Her allies include former Education Secretary William Bennett, co-founder of Empower America, the Parents' Music Resource Center, a pressure group co-founded by Tipper Gore in 1985, the NAACP, the Congressional Black Caucus, the National Baptist Convention, labor unions, churches and some elected officials. The fight is against what they describe as pornographic, misogynistic, anti-religious and often violent lyrics of rap artists such as the late Tupac Shakur, Snoop Doggy Dogg and the Dogg Pound and rock groups like Nine Inch Nails.

Tucker's message is a simple one. "I tell them stop calling our women 'ho's, bitches and sluts. When they say hos, they're talking about black women and the world is seeing that. These images of black young kids acting like gangstas go all around the world," Tucker said.

In 1994, Tucker brought her fight to Capitol Hill. Cardiss Collins chaired hearings on gangsta rap lyrics in the House of Representatives and Sen. Carol Moseley Braun chaired hearings on the Senate side. Then Tucker decided to attack gangsta rap not only on a political level but a corporate one. "Money is the driving force behind gangsta rap," she explained. Some people in the entertainment industry have told her that rappers have to use "gangsta" lyrics in order to get a contract, Tucker said. She started focusing her attack on record stores and Time Warner, then the distributor of one of the biggest gangsta rap labels, Interscope Records, and its subsidiary, Death Row Records. She bought stock in Time Warner and the right to speak as a stockholder at the company's annual meeting last year.

During the stockholders' meeting, she asked during her 17-minute statement: "How long will Time Warner continue to put profit before principle? How long will it continue to turn its back on the thousands of young people who are dying spiritually and physically due to the violence perpetuated in these recordings?" She challenged company executives to read the lyrics out loud. They refused. Since then the company has sold its $115 million interest in Interscope.

Tucker insists that she is not against the rappers themselves or even rap music. She said she simply wants the image of black men to be a positive one. "Rap music is wonderful. They have perverted it. Gangsta rap is a form of rap that is teaching our children to be criminals," she said. "People are viewing us and black males in this image. That we're thugs and rapists. This issue of gangsta rap transcends politics, race, religion. It's a human issue."

The lawsuits filed by Interscope Records and Death Row Records charge Tucker with conspiracy and extortion. The suits contend that last year Tucker tried to persuade Marion "Suge" Knight, head of Death Row Records, to take his business from Interscope, a distributor. The suits say that Tucker offered to distribute Knight's records through a new company that Tucker would control.

Tucker describes a more innocent scene. Tucker said that she agreed to meet Knight along with singers Melba Moore and Dionne Warwick, who had brought gangsta rap to Tucker's attention four years ago at the brunch of the National Political Congress of Black Women. "When I talked to Suge Knight,

I took his face in my hands and I said, 'I'm so happy to see you.' I said you hold in your hands two of the greatest role models of our children. They love the beat. But why can't you put positive messages about the Mandelas inside of them, about who they are? He said, 'I can,' " Tucker said. "He said these guys are not that bad, but in order to make them genuine to those who are we have to go overboard."

Tucker said Knight told her he would need distribution to produce positive music. Tucker said she simply asked Warwick and Moore to identify women in the business who might be interested. "My faith is so strong and it sustains me in everything that I do," Tucker said. "I don't fear anything at all."

Tucker and her husband, William, who have no children, have lavished their love and finances on three generations of nieces and nephews. Her concern for children is one of the reasons Tucker fights so hard against gangsta rap. "We have protected children. We have protected them from liquor. We have protected owls, rivers. We protect animals. We have to protect children," Tucker said. "This music is porno rap music. It should be put in a porno shop. That's my position. That parent's advisory doesn't mean a thing. It just tells them which one they should buy."

What about First Amendment rights and free speech? Tucker points out that newspapers that have First Amendment rights won't print the lyrics that are full of four letter words.

A tall woman, Tucker wears a large diamond ring and usually sports her trademark turban and elegant suits. Her speech is peppered with scriptures and references to God. Her father was a Philadelphia minister who immigrated from the Bahamas. The 10th of 11 children, Tucker was raised in the church, directing the choir and playing the organ. One of her favorite scriptures is found in the Old Testament book of Micah. The prophet asks the Lord what is required of him and the answer was to do good to everybody, to love mercy and to walk humbly with God. "Throughout my life that's what I've tried to do," Tucker said.

Her parents imparted such a strong self-image to their daughter she said she was surprised when she first encountered racism and segregation. When she was 19, her father took her to the Bahamas. When she found out the black passengers had to ride in the bottom of the ship, she refused to go and slept all night on deck. As a result she developed tuberculosis, she said. "I refused to yield to something that I felt was improper for me as a person."

She became involved in politics through the NAACP and as a teen, she helped register black voters. Now she is a member of the NAACP board of trustees. She is a fundraiser for black causes. She has received more than 300 awards and honors, including the NAACP Thurgood Marshall Award. She has spoken at five Democratic conventions. She was formerly the chair of the Democratic National Committee Black Caucus. Tucker was the first African American to serve as president of the National Federation of Democratic Women.

As a member of the Democratic National Committee, Tucker organized a woman's caucus and served on a charter commission to ensure that women had a fair share of representation at all levels of the Democratic Party. Besides the National Political Congress of Black Women, which was founded 10 years ago, Tucker is also the president of the Bethune DuBois Fund, an organization that supports the cultural development of black youth. She also is the publisher of "Vital Issues: The Journal of African American Speeches."

Tucker's day starts early in the morning, around 5 or 6. She makes phone calls at that time so that if she needs to talk to someone like Jesse Jackson she can catch him before the day starts. Her days end between midnight and 1 A.M. most days. From the time she wakes up until she lays her head down at night, Tucker said, she is busy serving people. She answers every letter written to her and insists that whoever works for her treats everyone like they would treat their own mother.

She says she has only had one salaried job in her whole life. That was when she was the secretary of state for Pennsylvania from 1971 to 1977, the highest ranking black woman in state government in the country at that time. "I'm a servant of God and I serve people," Tucker said. "I don't charge. I give."

DISCUSSION QUESTIONS
1. Listen to a selection of regular rap music and a selection of gangsta rap. What do you think of each type of rap?
2. What is the importance of rap music in American society?
3. Should gangsta rap be boycotted or censored?

CHAPTER 5

FILM

Elaine Rivera, *Spike Lee Speaks His Mind*

Suzanne Fields, *Propaganda in the Guise of Truth: Oliver Stone's Movies Give Young Americans a Distorted View of History*

Gloria Steinem, *Hollywood Cleans Up* Hustler

S helton Jackson Lee, better known as "Spike," became the first African American filmmaker to win widespread acclaim both in the United States and abroad. His first big hit was *Do the Right Thing*, a 1989 film that deals with tensions between blacks and Italians in a New York City neighborhood. *Malcolm X*, a 1992 movie about the late African American leader, is probably Lee's most important film. In the first reading of this chapter, Lee discusses how the film was made and what he believes its importance is to both African Americans and white Americans.

Oliver Stone is another successful director whose credits include personal Oscars for *Platoon* and *Born on the Fourth of July*, two films about Vietnam. In the second reading, a critic argues that Stone's movies—many of which center on historical events and individuals—are not always accurate. Some people complain that Stone presents merely his view of the world in his movies, for example, in *JFK* endorsing the theory that John F. Kennedy was killed by a group of conspirators rather than by a lone assassin.

The third reading, written by feminist Gloria Steinem, criticizes the film *The People versus Larry Flynt*, which Stone produced and Oscar-winner Milos Forman directed. The movie centers on Flynt, the publisher of *Hustler* magazine, and his court battle to uphold his right to publish a tasteless satire of political and religious leader Jerry Falwell. Steinem argues that the film portrays Flynt in a far better light than he deserves.

SPIKE LEE
SPEAKS HIS MIND

Elaine Rivera

■

$\mathbf{A}$s soon as Spike Lee started angling to direct "Malcolm X," the controversies began. There was carping about Lee's ability to be true to the ideals of the slain African American leader. When the film went over budget, it made news. And when a group of black superstars rallied to his cause with contributions, it made news again.

There were headlines when Lee battled for the right to use the Rodney King footage in the film. And more when Lee allegedly said students should skip school to see his film on opening day. And more again when it came out that he'd asked some publications to assign African American interviewers.

. . . Spike Lee sat down for an interview at Manhattan's Rihga Hotel. Dressed casually in a turquoise "X" cap, a blazer, jeans and purple and gray Nike sneakers, the always-outspoken Lee was direct and pointed, and at times displayed a sense of humor, as he spoke of Malcolm X, racism and the film industry.

Q: How did Malcolm X affect your own political development?

A: It had a great effect. I read the book in junior high school. It changed everything—the way I thought, the way I felt, the way I viewed the world. It made everything clear for me: the conditions of black people who live in this country, how it came to be that way, why it came to be that way, and what we must do as a people to deal with those things.

Q: Did you think one day you would be making a film about him?

A: It was probably subliminal. Each of my films, even "She's Gotta Have It," Malcolm X is mentioned. Nola Darling [the lead character in "She's Gotta . . ."] was born on May 19, which is also Malcolm's birthday. "School Daze," he's mentioned. He's a big part of "Do the Right Thing." But it wasn't until "Mo' Better Blues" that I began to really think about doing it. At that time, Norman Jewison was the director.

Q: You leveraged the film away from Norman Jewison, claiming it needed a black director. Since the film you've made is a straight bio-pic, why was it so important it have a black director?

A: White Americans will never know what it feels like to be an African American in this country. This is a story of Malcolm X whose life you might say is very symbolic of the whole African American experience in this country. I've said this again and again, that Francis Ford Coppola being Italian American definitely enhanced the "Godfather" films. Same thing with Martin Scorsese with "Mean Streets," "Raging Bull."

So why should those same things not enhance African Americans doing films about the African American struggle? At the same time, that's not saying that only white people can direct white films or black people can direct black films, but there are specific cases where you are from, your environment, will help.

Q: What, for instance, couldn't have been done if there wasn't a black director?

A: A tremendous amount of research had to be done for this film. Research meaning going to talk to people who knew Malcolm—relatives, people in the Nation, the OAAU [Malcolm X's Organization of Afro-American Unity], and they were not going to talk to no white man. They would never open up. Do you think [Minister Louis] Farrakhan would have invited a white director into his house and tell them that Malcolm was his mentor? Forget about it.

No white director could have gotten Nelson Mandela to be in his film. Hell no. They probably wouldn't even have thought about it or seen the connection between Malcolm and Mandela. Warner Bros. definitely didn't see the connection.

I don't think a white director could have gotten access to shoot Mecca. . . . Hell no. To shoot the sacred rite of Hajj. That's never been done before. Ever, ever, ever. These are the same people who sentenced Rushdie to death—the Highest Islamic court—they're the ones who gave us permission.

Q: So how did you get that?

A: Through Allah. (He smiles.)

Q: How did you decide which parts of the autobiography to use in the movie?

A: I relied on instinct and my gut feeling. I tried to get the essence of the man. There's no way you can tell the man's entire life in three hours—you can't do it in eight hours.

This is not a documentary. The words that came out of Denzel's mouth are not the same words Malcolm said. But you always have to ask yourself this question, are you being true to Malcolm, are you being truthful. That's all you can do.

Q: There was criticism on the part of [poet and playwright] Amiri Baraka about starting the film with Malcolm's gangster days. Why was it so important to open with that and to devote nearly an hour to that period?

A: It's not so much time. We devoted an adequate amount of time. That's why the film is the length it is. I don't think we can do a three-hour film on one Malcolm X. There's the one Amiri Baraka wanted, and the one the black nationalists wanted, but he was not always at that place. He had to do a whole lot of things, he had to live a life to get to that point. That's what makes it interesting to see that evolution and change, to see Malcolm evolving, to see him get to the point where he got.

And he doesn't start out as a gangster. In that first hour, twenty minutes of that is flashbacks as Malcolm as a young boy and his family.

Q: This is the first time you've done a film based on a factual story. Did this affect your style or approach?

A: Yeah, it had to. Malcolm X was a person who lived, breathed, walked on this earth, so I could not just do anything I wanted to do. I didn't feel constrained, I just felt I had to find a way to be respectful of Malcolm X, yet still make it a personal film. I think I found that. I think you can look at this film and tell that I did it. It has the flavoring of a Spike Lee film. The use of music, cinematography, the editing, the opening credits.

Q: Why do you think Hollywood decided to make this film now versus ten, twenty years ago?

A: Malcolm is not as feared as he was back then. Also, they can make some money, and there is nothing wrong with that. That's why they make any movie.

Q: The implication from the movie is that the Nation of Islam was behind the shooting. Do you think Elijah Muhammad ordered Malcolm's killing?

A: They had a lot to do with it. If it wasn't him, it was someone directly under him in Chicago.

Q: Does white suburban America have an understanding of what Malcolm X was about, or do you think he's still seen as that militant black guy who talked about the white man as the devil?

A: Yeah, still today, but I think this film will help toward a better understanding—if one is open to it.

Q: Can white America embrace Malcolm X as an American leader versus a black leader?

A: Open-minded white America can.

Q: Do you think people will really understand Malcolm after seeing the movie?

A: I think there's varying degrees of intelligence among the movie-going audience. All you can do is make the best film.

Q: Why hasn't Martin Luther King achieved the popularity among young people that Malcolm X has?

A: You have to look at this in a historical context. It's only very recently that we've had this flip flop. There's no Malcolm X day in America, no national holiday.

Malcolm X appeals more to young America today because of his militant, no-sellout stance and kids can't get into that complete non-violence stance. They know that the turn-the-other-cheek approach doesn't work. They live in this world.

Q: What do you think he means to young people of color?

A: He's a hero. Ossie Davis said it the best. He said Malcolm was our manhood, our shining black prince, and young black males don't have any role models who are as strong as Malcolm.

Q: What is Malcolm's message?

A: What Malcolm are you talking about? What people have to realize is that there were many different Malcolms. You have to specify which Malcolm you're talking about because he was constantly redefining where he was politically. The Malcolm before Mecca was not the same Malcolm who came back from Mecca. The one big misconception is that when Malcolm came back from Mecca he repudiated black self-defense; he never did that. Never, ever did that. He felt that way to his grave.

I don't think we diluted his message.

Q: Why did you ask the *Los Angeles Times* to assign an African American writer to interview you?

A: Why? Because I don't get hatchet jobs done on me. African American journalists aren't going to ask me, "Spike, so do you have any white friends?" What kind of ——— questions are those. Stupid.

DISCUSSION QUESTIONS

1. Watch the movie Malcolm X and write down what you think about the film. Does your opinion of the film differ from that of your classmates?
2. Do you agree with Spike Lee that only an African American could direct the film? Why?
3. What do you think about Spike Lee's desire that only African American reporters interview him?

PROPAGANDA IN THE GUISE OF TRUTH: OLIVER STONE'S MOVIES GIVE YOUNG AMERICANS A DISTORTED VIEW OF HISTORY

Suzanne Fields

∎

O liver Stone, movie director, is an easy target for the sharpened pens of criticism. He deserves the slings and arrows for creating sinister portraits of politicians he doesn't like, usually more fiction than fact.

As a result of his movies, a generation of young adults is coming of age with distorted propaganda in the guise of history. But Oliver Stone is not the real problem. The real problem resides in the pseudo-education of our children. We are disarming them by slick narratives packaged as truth. They aren't forearmed with intellectual curiosity about their country's history. If they were, they could identify the fictive lies themselves.

I once defended fictional biographies of artists, thinking they were thus easily accessible to readers who might not yet know much about fine art, but who might be lured into a larger audience for painting and sculpture. But now I recognize that defense as the beginning of the slippery slope. Educating through condescension nearly always fails.

Now that movies, TV and cozy computer chat-rooms often replace the printed word as a major source of knowledge, lies can pass for truth. The printed word and even some of the more sophisticated talk shows are alive with historical errors. The often sugarcoated narratives seep swiftly into the consciousness of a generation of adults who have no historical memory.

Plato, we can be sure, is spinning in his grave repeating a scolding phrase, "I told you so." He knew that the power of the poet to cast fanciful illusions would lend him the greater weight for good or for ill than all the philosophers together. Hence he warns that an appeal to the senses through poetry, delightful as that may be, can dangerously mislead.

How much greater that power today as epics on the big screen—and on the little screen—seduce us into believing a mixture of fact and fiction as the real story, tantalizing us with chocolate-covered factoids.

Oliver Stone hides behind poetic license to distort facts in creating his movies "Nixon" and "JFK." He freely admits that he makes movies to "re-shape" the world.

Oliver Stone should not be prevented from creating his goofy history. Poets, novelists, playwrights and other weavers of illusions have often dabbled in historical revisionism.

But in the 20th century, when popular artists are accorded more prestige than historians or playwrights, a moviemaker like Oliver Stone is regarded as deadly in an Orwellian sense, becoming Big Brother interpreting contemporary history.

Socrates' admonition to the Athenians, as described by Plato in "The Republic," is relevant. Socrates likens artists who express moral deformity as a menace to the upbringing of young citizens, who must after all grow "as in some foul pasture, where browsing day by day on many a weed, little by little, they gather without realizing it a great mass of corruption in their souls."

Plato's citizens, like citizens of today, are denied an education when they are spoon-fed lies as illumination. Mendacity at the movies as a pretense of history reduces reason to rot and musing to mush. If we didn't learn that from Plato in intellectual argument, we can see it in action in a movie by Oliver Stone.

DISCUSSION QUESTIONS
1. Watch a movie by Oliver Stone. How effectively does his directing convince you of the point of view of the movie?
2. Research the facts about the story in the movie. How well does the movie portray those facts?
3. Do you think a movie should be accurate about historical facts? Why, or why not?

HOLLYWOOD CLEANS
UP *HUSTLER*

Gloria Steinem

■

L arry Flynt the Movie is even more cynical than Larry Flynt the Man.
"The People vs. Larry Flynt" claims that the creator of *Hustler* magazine is a
champion of the First Amendment, deserving our respect. That isn't true.

Let's be clear: A pornographer is not a hero, no more than a publisher of
Ku Klux Klan books or a Nazi on the Internet, no matter what constitutional
protection he secures. And Mr. Flynt didn't secure much.

The Rev. Jerry Falwell sued him over a *Hustler* parody that depicted Mr.
Falwell in a drunken, incestuous encounter with his mother. Mr. Flynt's victory
only confirmed the right to parody public figures (if the result can't be taken
as fact) and prevented plaintiffs from doing an end run around the First
Amendment by claiming they suffered "emotional distress."

In fact, the Nazis who marched in Skokie, Ill., and the Klansman who advocated violence in Ohio achieved more substantive First Amendment victo-
ries than did Mr. Flynt. Yet no Hollywood movie would glamorize a Klansman
or a Nazi as a champion of free speech, much less describe him in studio press
releases as "the era's last crusader," which is how Columbia Pictures describes
Mr. Flynt.

In this film, produced by Oliver Stone and directed by Milos Forman,
Hustler is depicted as tacky at worst, and maybe even honest for showing full nu-
dity. What's left out are the magazine's images of women being beaten, tortured
and raped, women subject to degradations from bestiality to sexual slavery.

Filmgoers don't see such *Hustler* features as "Dirty Pool," which in January 1983 depicted a woman being gang-raped on a pool table. A few months
after those pictures were published, a woman was gang-raped on a pool table
in New Bedford, Mass. Mr. Flynt's response to the crime was to publish a
postcard of another nude woman on a pool table, this time with the inscription

71

"Greetings from New Bedford, Mass. The Portuguese Gang-Rape Capital of America."

Nor do you see such typical *Hustler* photo stories as a naked woman in handcuffs who is shaved, raped and apparently killed by guards in a concentration-camp-like setting. You won't meet "Chester the Molester," the famous *Hustler* cartoon character who sexually stalks girls.

You certainly don't see such *Hustler* illustrations as a charred expanse of what looks like human skin, with photos of dead and dismembered women pinned to it.

On the contrary, the Hollywood version of Larry Flynt, played by the charming Woody Harrelson, is opposed to violence. At an anti-censorship rally, he stands against a backdrop of beautiful images of nude women that are intercut with scenes of Hiroshima, marching Nazis and the My Lai massacre. "Which is more obscene," the Flynt character asks, "sex or war?" Viewers who know *Hustler*'s real content might ask, "Why can't Larry Flynt tell the difference?"

Mr. Flynt's daughter Tonya, 31, is so alarmed by this film's dishonesty that she joined women who picketed its opening in San Francisco. She also publicly accused Mr. Flynt of having sexually abused her when she was a child, a charge he vehemently denies and attributes to her "mental problems."

"I'm upset about this film because it supports my dad's argument that pornography does no harm," she has said. "If you want to see a victim of pornography, just look at me."

Unlike his film character, the real Mr. Flynt is hardly an unwavering advocate of free speech. Indeed, other feminists and I have been attacked in *Hustler* for using our First Amendment rights to protest pornography. In my case, that meant calling me dangerous and putting my picture on a "Most Wanted" poster. I was also depicted as the main character in a photo story that ended in my sexual mutilation. Given the number of crimes that seem to imitate pornography, this kind of attack does tend to get your attention.

So, no, I am not grateful to Mr. Flynt for protecting my freedom, as the film and its enthusiasts suggest I should be. No more than I would be to a racist or fascist publisher whose speech is protected by the Constitution.

My question is, Would men be portrayed as inviting, deserving and even enjoying their own pain and degradation, as women are in Mr. Flynt's life work?

Suppose Mr. Flynt specialized in such images as a young African American man trussed up like a deer and tied to the luggage rack of a white hunter's car. Or a nude white man being fed into a meat grinder. (Those are some of the milder ways in which *Hustler* portrays women.)

Would Oliver Stone—who rarely lets powerful men emerge unscathed—bowdlerize and flatter that kind of man, too? Would Woody Harrelson, who supports animal rights and protests the cutting of trees, pose happily next to that Larry Flynt? Would Milos Forman defend that film by citing his memories of censorship under the Nazis?

What if the film praised an anti-Semitic publisher? Would it be nominated for five Golden Globe awards? Would there be cameos by Donna Hanover Giuliani, the wife of New York City's Mayor; Burt Neuborne, a New York University law professor; Judge D'Army Bailey of the Memphis Circuit Court; or James Carville, President Clinton's former political consultant? I don't think so.

The truth is, if Larry Flynt had published the same cruel images even of animals, this movie would never have been made.

Fortunately, each of us has the First Amendment right to protest.

DISCUSSION QUESTIONS

1. Read the First Amendment to the U.S. Constitution and the decision made by the U.S. Supreme Court concerning the Larry Flynt case. What do you think of the Court's decision?
2. Watch the film *The People vs. Larry Flynt*. What is your opinion about the portrayal of Larry Flynt in the film?
3. Does Gloria Steinem have a valid point about the praise for Larry Flynt and this film? Why, or why not?

CHAPTER 6

BOOKS

Richard B. Woodward, *Books Are Dead! Long Live Books! How
an Outdated Piece of Hardware Just Keeps on Going and Going
and . . .*

D. T. Max, *The End of the Book?*

Joseph Deitch, *Portrait of a Book Reviewer: Christopher
Lehmann-Haupt*

Fighthor most of the past 1,400 years, the Armenians had no country of their
own. During that time, the Persians, Mongols, Arabs, Turks, and Russians
slaughtered and subjugated the Armenian people.

Early in the fifth century, a monk named Mashtots devised the Armenian alphabet. Scribes then began to document Armenian history, philosophy,
and laws. Today, more than twenty-five thousand of these manuscripts have
survived—some ten thousand alone in Yerevan, the capital of Armenia. Today,
the Armenians finally have a country in the former Soviet Union, and their culture has survived because of their books.

In the 1450s, Johann Gutenberg's invention of the printing press made
it possible for many people to have access to the ideas of the world. Today, an
estimated 50,000 new book titles are published each year in the United States
alone. Still, increasing numbers of books—from children's texts to classical
literature—are being transferred to audiocassette. Reference books such as
encyclopedias are being placed on computer disks.

Some think the printed book may be dying as we enter the new millennium. The first two readings, by Richard B. Woodward of the *Village Voice* and
D. T. Max in the *Atlantic Monthly*, turn conventional wisdom on its head. The
third reading features a profile of Christopher Lehmann-Haupt, the book
critic for the *New York Times*, and of what he does.

Books Are Dead! Long Live Books! How an Outdated Piece of Hardware Justs Keeps on Going and Going and . . .

Richard B. Woodward

·

Rabbit was rueful. Gazing out at the hall from his podium onstage, flanked by the tiers of aged eminences that comprise the American Academy of Arts and Letters, he cast his eyes at the horizon and feared what he foresaw. The end. His own redundancy and extinction. Not enough.

He was up there on upper Broadway last May for the annual award-mongering and cocktail party, and to receive a fat prize himself: the William Dean Howells Medal, given to *Rabbit at Rest* as the best novel of the last five years. But in accepting, he chose to make a mournful speech more reminiscent of Sydney Carton at the guillotine than a hallowed establishmentarian being festooned with honors by his peers. Resigned rather than bitter, he spoke in a dying sigh. The novel, as he had seen fit to define, crown, and embody it, was through.

"What looms is not a mere change of literary fashion or shift of genres, but a loss of literature itself, rendered passé by the bright flickering tongues of the electronic modes of entertainment and instruction," he asserted in a voice whose authority was amplified by its mild manner.

"Young students, it is reported from academia, are less and less willing and able to read, and the language of even as limpid a 19th-century style as that of Hawthorne is impenetrable to them. Those of us who grew up on a diet of the modernist masterpieces, and have tried to write works that would enchant and challenge readers such as we were, may be like those Renaissance poets who mastered the art of Latin verse, in quixotic or elitist defiance of a widespread linguistic death. We are writing for an audience that less and less exists, and a posterity that will not exist."

Even if this was your boilerplate Death of the Novel speech updated

---

This article has been adapted.

with some '90s allusions, the audience listened as though hearing bad news for the first time. Howells had once chastised his fellow Americans for preferring the "foolish joys" of romantic escapism to the hard knocks of realism, but Updike went further in his sermon, for, as he said, "the situation now is more drastic." He wasn't just arguing for one kind of fiction over another: he was announcing the imminent demise of thoughtful reading and writing altogether.

The hall attended closely to his words. I know I was not alone in my shame at never having finished *Rabbit Redux*. But being disciplined by Updike is like being flogged exquisitely with a cashmere cat-'o-nine. You want the punishment to continue if only to feel more deeply your own unworthiness in the face of his soothing verbal command.

What's more, his anguish was a moving sight. Even if he enjoys the luxury of knowing that publishers around the world will print his every thought on any subject, from golf to Degas to oral sex, it can't be fun to try a new tack in your fiction and be blistered by critics and ignored by readers, as occurred with *Brazil*. He seemed to be speaking for several generations of long-in-the-tooth postwar male literary lions—Mailer, Bellow, Heller, Gaddis, Berger, Barth—once regnant as America's most celebrated and daring writers now of diminished relevance to current tastes in the novel.

But the speech was also weirdly self-pitying and trendy. The narcissistic undertone of Updike's lament seemed to be: Literature must be dead because I'm unread. Was he speaking up for a hitherto unknown class of victims in America's culture wars? Or just being a John-come-lately on the profitable neo-con bandwagon? (It pays to be in the apocalypse racket these days because we're all sinners and no one is ever too upset if the worst-case scenario turns out to be dead wrong. Just ask William Bennett and Gertrude Himmelfarb.) Had Updike checked some publishing statistics against his morbid hunch or waited a couple of weeks and read a *Wall Street Journal* story ("Book-Buying Is at New Highs, Survey Says," June 2, 1995), he might have felt better about his award.

If the audience for literature has followed the novel to the grave, the news has so far not reached many outstanding writers still above ground like E. Annie Proulx, Cormac McCarthy, Toni Morrison, Jane Smiley, William Trevor, or David Foster Wallace never mind those long gone, like Robert Musil, Dante, Zora Neale Hurston, Edith Wharton, and Ulysses S. Grant.

Some of the numbers put up by these authors are mighty impressive. Trade paperback sales of *The Shipping News*, by no means lite reading, have topped one million. Knopf's initial print-run of 200,000 copies for *The Crossing* was insufficient to meet last year's demand; twice it went back to press, each time for another 25,000. *Jazz* was the sixth straight fiction bestseller for the Nobel Prize winner (close to 180,000 in hardcover) and *A Thousand Acres* did almost as well (175,000). Although *Felicia's Journey* did not post these kinds of figures, its sales last year were four times that of any previous Trevor title. Everyone's favorite wristbuster, *Infinite Jest*, is in its fourth printing.

Nor have dead white males been consigned to the ash heap in the multicultural information age. Robert Pinsky's translation of *The Inferno*, which restores the poem as ripping yarn and makes Hell a palpable Horror, has 25,000 copies in print; while the new English translation of *The Man without Qualities*, the most authoritative yet, went back to press three times, and has sold 13,000 copies despite a hefty price tag of $60 for the boxed, two-volume set.

Sales for the Everyman's Library, which now has esteemed writers present (Achebe, Naipaul, Rushdie, Solzhenitsyn) and past (Bulgakov, Kafka, Borges, Cather) were up 60 percent last year. The Library of America had its best year in the 14-year history of the program and has doubled its sales in the last six years, and not just to libraries. "People would be surprised that the bulk of our business is with individuals," says publisher Max Rudin. "There is a group of 20,000 subscribers who review everything we publish. And that doesn't include bookstore buyers."

Why then is the feeling widespread among culture watchers that serious books are dead? Updike was only harmonizing the dirge sung by essayist–book critic Sven Birkerts, whose *The Gutenberg Elegies* (1994) bemoans the end of civilized reading as we've—or at least he's—come to know it.

Are throbbing pixels on computer screens sexier to Americans than dull, opaque pages of print, as Updike and his cohorts seem to think? To judge from the number of stories—in this paper as well—about the Web in the last year, it would certainly appear so. There is a nagging fear that the new communications technology will render all old forms obsolete. Every capitalist child lives in dread of missing a trend; and the money to be made from start-up companies, and the stakes in promoting fear of being passed by, are enormous.

The heady thrill of sightseeing along the information superhighway, however, has led to blurred vision. The evidence is convincing that books are resiliently popular, as central to American life as in the past, and likely to be for the foreseeable future. Television in the '50s and the VCR in the '80s were supposed to kill off movies; and before that it was "inevitable" that radio would die out. For a century now these electronic distractions have been leading people astray who presumably would have been racing through the Harvard classics.

It's not as if the doomsayers don't have a good historical case. New technologies can come along that in a few years make careers and lives redundant. Employees or stockholders of Smith-Corona, IBM, and Apple would seem to have more to worry about in this regard than novelists, but TV did put an end to radio drama and comedy (in America at any rate). Who can argue that illiteracy remains a virulent problem and threatens to become worse, not better? If the well-documented ignorance of grammar, elementary history, and geography is deep-rooted, the class of people without access to the new tools is now doubly alienated.

It wouldn't appear to be a good time to be a serious writer either. The media seem to have written off challenging fiction as irrelevant to Americans. I can't recall a prominent news magazine in the '90s devoting a cover to a novelist simply because his or her writing was superb. Clancy, Crichton, Grisham,

King, or Rice seem to be the only ones to rate exposure—as business stories. The absence of a visible group of young American novelists is discouraging, and the unwillingness of newspapers or television to discuss books at length (except Brian Lamb's lonely Sunday night show on C-SPAN) is an American disgrace.

Given a choice between the radiant electronic horizon as paintboxed, by Bill Gates and Nicholas Negroponte, and the dark ages of literature imagined by Updike and Birkerts, I'll side with the reactionary nostalgists, if only because they appear less profit-oriented. I'd rather live in their messy book-lined caves than inhabit a pristine mansion outside Seattle where a searchlight tracks my every move and everything I read or study is beamed to me on an Orwellian screen.

These are the self-annihilating visions of extremists. Signs of both a digitalized, virtual reality dawn and of a *12 Monkeys* dystopia are written on the walls for those who choose to read that way. But the explosion of superstores, the quiet, uncorporate spread of reading groups, the current red-hot literary market for quality fiction, and the brave if hopelessly muddled attempt by *Granta* magazine to boost the careers of young writers are also signs of the times, and easier to decipher.

As the millennium slouches to be born, it might help to sort out conflicting claims on the future by looking more closely at the present. For the time being, that's where most of us have to live.

The cult of the book has in many ways never attracted a more motley crowd of unlikely devotees. The joke is that everyone in L.A. or New York is at work on a screenplay; the reality seems to be that just about anyone who has ever been microwaved in the media has published a book. The TV, film, radio, music, sports, business, political (and now judicial) stars—genuine, wannabes, hasbeens, never-weres—whose ghostwritten memoirs, wry musings on how socks disappear, and inspirational "Art of War" approaches to life choke airport shops and mail-order catalogues across the country should be an example to would-be writers everywhere. If Scott O'Grady can publish a book, you can, too.

Slow, costly, unwieldy to produce and sell, books are still necessary cogs in the machinery of fame. They may enhance rather than make a reputation nowadays, but they allow anyone to don the mantle of gravity once worn by Cicero and Milton that only writers are supposed to wear. It is as though renown for Jerry, Ellen, Tim, Paul, Rush, Bill, Roseanne, Kelsey, Mary, Loni, Oprah, Ricki, Montel, Kathy Lee, and Regis were a mirage until manifest between hardcovers that can be held by those unknowable Nielsen families. Unlike a ratings share, books are solid objects. Viewers can take one home, a piece of someone who is otherwise a flat and fleeting image.

Autobiographies let celebrities step out of character without makeup, confess to an addiction or troubled past, and settle scores with other celebrities (or unauthorized biographers). Howard Stern loves to ridicule Hollywood "phonies," but Miss America is a supermodel of this time-honored and still booming showbiz genre. A book may have once been a substitute but is more often now the pretext for a Barbara Walters special.

Publishers make "writing" for these nonwriters as painless as possible, setting them up with ghosts and, after a few weeks of rambling into a tape recorder, voila, a new revenue stream. It's only when celebrities actually try to punctuate their own sentences that all hell breaks loose, as Random House and Joan Collins have testified.

The special aura that books still cast was never more apparent than in '95, when publications right, left, and center took addresses on the WWW and the Trial of the Century saturated TV news. It was a year when the sober confessions of a retired general nearly became the launching pad for a moonshot at the presidency, a feat many believe—judging by the long lines at book signings—he could have pulled off. *Time*'s "Man of the Year" and cheerleader for the cyber-future has his own television classroom and probably got more ink and airtime than anyone except O.J. But to prove that he was not just a crackpot sociologist, he needed to write a book. Even the Devil himself, in mapping the road ahead for the masses now in thrall to Microsoft (and taking another opportunity to promote his products), had to rely on a 500-year-old piece of technology to convey his message.

You prefer classics? *Last of the Mohicans, The Age of Innocence, Middlemarch, Persuasion,* and *Sense and Sensibility* are subway reading again. Publishers have learned how to bumper-surf on movies and PBS. The Library of America timed the release of Grant's and Sherman's memoirs to coincide with Ken Burns's Civil War series and its collection of war reporting with the anniversary of the Second World War's end. The market for children's books, thanks to boomers having babies, has been on an upswing for 10 years.

The portability of books and newspapers ensures their immediate survival into the next generation. I don't know anyone who takes their laptops to bed, to the beach, or on the bus. And were they one day flexible and light enough to be perused easily while eating Wheat Chex or stretched out on a sofa—and who doubts they won't be?—will people want to read fiction on a screen? The CD-ROM companies like Voyager that were loudly predicting as much a couple of years ago have been forced to eat their words.

"If you're just going to put words on a screen and expect people to read them, you're going to be disappointed," says Randi Benton, president of Random House New Media. "That's been proven in the marketplace. There was this hysteria for a while that all you had to do was take this material and move it from here to there. That doesn't work. Interactivity? I don't want to go to a movie and decide how it will end. Storytelling is an art. We need to find new ways of telling stories on computer. The book is a very effective storytelling tool."

In the long run, the price of materials and the vastness of cyberspace might very well tip the balance to computers. The jump in pulp paper costs this past year took a nasty bite out of every publisher's budget. The speed of data transmission and storage capacity of digital technology, which has already sent many print mechanisms to the junk heap, will only improve, while the book has reached evolutionary stasis. Benton looks forward to a handheld device that could be carried on vacation, instead of four hardcovers, and on which type-size could be adjusted. The Newton is a crude prototype of just such an invention.

When Gates was asked recently during a book-tour speech at the National Press Club if companies like his would kill off newspapers, he was careful not to boast or spook his listeners. He envisioned a long-term need for smart reporters and well-edited information—everyone was thrilled, of course, that he meant them.

Discussion Questions

1. What's your reaction to the statement that modern-day students are less willing than their predecessors to read books for intellectual stimulation?
2. What books do you read outside of course work and why?
3. How much time each day do you spend reading books versus using other media, including newspapers, television, radio, and magazines?

THE END OF
THE BOOK?

D. T. Max

■

"We'll teach you about multimedia before your kids have to."
—Billboard on Route 101 near Silicon Valley

An office-party atmosphere pervaded the headquarters of *Wired* magazine, the newly created oracle of the computer-literate generation. *Wired* is housed on the third floor of a flat, low brick building with plain-pine interiors in an industrial section of San Francisco south of Market Street. The area is known as Multimedia Gulch, for the scores of small companies working in the neighborhood which mix sound, video, and text into experimental interactive multimedia computer products that they hope will one day sell millions of copies. *Wired* is not an ordinary computer magazine: It promises the faithful reader not mere computing power—something available from a grown-up computer magazine like *Macworld*, which happens to be across the street—but, more important, hipness, the same sense of being ahead of the curve that once attached to a new Bob Dylan album or Richard Brautigan book.

The weekday afternoon I was there, hero sandwiches lay on the table, the magazine's pet gray parrot was hanging outside its cage, and young men and women with sophisticated eyewear sat rapt before their computer screens. The reference folders and layout paraphernalia common to magazine editorial departments were scattered around. The ringing of the phones was constant. When I had first called *Wired*'s co-founder, Louis Rossetto, in the summer of 1993, I got through to him immediately, and he had, if anything, too much time to speculate about the shape of things to come. Several months later I had to go through a secretary and a publicist for my interview, and once I arrived, I was made to wait while more urgent calls were put through. What happened in the interim is that the information highway became a hot subject. Rossetto was now every media journalist's and Hollywood agent's first call.

What I wanted from Louis Rossetto was his opinion on whether the rise of the computer culture that his magazine covered would end with the elimination by CD-ROMs and networked computer databases of the hardcover, the paperback, and the world of libraries and literate culture that had grown up alongside them. Was print on its way out? And if it was, what would happen to the publishers who had for generations put out books, and to the writers who had written them? Or was there something special about the book that would ensure that no technical innovation could ever supplant it? Would the book resist the CD-ROM and the Internet just as it has resisted radio, television, and the movies?

Finally I was taken into the sunlit confines of his office. Bookshelves ran along one wall. A forty-five-year-old career journalist with shoulder-grazing gray hair, Rossetto is a late convert to computers. He spent much of the 1980s in Europe, and gives off a mild sense of disengagement—there is a touch of the sixties about him, as there is about much else in the Gulch. Now he set out his vision of a fast-changing computerized, paperless, nearly book-free society, and did so with a certainty that would frighten even someone whose sense of equilibrium, unlike mine, did not involve visits to bookstores or the belief that last year's laptop is basically good enough. "The changes going on in the world now are literally a revolution in progress, a revolution that makes political revolution seem like a game," Rossetto, who recently sold a minority interest in his magazine to Condé Nast, said. "It will revolutionize how people work, how they communicate, and how they entertain themselves, and it is the biggest engine for change in our world today. We're looking at the end of a twenty- or thirty- or forty-year process, from the invention of tubes to transistors to fiber-optic and cable to the development of cable networks, until we've reached critical mass today."

I asked if there was no downside, no tradeoff for all that information in the world that was to come. "It doesn't keep me up at night, I admit," he said. "Written information is a relatively new phenomenon. Depositing it and being able to reference it centuries later is not common human experience. In some ways what is happening with online is a return to our earlier oral tradition. In other ways, it is utterly new, a direct connection of minds. Humans have always been isolated, and now we're starting to see electronic connections generating an intellectual organism of their own, literally a quantum leap beyond our experience with consciousness."

This is classic 1990s cybervisionarism, repeated up and down the halls of *Wired* and echoed throughout the Bay area, and it derives directly from the teenage-male personalities of the hackers who created the computer industry: Cyberspace will be like a better kind of school.

There are three principal articles of faith behind this vision. 1) The classroom will be huge: The linking of information worldwide will cause a democratic explosion in the accessibility of knowledge. 2) The classroom will be messy: The sense of information as an orderly and retrievable quantity will decline, and you won't necessarily be able to find what you're looking for in cyberspace at any given time. 3) There will be no teachers: The "controllers of information"—censors, editors, and studio executives—will disappear, and the gates of public discourse will swing open before everyone who can get online. Anyone can publish; anyone can read what is published; anyone can comment on what he or she has read. Rossetto had been delineating his vision for twenty minutes, but suddenly it was time to go. An assistant popped in to pull him into an editorial meeting. "I have a pretty cynical view of most of the American media," Rossetto said before leaving (read: "You'll get this wrong. You'll be hostile."). "Their jobs are at stake, because their businesses are threatened. Take *Time* magazine. What function would it have in the modern world?"

One look at *Wired* suggests a gap between message and messenger. *Wired* looks more radical than it is. It cheerleads and debunks its subjects using editorial formulas that came in with the nineteenth-century magazine—a fictional takeoff on Microsoft, written by Douglas Coupland, the author of *Generation X*; a classic star cover on Laurie Anderson, "America's multimediatrix"—rather than harnessing any global back-and-forth among literate minds. Although *Wired* communicates extensively by e-mail with its readers, conducts forums, and makes back issues available online, its much-repeated goal of creating a magazine—currently called *HotWired*—that is especially designed to exist electronically remains fuzzy. For the moment this is no open democracy, and *Wired* is no computer screen—its bright graphics would make a fashion magazine envious. *Wired* celebrates what doesn't yet exist by exploiting a format that does: It's as if a scribe copied out a manuscript extolling the beauty that would one day be print.

THE LIMITATIONS OF THE BOOK

Overhyped or not, interactive multimedia do hold vast potential for the companies that in the next decades back the right products in the right formats. Multimedia are not new—a child's pop-up book is one example, and an illustrated pre-Gutenberg Bible is another. But interactive multimedia as envisioned by the computer industry (especially if television cables or telephone wires are reconfigured to accommodate two-way high-quality video digital transmissions—technologies that may be in place on a national scale sometime around the millennium) have great potential, because they would persuade consumers to bring software into their homes as they brought it into their offices in the 1980s. Who wouldn't want a screen that accessed all currently existing forms of information, from mail to movies, and did so with great convenience and flexibility?

Even if this vision is only partly realized, the book, the newspaper, and the video will be hard-pressed to maintain their place in our culture. Look at the book without sentiment and its limitations are evident: Books can excite the imagination, but they can't literally make you see and hear. "What is the use of a book without pictures or conversations?" Lewis Carroll's Alice grouses, before tumbling down the rabbit hole into the more absorbing precincts of Wonderland, in one of the favorite texts of hackers. Interactive-multimedia designers, with their brew of sights, sounds, and words, believe that they could keep Alice (her age puts her very much in their target group) above-ground and interested. Or a multimedia designer could expand the book's plot line, giving the reader the choice of whether Alice goes down the hole or decides to stick around and read alongside her sister on the river bank. The reader could hear Alice's voice, or ask her questions about herself, the answers to which are only implicit in the book.

When something intrigues the readers of a printed book, they have to wrestle with an index and then, perhaps, go to a library to find out more about the subject; they can't just hit a search button to log on to a database attached to the book and read something else on the same subject, as they can on a computer. "I decided books were obsolete thirty-four years ago," says Ted Nelson, an early computer hacker who coined the word *hypertext* in the early sixties to describe how knowledge would be accessed if all information were available simultaneously. "I have thousands of books and I love them. It's only intertwining I want more of."

But such intertwining—a vast linkage of electronic text across databases worldwide—would inevitably push the printed word to the margins and replace it with sleeker, more efficient text conveyers. It is not the viability of text itself that is in question. On the contrary, whether paper gives way to the computer screen or not, there is little question that words as the cornerstone of communication are safe. *"Littera scripta manet,"* an anonymous Roman wrote: "The written word endures." This is a comforting quotation—typically if erroneously attributed to the poet Horace—that writers about multimedia are fond of using. In fact, words are multiplying wildly. In the world of computers they are a bargain compared with images: cheap to transport and easy to store. Probably more words are put out in a week by the twenty million people who use the loosely strung computer networks that constitute the Internet than are published by all major American publishing companies in a year. There's a "Poetry Corner" and bulletin boards where new novels get posted constantly. In a recent announcement a nonprofit organization called Project Gutenberg, run out of a university in Illinois, presented as its mysteriously precise goal "To Give Away One Trillion E[lectronic] Text Files [of classic books] by December 21, 2001." When I mentioned the scope of fiction on the Internet to the novelist John Updike, he said lightly, "I imagine most of that stuff on the information highway is roadkill anyway." And of course he is right. But his is a minority opinion outside the circles of tastemakers.

VAPORWARE INTIMIDATION

Text and books are not, however, joined at the hip—words don't need print. "Books on paper are a medium unto themselves," Louis Rossetto says, "and my sense is that anything that is stand-alone is a dead end." But even to Rossetto a world completely without books seems unlikely. One view is that the book will become the equivalent of the horse after the invention of the automobile or the phonograph record after the arrival of the compact disc—a thing for eccentrics, hobbyists, and historians. It will not disappear, but it will become obsolete. Multimedia programmers themselves disagree sharply on whether this will come to pass in five years, ten years, or never. One question is whether there is money to be made in the production of multimedia. Another is how good multimedia products will ever be, for by industry admission they are not very good now. The great majority of the three thousand multimedia products launched last year were little more than rudimentary efforts. "I think that there are fewer than thirty titles with good, solid, deep information out there," Rick Fischer, the director of product development at Sony Electronic Publishing, says. "The majority of titles are kind of pseudomultimedia. People are still learning how to do this." Besides, computer companies are not as excited by books as they are by games, which represent an ever-increasing share of the market. Sony, for example, has backed an interactive game version of its movie *Bram Stoker's Dracula*—Harker races against rats, wolves, and flaming torches to slay the Prince of Darkness—rather than the book *Dracula*, three hundred pages of print that could be augmented with perhaps a moving illustration or two.

Publishers are terrified. They have read a thousand times that one day we will play games, shop, watch movies, read books, and do research all on our computer or television screens. Computer companies are skillful at bluffing one another, forever claiming that they are nearly ready to release a hot new product, which is in truth barely in prototype. This kind of nonproduct has the nickname "vaporware" within the industry. But publishers, unfamiliar with computer culture, believe the hype. In the past year *Publishers Weekly* ran six major stories on how CD-ROM and the Internet will remake publishing. The comments of Laurence Kirshbaum, the president of Warner Books, a subsidiary of Time Warner, were not untypical: "I don't know if there's the smell of crisis in the air, but there should be. Publishers should be sleeping badly these days. They have to be prepared to compete with software giants like [Microsoft's chairman] Bill Gates." Publishers are most of all afraid of doing nothing—as hardback publishers did when they ignored the paperback explosion of the 1960s and 1970s. So they are rushing to form electronic-publishing divisions and to find partners in the software business. "Eighteen months ago no one was talking about multimedia and CD-ROMs seriously, and now everyone is deeply involved and deeply conscious of them," says Alberto Vitale, the chairman of the normally cautious Random House, Inc., which has signed a co-venture deal with Broderbund, a leading children's software developer in Novato, California, to create children's interactive multimedia. Putting Dr. Seuss on CD-ROM is one of their first efforts. The Palo Alto "media kitchen" owned by Viacom, where the company's film, television, and book divisions cooperate—at least theoretically—on interactive-multimedia research, is designing new travel guides: why actually go to San Francisco when by 1995 you will be able to take a virtual walking tour on a Frommer CD-ROM? Interest has even percolated into the last redoubt of traditional publishing, the firm of Alfred A. Knopf. Since its inception Knopf has placed great emphasis on the book as handsome object. But Knopf's president attended the first International Illustrated Book and New Media Publishing Market fair, held earlier this year, which was designed to introduce multimedia's various content providers to one another. (The fact that the fair was in Cannes probably did not hurt attendance.)

Behind the stampede into electronic publishing is doubtless a widespread feeling among those in conventional publishing that the industry is in dire, if ill-defined, trouble. A decade-long trend among major publishers toward publishing fewer trade books recently had an impact on four imprints in just two months, most notably a near-total cutback of Harcourt, Brace's trade department (the publishers of T. S. Eliot, Virginia Woolf, and Alice Walker) and the closing of Ticknor & Fields adult books, a Houghton Mifflin imprint (which included William Gass and Robert Stone among its authors). Aggressive marketing has allowed publishers to sell more copies of their top titles, creating the illusion of pink-cheeked health in some years. But after decades of competition from radio, television, movies, videos, and Americans' increasingly long workdays, it is hard to imagine how the publishers of mainstream fiction and nonfiction in book form will ever again publish as many titles as they did in the past; after all, popular fiction magazines never recovered from the advent of radio serials. Giants like Doubleday and Putnam publish perhaps a third as many hardcover books as they did ten years ago, and McGraw-Hill, once the publisher of Vladimir Nabokov and hundreds of other authors, is out of the new-trade-book business altogether. Recently, Random House sent a glass-is-half-full letter to book-review editors, letting them know that the company would be making their jobs easier by publishing fewer books. According to a 1993 survey by Dataquest, a San Jose information-technology market-research firm, most employees in the multimedia-content industry come from traditional print backgrounds. And the extremely rudimentary employment statistics that exist for the publishing industry show a decline since the late 1980s in New York–based publishing jobs, though it is hardly enough of one to confirm a sea change in publishing's fortunes, or to suggest that Armageddon is around the corner. Last year, nearly fifty thousand new titles destined for bookstores were published, and total consumer-reference CD-ROM software sales amounted to only about 3 percent of trade-book sales.

Besides, the computer industry acknowledges that what most readers think of as books—that is, novels and nonfiction text—gain nothing from being on screen; the appeal of the product depends on the quality of the prose and the research, neither of which is enhanced by current screens. Whether you scroll down a screen or turn a page to read *The Bridges of Madison County* makes a great deal of difference in the quality of the reading experience. "I just don't personally believe in reading novels on a computer screen," says Olaf Olafsson, the president of Sony Electronic Publishing and the author of *Absolution*, a novel published in March by Pantheon Books. He says that he would never want to see his own work on a computer: "There's a lot of content that's now being delivered on paper that's fine on paper." The book has great advantages over the computer: It's light and it's cheap. That it has changed little in four hundred years suggests an uncommonly apt design. John Updike says, "It seems to me the book has not just aesthetic values—the charming little clothy box of the thing, the smell of the glue, even the print, which has its own beauty. But there's something about the sensation of ink on paper that is in some sense a thing, a phenomenon rather than an epiphenomenon. I can't break the association of electric trash with the computer screen. Words on the screen give the sense of being just another passing electronic wriggle." You can drop a book in the bathtub, dry it out on the radiator, and still read it. You can put it in the attic, pull it out two hundred years later, and probably decipher the words. You can curl up in bed with it or get suntan lotion on it. These are definitely not possibilities suggested by the computer. A well-thumbed paperback copy of John Grisham blowing in a beach breeze represents a technological stronghold the computer may never invade.

A SOLUTION IN SEARCH
OF A PROBLEM

Lovers of literature (and schlock) may not see much change, then, but that doesn't mean publishers are in for an easy ride. Novels, nonfiction, and belles lettres are a prestige sideshow for publishers—they amount to only a few billion dollars in a roughly $18 billion book industry. Take dictionaries and encyclopedias, which are in effect databases in book form. The hand cannot match a computer chip in accessing given references, which constitutes the primary function of such works. Last year, the 1989 edition of the *Oxford English Dictionary*, the flagship publication of the four hundred-year-old university press, sold four times as many copies in a new CD-ROM version as in its traditional twenty-volume book form. The company has said that the next print edition, due in a decade, may well be the last. At an October 1993 celebration at the New York Public Library in honor of the publication of the fifth edition of the *Columbia Encyclopedia* in both book form and (a year hence) on CD-ROM, one guest speaker commented that the next edition, whenever it was ready, might well not have a paper counterpart. There was barely an objection from the audience.

Publishers are divided over the fate of so-called soft reference titles—cookbooks and how-to books—and children's books. These are huge markets, and the question is whether electronic books will capture them or expand on them. "My generation may be the last . . . to have a strong visceral affection for books," Janet Wikler, a former director of advanced media at HarperCollins, told *Publishers Weekly* last year.

What publishers have not stopped to consider is whether consumers like CD-ROMs in the first place—or how comfortable they will ever be with networked, digitalized, downloaded books when they become available. It may be a question of technical proficiency: How many families possess the sophistication to use Microsoft's new CD-ROM Musical Instruments—a charming visual and audio tour of the instruments of the world which is perfect for six-year-olds? The product requires either a multimedia computer or "a Multimedia PC upgrade kit, which includes CD-ROM drive (with CD-DA outputs, sustained 150K/second transfer rate and a maximum seek time of one second while using no more than 40 percent of the CPU's processing power)." Electronic encyclopedias have all but driven print encyclopedias out of the market in large part because they are "bundled"—sold at a deep discount to computer-hardware manufacturers to be included free when the consumer buys a CD-ROM drive. This is roughly like giving the consumer a book if he will only buy a lamp. "Traditional publishers may be a Luddite[1] elite, but software publishers are arrogant sheep," says Michael Mellin, a multimedia executive who until last year was the publisher of Random House's electronic-publishing division. "One thing publishers don't realize is that there hasn't been a comparable kick in sales of CD-ROM multimedia titles given the rise in the number of CD-ROM drives installed." In other words, books on CD-ROM don't sell—at least not yet. A study of the industry last year found that of those people who had bought a CD-ROM drive, fewer than half had returned to the computer store to buy new discs. Compare this with the way the compact-disc player caught on in the mid-1980s. Interactive multimedia may turn out to be the biggest bust since the paperless office. One former industry executive describes multimedia as "a solution in search of a problem, doing what other things do already, only slightly less well."

Publishers derive their impressions of the awesome potential of multimedia from products like Microsoft's much publicized Encarta CD-ROM, a magnificent encyclopedia with text drawn from Funk & Wagnalls's twenty-nine-volume encyclopedia and augmented by hundreds of video and audio clips. Alice would have fun with this: She could listen to bird calls and African drums, or experiment with changing the moon's orbit. (She could also click on

---

[1]Luddite: Someone who resists technology, especially in the form of automation (named after the farm laborers, said to be followers of "Ned Ludd," who rioted against mechanization in early nineteenth-century England).—Ed.

Bill Gates's name and hear his nasal assurance that Microsoft "has never wavered from the vision" of a personal computer "on every desk and in every home." This was not part of Funk & Wagnalls's original text.) But having been five years in development, employing a hundred people at its peak, and reportedly costing Microsoft well upward of $5 million, Encarta may be something of a Potemkin Village,[2] meant for credulous competitors to marvel at. The company has dropped the price from $395 to $139 to try to get consumers to buy it.

THE LIMITATIONS OF THE COMPUTER

Paper has limitations, but the computer may have more. As a physical object, it is hardly comforting. "Who'd want to go to bed with a Powerbook?" John Baker, a vice president at Broderbund, asks. And even if the laptop goes on shrinking, its screen, whose components represent nearly all the machine's cost, remains at best a chore to read. At the Xerox Palo Alto Research Center (where the receptionist's cubicle still houses an IBM Selectric typewriter) is a display room with half a dozen prototype six-million-pixel AMLCD screens. The quiet hum of the room, the bright white lighting, the clean, flat antiseptic surfaces, give the impression of an aspirin commercial. "It was clear to us that no reader was going to read a book off any of the current screens for more than ten minutes," says Malcolm Thompson, the chief technologist. "We hoped to change that." A large annotated poster on the wall illustrates point for point the screen's superiority to paper, as in an old-fashioned magazine ad. This flat panel display is indeed better than commercial screens, but it is neither as flexible nor as mobile as a book, and it still depends on fickle battery power. A twentysomething software marketer who began as an editorial assistant in book publishing points out, "A book requires one good eye, one good light source, and one good finger."

LOST IN CYBERSPACE

In the heart of official Washington, D.C., down the street from the Capitol and at the same intersection as the Supreme Court and the Library of Congress, stands an incongruous statue of Puck, whom the *Oxford Companion to English Literature*, soon to be issued on CD-ROM, defines as "a goblin," and whom Microsoft Encarta passes over in favor of "puck," which it defines solely as a mouselike device with crosshairs printed on it, used in engineering applications. The 1930s building next to the statue is the Folger Shakespeare Li-

---

[2]Potemkin Village: Grigori Aleksandrovich Potemkin (1739–1791) constructed elaborate fake villages to impress Russian Empress Catherine the Great when she toured the Ukraine and the Crimea.—Ed.

brary. Two flights below the reading room, designed in the style of a Tudor banquet hall, next to which librarians and scholars click quietly on laptops and log on to the Internet's Shaksper reference group for the latest scholarly chatter, is a locked bank gate. Behind it is what librarians call a "short-title catalogue vault"—in other words, a very-rare-book room. This main room—there is another—is rectangular, carpeted in red, and kept permanently at 68 degrees. Sprinkler valves are interspersed among eight evenly spaced shelves of books dating from 1475 to 1640 and lit by harsh institutional light. Of these books 180 are the only copies of their titles left in the world: You can spot them by the small blue slips reading "Unique" which modestly poke out from their tops. At the end of the room is a long shelf on which stacks of oversize volumes rest on their sides: These are nearly a third of the surviving First Folio editions of the plays of William Shakespeare. When the First Folios were printed, in the 1620s, printing was still an inexact art. Each page had to be checked by hand, and the volumes are full of mistakes: backward type, ill-cut pages, and variant lines. Several copies lack the 1602 tragedy *Troilus and Cressida*, owing to a copyright dispute. And yet, 370 years after they came off the printing press, you can still pull down these books and read them. The pages are often lightly cockled and foxed,[3] because the folio was printed on mid-priced rag paper, but the type is still bright and the volume falls open easily. You can balance it on your lap and run your finger along the page to feel the paper grain in that sensuous gesture known to centuries of book readers: Here is knowledge.

In 1620 Francis Bacon ranked printing, along with gunpowder and the compass, as one of the three inventions that had "changed the appearance and state of the whole world." Indeed, the existence of multiple identical copies of texts that are nearly indelibly recorded, permanently retrievable, and widely decipherable has determined so much of modern history that what the world would be like without printing can only be guessed at. More books likely came into existence in the fifty years after the Gutenberg Bible than in the millennium that preceded it. "Printing was a huge change for Western culture," says Paul Saffo, who studies the effect of technology on society at the Institute for the Future, in Menlo Park (where the receptionist also uses an IBM Selectric). "The dominant intellectual skill before the age of print was the art of memory." And now we may be going back.

For the question may not be whether, given enough time, CD-ROMs and the Internet can replace books, but whether they should. Ours is a culture that has made a fetish of impermanence. Paperbacks disintegrate, Polaroids fade, video images wear out. Perhaps the first novel ever written specifically to be read on a computer and to take advantage of the concept of hypertext—the structuring of written passages to allow the reader to take different paths

---

[3]Over time, books and manuscripts can become wrinkled or puckered (cockled) as well as discolored (foxed) from acid residues in the paper.—Ed.

through the story—was Rob Swigart's *Portal*, published in 1986 and designed for the Apple Macintosh, among other computers of its day. The Apple Macintosh was superseded months later by the more sophisticated Macintosh SE, which, according to Swigart, could not run his hypertext novel. Over time people threw out their old computers (fewer and fewer new programs could be run on them), and so *Portal* became for the most part unreadable. A similar fate will befall literary works of the future if they are committed not to paper but to transitional technology like diskettes, CD-ROMs, and UNIX tapes—candidates, with eight-track tapes, Betamax, and the Apple Macintosh, for rapid obscurity. "It's not clear, with fifty incompatible standards around, what will survive," says Ted Nelson, the computer pioneer, who has grown disenchanted with the forces commercializing the Internet. "The so-called information age is really the age of information lost." Software companies don't care—early moviemakers didn't worry that they were filming on volatile stock. In a graphic dramatization of this mad dash to obsolescence, in 1992 the author William Gibson, who coined the term "cyberspace," created an autobiographical story on computer disc called "Agrippa." "Agrippa" is encoded to erase itself entirely as the purchaser plays the story. Only thirty-five copies were printed, and those who bought it left it intact. One copy was somehow pirated and sent out onto the Internet, where anyone could copy it. Many users did, but who and where is not consistently indexed, nor are the copies permanent—the Internet is anarchic. "The original disc is already almost obsolete on Macintoshes," says Kevin Begos, the publisher of "Agrippa." "Within four or five years it will get very hard to find a machine that will run it." Collectors will soon find Gibson's story gone before they can destroy it themselves.

DISCUSSION QUESTIONS

1. What, if any, books have been important in your life? Why?
2. What importance do books play in our society as a whole?
3. Do you think books are dead or becoming obsolete? Why, or why not?

PORTRAIT OF A BOOK REVIEWER: CHRISTOPHER LEHMANN-HAUPT

Joseph Deitch

•

An avid baseball fan who is an insatiable reader once spent a year in search of his sport's gods. He ended up with a bat in his hands facing Goose Gossage, the fireball pitcher for the New York Yankees. The confrontation took place on a late afternoon in Yankee Stadium. Shaking in fear, the fan waited for the pitch. It and others came with blinding speed and, much to his surprise, he connected each time. His saga concludes: "Gossage throws again, and this time I put some muscle in my swing. The crack of the bat feels sweet. The ball is rising in the night sky. Lara [Yankee batting coach] is whistling. [Manager Billy] Martin steps onto the field. Somebody is even cheering."

None of this happened, of course. The batter was, of all people, Christopher Lehmann-Haupt, the senior daily book critic of the *New York Times*. His adventures and misadventures and daydreamed encounter with Gossage are recalled in *Me and DiMaggio*, published last year by Simon & Schuster.

Lehmann-Haupt's chief baseball divinity is "Joltin' Joe," also called DiMaggio, who, in addition to superb fielding, hit safely in fifty-six consecutive games, including three fan-hysterical home runs in one game. For the first time, the man who had written reviews of two thousand books was himself reviewed last year. If anything, *Me and DiMaggio* enabled him to feel what a couple of thousand other authors felt as they awaited verdicts from one of the most influential book critics in the country.

In an interview at his home in the Riverdale section of the Bronx, Lehmann-Haupt seemed content with the book's critical reception. It received a good number of favorable reviews and a few bad ones. "What I missed was an intelligent bad review from someone who knew what I was trying to do," he said. "Many of the good reviews understood this. I did not mind the bad reviews, but most of them were stupid."

92

Book reviewing is done with widely assorted degrees of responsibility, seriousness, and competence in thousands of newspapers, magazines, professional journals, and in broadcasting. It is becoming recognized that a book—or play, opera, pianist, dancer, actor, TV show, painter, monologist, or zitherist—may get rave notices elsewhere, but if the *New York Times* doesn't like the way these cultural commodities are handled, the customers are apt to stay away in droves. Especially if it is books.

A kind word about a book from the *Times* alone may get it on somebody's best-seller list. An adverse, or bad, review could consign it to oblivion, even though other papers praised the book. Aware of its influence, the *Times* takes the quality of its criticism and its critical standards most seriously.

For many, *Times* criticism—in authority, experience, and objectivity—is about the best in world journalism. Much of it can give the best academic criticism a run for its money. What, I recently wondered, goes on behind the scenes for a *Times* daily book review—for "Books of the *Times*," as this column is titled? Do Lehmann-Haupt and his daily-reviewer colleagues, John Gross and Michiko Kakutani, arrive in the morning, put their feet up on desks, and start reading, break for lunch, return, put their feet up on desks again and read till five, come in next morning and tap out their reviews—then repeat the process for the next books?

The reviewing procedure for Lehmann-Haupt (probably much the same way for his colleagues) is carried out in two-day cycles, working at home. It begins, of course, with picking books for review. Lehmann-Haupt receives about five thousand books a year—those sold in bookstores for off-the-street trade; no textbooks. Books come to his desk for review at the rate of a hundred or so a week—more at the height of the publishing seasons in spring and fall.

He opens the book packages himself. By doing so, he weeds out 90 percent of what comes in. He can tell by the titles which books do not belong in "Books of the *Times*." Immediately rejected are books on specialized subjects and most cookbooks. Books that seem to deserve review go into his study. "I have been doing this for so long, it is hard to articulate, anymore, why I choose among these for review." In general, the criteria are that books have to do with the news—directly, like the new Bob Woodward book, *Veil: The Secret Wars of the CIA 1981–87*. New books by prominent writers constitute news of this kind.

Lehmann-Haupt often works under deadlines. *Veil* was an example. He had to produce his review for publication the same day, September 30, 1987, as a *Times* news story on the book out of Washington. Lehmann-Haupt got the book at 4:30 P.M. on September 28. His deadline was 4 P.M. the next day. He met the deadline by reading the 543-page book and writing his approximately one thousand-word review in less than twenty-four hours.

Another type of major book news, in contrast to books whose contents make news, is the sale of a paperback for millions of dollars. "People become curious about what such a book is like, and buy it," Lehmann-Haupt said. Asked if the new book by John Kenneth Galbraith, *Economics in Perspective,* might be reviewed for news value, he said the author's name and reputation and his role in economic history for fifty years would warrant attention in "Books of the *Times.*"

Even from the ten out of a hundred books that become candidates for the column every week, the *Times* senior reviewer has to "pick and choose before admitting two of them to my column every week." Great care goes into selection "because I only do two reviews a week for the thousands of books we receive—only," he added with some irony, as if those two reading, judging, and writing chores were enough.

Although he gets some books a month or so before publication dates, he does not read ahead, he said. "If I do, I tend to forget what I read in advance by the time I get around to giving the book full attention."

He would normally start reading the Woodward book on Sunday night—Lehmann-Haupt was interviewed on Saturday afternoon. The book was not available until Monday, which meant that he would have to read "very fast" for a Wednesday morning appearance in "Books of the *Times*" in conjunction with the *Times* Washington bureau story on newsworthy revelations in the book. Usually, his reviews are due late Tuesday night or Wednesday morning. But the need to read a book in a day or less does not come up often.

Why the occasional need for speed?

The paper wants to be among the first to report on a book with news potential, and the review itself becomes a kind of news story, with evaluation of content. The *Times* had assigned someone to search the book for news. "My job is to report what *Veil* is like as a book: Is it an interesting story? The question on everybody's mind is, What did Woodward discover that is worth 543 pages?" A lot of newsworthy stories but much else, according to Lehmann-Haupt's review, that was "irrelevant," "morally neutral," "lacking in narrative punch," "a great deal taken on faith," and failure to identify most of the 250 people Woodward said he interviewed.

" 'Books of the *Times*' is supposed to come out with the first reviews of books, but it isn't always first by any means," Lehmann-Haupt said. It competes, most of all, with Sunday's *Times Book Review*, which has much more space. As preparation for his reviews and as a professional reader and critic, Lehmann-Haupt takes extensive notes and makes marginal notes for his eight hundred- to one thousand-word critiques.

After finishing a book, he goes over his notes and underlines, in red, the high points, which he has already "asterisked." Then he draws a line down the middle of an 8½-by-11-inch sheet of paper. On the left side of the line, he makes a list of points he wants to include in the review. On the right side, he outlines the review—the most difficult and creative part of the process, he said. He adheres "pretty strictly" to the outline.

You might think that Lehmann-Haupt and other professional readers and book critics must be among the world's fastest readers. Lehmann-Haupt is not a particularly fast reader. He can read speedily if he has to. His normal rate is rather slow. He likes to savor what he reads and to "exercise his imagination." By imagination, he means the link between words and the pictures they conjure up. It takes slower reading to form pictures, he said.

He waits for a book to impact on him and even to justify its existence. He does not do research on a book's subject. He might check to see what the author's earlier books were about and how the new book fits in. Beyond that, he does not delve deeply into a book's subject in advance or while reading it. "There just isn't time on a daily paper," he said. "I take the background for it out of my head"—a reference library of world affairs, events, and people, drawn on as needed.

He added: "In reading and reviewing the Galbraith book, I did not fancy myself an economist who could say that he is wrong about this and right about that. The two things I had to tell was first, the satisfaction of getting a sense of everything in its place. The other was to convey the clarification I got—after reading about it over and over again, like the ideas of classical economists—about the book's governing principle. This was the notion of perspective that allowed the author to select only what he thinks is important and to be critical of ideas he does not agree with from his perspective."

Lehmann-Haupt made a distinction between reviewing and criticism. To begin with, the daily *New York Times* reports the news. The Sunday edition, including the "Book Review," has more time and space to reflect on the news. Many books reviewed by Lehmann-Haupt are in the context of the day's news or of the recent past.

"Sunday book critics are presumably experts on their subjects, and the three of us who do 'Books of the *Times*' are not," Lehmann-Haupt said. The daily reviews are often part of each day's news mainstream.

"We are intelligent ombudsmen for the reader who is going to tell other people what the experience of reading a book is like. The Sunday reviewer comes along and says the book may be fun to read, as the daily reviewer has already said, but adds his own perspectives. Ideally, the reader reads the two reviews back to back and learns one thing from the daily and something else from the Sunday review."

Lehmann-Haupt reads as fast as the book demands. Where the writing and content are important, he reads slowly, he said. Where a book conveys a lot of information, he will read it faster. "If you have been around books, professionally, long enough, you know how to read them. You know where you can skim or will have to read every word. The first will give you a better sense of a book's structure. If you have to skim, chapter headings, bibliography—even the rhythm of the prose and sentence structure—can more quickly help determine the author's main points. But this is a matter of experience.

"So my advice is that the more you read, the better you get at it."

Letters from readers praise, criticize, or offer information and insight. Generally, they get a form response—"there isn't time to do more, except for letters from distinguished people in their fields from whom I learn something. They get personal letters."

Authors who complain, in print, about bad reviews given them in *The New York Times Book Review* and in other book sections play a risky game. Below their usually long letters to the editor wondering, for example, if the reviewers really read their books, the reviewers are given a chance to respond. Reviewers are apt to reply that they reread the complaining author's book and not only stand by their initial criticisms but found the book even worse on a second reading.

The *Times*'s senior book critic got a complaining letter sent to Arthur Gelb, one of the paper's news executives. It was from Joan Peyser, author of a biography of Leonard Bernstein, the conductor. Lehmann-Haupt did not like the book. The letter noted that he had once been a tenant of hers in a building she owned and that he should not have been allowed to review a book by his former landlord.

"She said it was not fair, implying that the experience of being a tenant would dispose me not to like her book," Lehmann-Haupt said. "She also said that I had snatched the book from another reviewer to get revenge on her [by panning her book]." All this happened some twenty years ago, at about the time he went to work for the *Times*.

"The irony is that I never disliked her at all. In fact, she always treated me as if she was dying for me to review her. It was amusing, to us, that she turned everything around after she got the negative review."

Lehmann-Haupt did a hitch in the army and trained as an artilleryman at Fort Sill, Oklahoma. He played a lot of golf at the fort's links, "where enlisted men and officers were equal." He holds a master's degree from the Yale University Drama School. Married, he has two children, Rachel and Noah, to whom—with Natalie, his wife—he dedicated *Me and DiMaggio*. They "cheered," the dedicatory note says.

His venture into fantasy in the book's last chapter—Billy Martin leaves the Yankee dugout to see who hit that long fly ball—displays a gift for fiction. He is, in fact, writing a novel, which led me to ask, "As a book critic, what do you expect of a novel?"

He has no rules, "except that it engage me at some level of intellect or emotion and that it do something to me. It doesn't have to be a story, which is often totally lacking in modern fiction, yet, through some magic, you are moved to feel or think. I try hard to review novels on their own terms: What is it trying to do and does it succeed?"

Lehmann-Haupt tends not to use sweeping adjectives, pro or con. About as far as he has gone on the favorable end was to call Philip Roth's *Portnoy's Complaint* a "technical masterpiece" and "tour de force," but he uses these terms very sparingly, he said.

Doesn't all reviewing boil down to letting readers know whether they should buy or, in any case, read a book?

"No. Many readers merely want to know about the book so they don't have to buy or read it. They want to be able to talk about it at cocktail parties. Reviews enable them to do that.

"There's only so much time we can give to reading these days. Even I read half of what I should read. I would like people to get from my reviews a sense of what a book is about and where to put it in their minds."

Does he tire of the endless stream of "definitive" biographies—of Thomas Wolfe, Faulkner, Hemingway, H. G. Wells, Dostoyevski, among others? "You mean the bios that, in Hemingway's case, minutely describe every duck he shot and every bottle of wine he drank," Lehmann-Haupt said. "Their value is that they enable more selective writers to winnow through them for everything they might want to know for their biographies."

This and a publishing incident in Wolfe's *Of Time and the River* that I mentioned reminded Lehmann-Haupt of the publisher he worked for who appeared not to read manuscripts but "rippled through them to make sure there was print on each page and then said, 'Yes, we'll publish this.' "

The greater a book's challenge, the greater the excitement for the *Times*'s senior book critic. One of the most challenging in several years was Allan Bloom's *The Closing of the American Mind*, "an outstanding book that hits," he said, quoting an ad for the book, "with the approximate effect of electric shock therapy."

The great British critic George Saintsbury called book reviewing the "difficult art." "Any art is difficult: difficult to do well," Lehmann-Haupt said. "Even after doing it for twenty years, I can hit only one out of ten, and I am being generous to myself. Only one book in ten isn't routine. And it doesn't matter whether it is, as you say, quite a good book. It is the one that not only compels you to write a good review of it, but it transcends itself not only by saying something worthwhile about its subject but about life.

"That's where reviewing becomes art—everything comes together for the review, like a batter focusing himself to hit a baseball. Even so, he will hit a home run in maybe seven or eight times at bat."

The failure of such twentieth-century literary titans as Proust, Henry James, James Joyce, and Nabokov to win Nobel Prizes greatly lessened Lehmann-Haupt's respect for that award. The Pulitzer Prize for fiction "invariably goes to a mediocre book," he said.

Sitting at ease in his living room amid family pictures, it seemed, for a moment, hard to reconcile Lehmann-Haupt with the power and influence he could wield as the *Times* senior book reviewer. A word or two from the *Times*, or so popular perception might indicate, could make or break a book. "Not really," he said. Book critics "are not as powerful as *Times*'s theater criticism, which can close down a show. Fortunately, we are not as powerful as that." But the *Times* does better, more convincing criticism—"Perhaps more influential; I am not sure about better.

"I try not to be conscious of 'power.' Any review sort of legitimizes a book in a way that an unreviewed book is not. Certain reviews are capable of selling large numbers of books and, in certain cases, negative reviews hurt books." Suggestions of power and influence "are not relevant to reading and reviewing. What you try to do is your job."

DISCUSSION QUESTIONS
1. Do you read book reviews? Why, or why not?
2. What do expect from a book reviewer?
3. Do you think that book reviewers have too much power in determining whether an author will be successful? Why, or why not?

CHAPTER 7

NEWSPAPERS

David Noack, *Gathering News Online*

Jay Rosen, *Public Journalism: A Case for Public Scholarship*

Edwin Diamond and Gregg Geller, *Campaigns, Elections, and "Public Journalism": Civic-Mindedness or Mindless Cheerleading?*

Anewspaper, in a broad sense, is an unbound publication issued at regular intervals that seeks to inform, analyze, influence, and entertain. For the most part, the purpose of the newspaper has been to reach as many people as possible at a reasonable cost.

The earliest newspapers were handwritten notices in ancient Rome. The first newspaper in America was a Boston newssheet entitled "Publick Occurrenses Both Forreign and Domestick," published in 1690. It appeared only once. America's first regularly published newspaper was the *Boston News-Letter* in 1704.

An estimated 60,000 newspapers exist worldwide today with a combined circulation of nearly 500 million. About a third of all newspapers are published in North America, which has about 125 million readers.

There are a variety of pressures on today's newspapers. One important change is the Internet and its role as a source of information. The first reading in this chapter looks at how journalists are using the Internet as a means of obtaining information. Another concern of newspapers today is the belief that many publications may be out of touch with their readers. The second and third readings focus on the issue of public journalism—an attempt by some newspapers to become more actively engaged in their community. The second reading is by one of public journalism's leading advocates, and the third by one of its harshest critics—both former colleagues at New York University. These authors are Jay Rosen, the intellectual leader of the public journalism movement, and Edwin Diamond, the late editor, author, and media critic who regarded this movement as public "relations" journalism.

GATHERING NEWS ONLINE
David Noack

•

Heather Newman was in a situation most reporters know all too well. The DuPont plant in Nashville had struggled to make a particular line of synthetic fibers profitable in the hopes that corporate management would approve a plant expansion. However, when word finally got out—through unofficial sources and after working hours—that the multinational corporation decided instead to enlarge a factory in Spain, the race for information was on. "I was suddenly faced with the need to know everything about DuPont's Spain operations—after hours. Local executives were out. I was on deadline," recalled Newman, a business reporter for the *Tennessean*.

So she conducted a quick electronic search using the Securities and Exchange Commission's EDGAR archives and found the company's public filings, downloaded what she needed and used a simple word processor to run a key word search for references to "Spain."

"I had all I needed to know in 10 minutes, and I never would have been able to track it down that night by conventional means," she said. That example points up the power and versatility of the Internet to provide accurate information quickly.

But finding information on the Internet is an acquired skill. "Learn the resources first if you expect to use them quickly," advised Newman, who encourages reporters to sign up for mailing lists, which are discussion lists via e-mail.

One thing Newman avoids, if possible, is extended interviews online. "People are much more stiff in print than they are in person, or even over the phone," she said. "It's much more difficult to wander off on those conversational tangents that can be better than the original question and answer," said Newman.

Patrick Lee, a business reporter for the *Los Angeles Times*, finds the Internet a useful resource, not only for SEC documents on EDGAR (Electronic Data Gathering, Analysis, and Retrieval, http://www.sec.gov/edgarhp.htm/), but also for government economic, employment and census data.

When writing about a recent U.S.–China trade dispute, he was able to download export-import information from the International Trade Administration. And, for a story about electric utilities, he culled briefs and data from the California Public Utilities home page. "Pulling them off the Internet can save a lot of time. E-mail is also very useful, particularly if I persuade a source to send me a compressed data file," said Lee.

His advice for reporters seeking to "surf" the Internet when piecing together a story is to become familiar with a variety of search techniques, know what you're looking for, and rely on "primary sources of data from reputable sites: government, trade associations, academic institutions."

Lee said he generally doesn't use corporate or government press release sites. "I bypass press releases and canned statements and head straight for the statistics, official reports or full documents. The advantage of the Internet is that you can go to the primary sources directly without an intermediary," he said.

Gary Deckelnick, legal affairs editor for the *Asbury Park Press* and *Home News & Tribune* in New Jersey, cautions that using the Internet does not mean that journalistic standards can be relaxed. "Like anything else, the Internet provides good leads. Leads are the key. Anyone can sign on with any name and create their own home page and put up there what they want. That does not make it official. The more you know the person or group, the more you can rely on the most important premise: They are who they say they are," said Deckelnick.

Online services that tout experts on any number of topics shouldn't be treated any differently than other experts seeking to be quoted, he advised. "You weigh what they say, evaluate their credentials and act accordingly. There's no law requiring you to print everything you get from ProfNet or everything you get from interviewing the local mayor," he said. ProfNet links reporters to public affairs officers at universities, government agencies and corporations.

Neil Reisner, a training director of the National Institute for Computer-Assisted Reporting and adjunct professor at the Columbia University Graduate School of Journalism, called the Internet just another tool among many for journalists. "Use the same methods you use to verify any other source. It isn't different from the anonymous phone call, a document that comes in over the transom, a fax, or even a press release," he said.

A former database editor at the *Record* in Bergen County, N.J., Reisner said that getting raw data—such as census or labor information—and feeding it into a spreadsheet or database program yields results. "I've downloaded data, for example, to analyze teacher salaries in contrast to the inflation rate," he said about information from the Bureau of Labor Statistics.

The growing importance of the Internet and the World Wide Web as both a news and news-gathering source is bolstered by a recent survey. It found that 23% of editors report they or their staff used the Internet and commercial online services daily—up from 16% a year before. In addition, 56% of reporters say they want future dealings with companies and public relations firms to be online.

This survey, "The Media in Cyberspace," was conducted by Donald Middleberg, CEO of Middleberg & Associates, a New York PR firm and Steven S. Ross, an associate professor at the Columbia University Graduate School of Journalism. The 1995 study <http://www.mediasource.com/study/> reflects the views of more than 800 newspaper and magazine editors.

Today, members of the Fourth Estate can be found just about anywhere on the Internet. They are searching Web sites for stories, prowling news groups for sources and comments, downloading documents and discovering new story angles and spotting trends.

If you need to beef up or create an electronic Rolodex, here are some places to start.

Patrick Casey, an Associated Press reporter based in Oklahoma City, has created a Web page named The Reporters Internet Survivors Guide <http://www.qns.com/~casey/>. He has compiled a handy list of government, reference and search links. They include the Interior Department and FedWorld; references such as On-Line Medical Resources, On-Line News and popular directories and search engines such as Yahoo!, Lycos and Alta Vista.

Journalist Robert Niles has created Finding Data <http://www.probe.net/~niles/>, where you can find links to crime, population and economic statistics, and financial, health, military and nonprofit organizations.

The National Press Club <http://town.hall.org/places/npc/>, which provides links to government agencies, also offers extensive links to sites dealing with accounting, energy, higher education, pharmaceuticals and religion.

ProfNet <http://www.vyne.com/profnet/>, which links more than 2,100 public information officers (PIOs) at 800 colleges in 17 countries, offers access to academics and researchers.

BznetUSA <http://top.monad.net/~gehrung/> provides expert sources from the nation's top business schools. Information can be gleaned on national business trends, financial analysis, workplace trends and corporate culture.

The Yearbook of Experts, Authorities and Spokespersons site <http://www.yearbook.com/> provides a searchable database by topic and key word.

An all-in-one resource for reaching public affairs professionals is the Public Affairs Web <http://www.publicaffairsweb.com/>, with links to 14 categories of spokespersons from government, unions, nonprofits, the media, education, and politicians.

Recently, Counsel Connect, an online service for attorneys, launched Counsel Quote <http://www.counsel.com/counselquote/>, where reporters can post questions and get feedback regarding Supreme Court decisions or pending legislation.

Another source of experts is Tradeshow Central <http://www
.tscentral.com/>, a global database of more than 8,800 trade shows that provides leads to sources in a wide variety of fields.

Web sites for corporate news include PRESSline <http://www.press
line.com/>, which offers more than 20,000 press releases. There's a handy
FAQ (frequently asked questions) telling reporters on when releases can be retrieved and how to run key word searches.

Company News on Call <http://www.prnewswire.com/> provides news
releases from participating PR Newswire members. Here, you get the full text
of news releases moments after they are transmitted by PR Newswire. In addition, items are listed by industry: automotive, entertainment, health care,
technology and government.

Corporate Financials Online offers releases from more than 80 companies, all customers of Corporate Financials Online who first distribute releases
on the financial news wires and in other media. In addition, there are also
links to publicly traded companies <http://www.cfonews.com/>.

Project Vote Smart <http://www.vote-smart.org/>, a nonpartisan political research group in Corvallis, Ore., provides unbiased political research.
You'll find updated congressional voting records; presidential, congressional
and gubernatorial campaign information; and links to other key directories of
political information.

If you're looking for an all-in-one database site, then tap into Internet
Sleuth <http://www.intbc.com/sleuth/>, a compilation of more than 900 databases encompassing high-tech firms, news groups, the food and beverage industry, aviation and reference material.

DISCUSSION QUESTIONS

1. Do you generally trust what journalists report? Why, or why not?
2. Do you think that journalism will be better or worse in the age of digital reporting, or do you think it will stay the same? Why?
3. Digital journalism allows the reader to see original documents used by the
   reporter. Do you use that information or intend to use it? Why, or why not?

Public Journalism: A Case for Public Scholarship

Jay Rosen

∎

... [W]hat exactly is public journalism? It's at least three things. First, it's an argument about the proper task of the press. Second, it's a set of practices that are slowly spreading through American journalism. Third, it's a movement of people and institutions.

What the argument says is this: Journalism cannot remain valuable unless public life remains viable. If public life is in trouble in the United States, then journalism is in trouble. Therefore, journalists should do what they can to support public life. The press should help citizens participate and take them seriously when they do. It should nourish or create the sort of public talk that might get us somewhere, what some of us would call a deliberative dialogue. The press should change its focus on the public world so that citizens aren't reduced to spectators in a drama dominated by professionals and technicians. Most important, perhaps, journalists must learn to see hope as an essential resource that they cannot deplete indefinitely without tremendous costs to us and them.

The argument public journalism makes is derivative of academic theory. It is borrowed from the work of German philosopher Jurgen Habermas on the public sphere, from John Dewey's great book, *The Public and Its Problems*, and from the writings of James Carey, perhaps the leading journalism educator in the United States. What is distinctive about the argument is not the ideas in it, but the simple fact that journalists are helping to create the argument.

As an example, I offer my working relationship with Davis Merritt Jr., the editor of the *Wichita Eagle*. Merritt is my partner in crime. I consult with him weekly, we have shared many platforms together, and he is identified with the rise of public journalism to visibility within the profession. He has written a book on the approach and is trying to practice what he preaches. Merritt brings more than 30 years of journalism experience to the table and is persuasive to his colleagues in a way that I could never be. By doing something he's willing to call "public journalism," by urging his colleagues to try their own versions, he prevents the idea from becoming merely "academic."

Public journalism is also a set of practices, most of them experiments by local newspapers trying to connect with citizens in a more useful way. For example, the *Charlotte Observer* in 1992 abandoned the approach to election coverage known as the horse-race angle. Instead it sought to ground its coverage in what it called a "citizen's agenda," meaning a list of discussion priorities identified by area residents through the paper's own research. When candidates gave an important speech during the campaign, the contents were "mapped" against the citizen's agenda, so that it was easy to tell what was said about those concerns that ranked highest with citizens.

This may seem like a modest reform, but it involved a fundamental shift in the mission of campaign journalism. The master narrative changed from something like, "Candidates maneuver and manipulate in search of votes" to something like, "Citizens of Charlotte demand serious discussion." The Charlotte approach has become widely known and widely copied because it addresses long-standing frustrations with a campaign dialogue dominated by political professionals and the cynicism they engender.

A second kind of public journalism initiative is under way at the *Norfolk Virginian Pilot*. There, the editors have created something called the "public life team," which is a group of reporters assigned to cover politics and government in a "more public" way. Previously, these reporters would have been attached to institutions like city hall, and this attachment would have provided them with their lens on politics. The public life team is charged with inventing a more bottom-up orientation to public affairs reporting—one that includes city hall but doesn't originate there. Among the techniques they employ is the use of small deliberative forums, what they call "community conversations," not to ask people what they want to read, or to survey their opinions, but to discover how non-professionals name and frame issues. This then becomes the starting point for the paper's political reporting, replacing the usual sources—the machinations of insiders or the maneuvering of public officials.

In effect, Norfolk is trying to routinize the shift in narrative strategy that the *Charlotte Observer* undertook in its campaign coverage. As the public life team learns how public journalism is done—and they are very much inventing it as they go—they teach what they know to other teams of reporters. This past March, I assisted the editors of the *Virginian Pilot* in a weekend retreat intended to jump-start the process of changing routines. Fifty participants devoted three days to thinking through the shift in consciousness and technique that public journalism demands. The editors and I agreed on a price of admission to this retreat: a rather lengthy reading list of works in democratic theory and press scholarship, including essays by political scientist Robert Putnam of Harvard, along with excerpts from Daniel Yankelovich's important work, *Coming to Public Judgment*, and de Tocqueville's *Democracy in America*.

Officials of Landmark Communications, the company that owns the newspaper, chose to attend and they did the reading, too.

This retreat meant creating a public space for intellect within journalism. When 50 working journalists take time out to spend the weekend struggling with the implications of democratic theory and press criticism for their own work, when they do so under the expectation that they will reform their routines accordingly, when the executives within their company are joining them in this adventure, I hope you can see how a new kind of space has been created. As far as I know, nothing like it has been attempted in American journalism. This is public scholarship and public journalism brought together.

Other public journalism practices have involved creating public forums that show citizens engaged in deliberative dialogue. The forums, sponsored by a media partnership in Madison, Wisconsin, model democratic habits of mind and conversation. In several places, like Boulder, Colorado, and Olympia, Washington, newspapers have intervened in a lethargic public climate, bringing together civic leaders, experts, and groups of citizens to chart a long-term vision for a community, which is then published and debated in the newspaper. There have been various efforts to focus political reporting on the search for solutions to public problems; and a variety of measures have been adopted to heighten the visibility of citizens in the news by, for example, telling the story of individuals who get involved and make a difference. There have been campaigns to get people to vote, including some that allowed people to register in the lobby of the newspaper. There also have been other efforts to engage citizens as participants—for example a "Neighborhood Repair Kit" published by the *Star Tribune* in Minneapolis, which sought to give residents the information and incentive they needed to improve their neighborhoods.

The third form public journalism takes is as a movement. In the classic American tradition of public-spirited reform, this movement is trying to recall journalism to its deepest mission of public service. The movement is primarily drawn from professionals within the press, along with a smaller number from the academic world, and several institutional players. I would estimate its core membership at perhaps 200 or so, with several hundred others expressing sympathy with its general aims.

. . . So here is the accommodation we have come to: to acknowledge a political "identity" as a public journalist is to agree that you have a stake in public life—that you are a member of the community, and not a mechanism outside it. This does not mean that the press can become a partisan or advocate. But neither is it to withdraw into a stance of civic exile, where what's happening to the community somehow isn't happening to you as a professional.

Public journalists see themselves as conveners of public talk, aids to a more active citizenry, modelers of deliberative dialogue, supporters of a healthy public life. They are willing to assume a kind of political identity, but are not willing to join the struggles at the heart of left-right-center politics—except the very important struggle for a more vital public sphere, a better conversation, a public life that might earn our respect.

But isn't this the struggle we want the university to be engaged in? In this sense public journalism is very much an academic concern, but what it requires of the academic is to give up the one thing we often defend most vigorously: our claim to expertise. As soon as I become the expert in public journalism, I know I have failed, for public journalism has to be what journalists say it is, what they decide to do with it. I can try to persuade them that the interesting work lies in this or that direction; I can try to offer a vocabulary for their use. But the test of this vocabulary always lies with journalists themselves, and in a deeper sense, with the communities where public journalism is practiced.

DISCUSSION QUESTIONS

See Discussion Questions following the next reading, "Campaigns, Elections, and 'Public Journalism,'" by Edwin Diamond and Gregg Geller.

CAMPAIGNS, ELECTIONS, AND "PUBLIC JOURNALISM": CIVIC-MINDEDNESS OR MINDLESS CHEERLEADING?

Edwin Diamond and Gregg Geller

∎

The typical, big-time, tax-exempt American charitable foundation is, in the classic jokey definition, "an island of money surrounded on four sides by people who want some . . ."

The latest pile of tempting green stuff is being dispensed in the name of—ready?—"improving public discourse and journalism." The big giver: the Pew Charitable Trusts, a foundation built on the fortune of Joseph Pew, staunch Pennsylvania Republican and Big Oil man (Sun Oil Company). Early 20th century pirate capitalists whose fortunes now fund late-20th century do-good projects is an old story with interchangeable names, like Carnegie, Rockefeller, Mellon, Ford, et al. What's new in this latest money trail are the names of the supplicants.

Eye shades in hand, journalists who normally would cover the grant game are now suiting up in foundation uniforms and playing . . . all in the name of "the public interest," of course. But while some 100 newspapers, weeklies, radio and TV stations concentrated mainly in Southern and midwestern media markets have eagerly rushed in to claim $1.5 million in Pew money since 1993, other news organizations, by and large, national and big city, have remained aloof, high-minded, even hostile. So who's correct? Those who hold out their hands and say "Pew," or those who hold their noses and say "P.U."?

To hear the foundation beneficiaries tell it, the money "helps put the participatory back in participatory democracy," the civic duty back in journalism. According to Steve Smith, editor of the *Colorado Springs Gazette Telegraph*, civic journalism's detractors are—cover the kids' ears, here come the E words—Elitist and Establishment. But "Pew money" is an expletive to others. In this view, taking grants from foundations with "a very definite view of the road America should take"—as William Woo, former editor of the *St. Louis*

109

Post Dispatch, puts it—could drive a stake through the heart of whatever independent, swing-for-the-fences journalism still exists in late '90s America.

This is another new twist in the media narrative. Over the last few years, the threats to a free and feisty press appeared to be coming from the outside, from market-driven, Big Media conglomerates with multiple interests: Disney (ABC network, Mickey Mouse, theme parks), GE (NBC, nuclear reactors), Time Warner (CNN, magazines, movies, records). Now the danger seems within: in the name of grassroots democracy—giving the media consumer more of a "say" in news decision-making—a free press is assisting in its own death.

Of course, these latest newsroom suicide kits come wrapped with the nicest cover labels. What's more, some of the foundation Dr. Kevorkians are among the more likeable journalists in the land. During the 1996 campaign, for example, the Pew Center for Civic Journalism <http://www.pewcenter.org>, based in Washington and headed by Ed Fouhy, a former *CBS News* executive, served as a self-described funding "catalyst." The civic journalists' aims: "issues-based news coverage," "engaging the voter in the political process," "closing the gaps between people's lives and political discourse."

So far, so good. The elections-project packaging during campaign '96 was uniformly upbeat. "Your Voice, Your Vote" was the title of the "partnership" of 16 North Carolina newspapers and radio and TV stations that pooled their resources to cover the Helms–Gantt race for U.S. Senate "in a more positive way." Elsewhere, the citizens-first, feel-good language was similar. "Voice of the Voter," San Francisco; "We the People," Madison, Wisconsin; "Facing our Future," Binghamton, N.Y. And on and on: "The People's Forum," "Voices of Florida," "Front Porch Forum."

As Davis "Buzz" Merritt, a former Washington bureau chief for Knight-Ridder and now the ranking civic journalist at the *Wichita Eagle*, explains it, in recent political campaigns, "we asked the citizens what they wanted the candidates to discuss, rather than letting the candidates set the agenda." In one race, he said, the candidates didn't want to talk about abortion. But the voters did. And so when the candidates tried to "ignore the issue," editors threatened to run candidate photos with a blank space after the phrase "stand on abortion."

But do we really want to take the pol out of politics? Doesn't Power to the People have a certain 1960s deja-vu-all-over-again ring to it? Even though The People have become "Just Us Folks" (the desired consumers who may not be reading the paper or watching TV as much). How can newsrooms be so sure they know the public's will?

The answer is very '90s. Civic journalism–minded editors don't just ask their reporters what's going on out on the street. They bring together focus groups, just like Dick Morris for Bill Clinton and Madison Avenue for McDonalds fast food or Jeep Cherokees. Find out what the customers want, and serve it up to them. School uniforms and TV ratings? Put it in the State of the Union. Four wheel drive or more fries with a Big Mac? Have it your way.

According to Pew catalyst Fouhy, "the most common use of Pew money is to fund survey research or hire a community co-ordinator who knows how to reach out to the community."

In Manhattan, Kansas, for example, the Mercury (circulation: 12,500) covered the '96 campaign with the help of a focus group called "the Grand Jury"—some two dozen private citizens who met with editors "to share their thoughts, opinions, and solutions." According to executive editor Bill Felber, "jurors identified three local, eight state and 10 federal issues to watch. Those issues became [the Mercury's] agenda."

Too bad the paper had no Lincoln bedroom to rent out.

And so, just as political critics scorn Washington "leaders" who take a poll before deciding how they'll lead, so too do media critics put down civic journalists who use citizens' panels to determine news coverage. Journalists as "civic stenographers," in the cutting phrase of *New York Times* editorial page editor Howell Raines. "A variant of pandering," suggested Mike Hoyt of the *Columbia Journalism Review.* When you do focus groups, adds Carole Simpson of *ABC News,* "they say we're sick of hearing stories about the underclass. We don't want to see another story about public housing projects. Don't want to be bothered."

Hearing criticism like Simpson's, Buzz Merritt literally buries his head in his hands. All that the civic-minded advocates want, he insists, is for journalism to "move beyond the limited mission of 'telling the news' to a broader mission of helping public life go well." Adds Ed Fouhy: "focus groups are just one of several civic journalism tools. . . . Other outreaches are made: at one Dallas TV station, for example, every staffer must attend one outside community meeting every week. . . ." As for the unfriendly fire from what Fouhy calls the "fortresses of traditionalism"—AKA *New York Times* and the *Washington Post*—"they're at once arrogant and insular. . . ."

Insularity may be in the eye of the beholder. To clinch the civic journalists' case, Merritt cites . . . what else? . . . a poll. "Some 75 percent of the public believes journalism gets in the way of solving problems," he says. True, but large numbers of Americans also tell pollsters they're convinced the government is covering up the real story about TWA Flight 800 and that aliens have visited earth in this century.

Follow the polls far enough and you've exited the news business and entered "Twilight Zone" territory. That can't be what Joe Pew had in mind.

DISCUSSION QUESTIONS

1. Do you believe the American media are out of touch with their readers and viewers? Why, or why not?
2. What changes, if any, would you like to see in how the media cover news and information?
3. What do you think are the advantages and disadvantages of public journalism?

CHAPTER 8

MAGAZINES

Lisa Lockwood, *What Will You Read in 2006?*

L. A. Lorek, *E-Zines: The Once Fanciful Electronic Magazines Are Making Their Way into the Internet*

DM News, Wholehearted Commitment

More than 10,000 magazines and periodicals are published in the United States. Three out of every four adults in the United States buy one or more magazines each year. As a result of their popularity, magazines earn an estimated $6 billion in advertising.

The first magazine published in the colonies was Andrew Bradford's short-lived *American Magazine* issued in Philadelphia on February 13, 1741. Three days later, Benjamin Franklin opened *General Magazine*. Until the late nineteenth century, low circulation and little advertising prevented most magazines from surviving for more than a few years. Some, however, had greater longevity. *Harper's* magazine, which began publication in 1850, and the *Atlantic Monthly*, which began in 1857, are still in circulation today.

The period between the two world wars saw the establishment of the newsweekly *Time* and the picture weekly *Life*, the two magazines on which the publishing magnate Henry R. Luce founded his empire. Today, Time Warner offers different titles about health, gossip, sports, and myriad other subjects.

Since the 1960s the number of magazines devoted to narrow areas of interest, or niche markets, has grown enormously to reach diverse groups including ethnic organizations, stamp collectors, computer users, and gardeners. The first two readings in this chapter focus on the changing nature of magazines in a digital age, and the third is a profile of one magazine editor and what her work entails.

WHAT WILL YOU READ IN 2006?

Lisa Lockwood

■

Print: It's not dead yet.

The fact that magazines and newspapers are tactile, visually stimulating and portable will be their saving grace in the coming years, but the media world is spinning fast and electronic access to immediate, customized information is already changing the publishing landscape.

Who'll survive—and thrive—over the next 10 years? Agency pros and prognosticators are placing their bets on publications that cater to aging baby boomers' interest in personal finance, health, fashion, lifestyle, celebrities/entertainment, gourmet cooking, gardening and technology. And publications that secure even narrower niches—anything from alternative music to Latino lifestyles to cigar enthusiasts—will continue to grow, they said.

The big losers? Weekly news magazines are perceived as most vulnerable, with the proliferation of World Wide Web sites and cable channels providing up-to-the-minute news, 24 hours a day.

Here, some futurespeak. David Altschiller, chairman and chief creative officer, Hill, Holliday/Altschiller: By the year 2006, magazines that are very heavy in text information will have been replaced by the Internet and cable TV. "Oddly enough, the things that will continue to be important have to do with soft news and visuals. Frankly, style magazines that cover the home and clothing will continue very strongly. That kind of imagery won't be delivered by other media.

"People have to prepare for a much longer life. I think personal finance and retirement will be hot issues 10 years from now. The big bubble, the baby boomers, will be turning 60. I think we'll see gardening and home decorating magazines being important. And I think personal finance will be very important.

"The great fear of fashion magazines is that people will begin to buy on the Internet. If there's a lot more direct selling, there will be fewer advertisers in magazines." But, he said, "Ten years from now, there's going to be a tremendous shakeout. I think the Net will be used more for entertainment and less for information."

Altschiller says magazines that deal with children and parenting will become less important than they are now. "The reason for issues of parenting now is a major change in the construct of the household. Ten years from now, it will be taken in stride."

Peter Arnell, chairman and creative director, the Arnell Group: "Although I believe the Internet will take the place of much of the media that we now know as magazines, I believe the printed page will remain as a critical, portable, low tech delivery system of nonphotographic materials. Due to technology and three-dimensional visualization on computers, it will be hard for the printed page to survive with full multimedia capabilities delivering a full environment in which the content lives, versus a flat piece of art.

"For example, a simple Donna Karan print ad will be able to turn into a full runway display of a season's products. Publishers' language will change to reflect the new dictum set forth by electronic ink. All publishing will be interactive and connect you to the source of the content as well as allow you to have full purchasing power."

John Amodeo, partner, Amodeo & Petti: "I think it's more about the magazines that move along with the shift in the communications industry—those that reflect the various technologies will be important in the next millennium.

"I see it as a combination of *Allure* and *Wired*. With what's happening to the planet, *Allure* is addressing real needs and educating women and is more relevant to how the world is physically changing around us, such as ozone layers. What *Wired* is doing is directing the technology that's ruling our lives. These two magazines represent where we're going as people.

"With the ability of the World Wide Web to give us new information every hour, it will be difficult for magazines that have to plan three months in advance. Pressure will be on *Vogue* and *Harper's Bazaar* to figure out three months in advance what direction they're leading us in. Magazines going into CD-ROMs will be on a more timely basis. Magazines like *People* will survive—it will be a lot easier for a weekly.

"Technology is changing our expectations, and we've become much more immediate with our demands. Magazines of the future will be those that can inform, educate and service us. In fashion, they will tell the reader how to hook into more immediate information than waiting for your issue next month."

Steve Klein, partner and media director, Kirshenbaum, Bond & Partners: "Ten years from now, there will be a magazine like *TV Guide* for the Internet. News magazines will not be important. There are too many different ways to get up-to-the-minute news. There's CNN, a 24-hour news channel.

"Magazines that devote themselves to personal pastimes, such as cooking and gardening, will be influential. As the bulk of the baby boomers become 50 to 65 years old, magazines focused on gardening, personal finance and cooking will thrive. . . ."

DISCUSSION QUESTIONS

1. List the magazines you read on a regular basis. Why do you read these particular magazines?
2. Do you read general news magazines such as *Time*, *Newsweek*, or *U.S. News & World Report*? Why, or why not?
3. What type of news and information do you expect from a magazine? Is it different from what you expect from a newspaper or television? If so, why?

E-Zines: The Once Fanciful Electronic Magazines Are Making Their Way into the Internet

L. A. Lorek

∎

E ver hear of *Cyberconch, Roadkill, SmartKid* or *Scoop*? They are e-zines—electronic magazines—made in South Florida, among more than 1,000 nationwide. Like most things in cyberspace, e-zines are multiplying—and becoming more sophisticated. In the past, people created these low-budget electronic publications for fun and to have a voice in the on-line world.

The first grassroots e-zines often resembled fanzines—fan-produced tributes to the stars. They ranged in size from a single page to dozens of pages and often contained social commentary, manifestos, poetry and lots of opinion. But today's e-zines, like the Internet itself, have changed.

This year, big-league media players such as Microsoft in Redmond, Wash., and Turner Entertainment Network in Atlanta have launched high-budget e-zines—*Slate* and *Spiv*, respectively—to capture some of the advertising revenues and readers on-line. Often irrelevant, bizarre and esoteric, e-zines have not been considered mainstream publications and did not, until recently, contain advertisements. They were not targeted at a mass audience and were generally not produced to make a profit. But this new breed of e-zine is. The latest e-zines have business plans and marketing and research budgets, said Peter Krasilovsky, senior analyst at Arlen Communications, a Bethesda, Md., consultancy. The new e-zines plan to make money much like the cable television industry does, with dual revenue streams from advertisers and subscribers, he said.

While some media companies have poured millions of dollars into their e-zines, no one is making any money, Krasilovsky said. "There's no quick return on the Internet," he said. "Right now, people are building brand identity in hopes of cashing in on it in the future."

116

Fueled by the popularity of the Internet's World Wide Web and graphical browsers such as Netscape and Microsoft's Internet Explorer, the number of e-zines has skyrocketed. In 1993, only a handful of e-zines existed nationwide, but that figure has grown to more than 1,000 today, according to John Labovitz, a San Francisco–based computer consultant who keeps a list of e-zines at <http://www.nearnet.gnn.com/wix/lit.32.html>.

However, because the Internet is a new publishing medium, someone producing an e-zine from a home or dorm room could hit it big. Spending big bucks doesn't guarantee success, Krasilovsky said.

Microsoft's e-zine, *Slate*, has been a flop on the Internet. *Wired* magazine recently put *Slate* on its Internet Death Watch list. Microsoft launched *Slate* in July. It is edited by writer, editor and television pundit Michael Kinsley, who was hired away from Cable News Network's *Crossfire*. In his opening, 2,150-word statement introducing *Slate*, titled Read Me, Kinsley wrote, "There is a deadening conformity in the hipness of cyberspace culture in which we don't intend to participate. Part of our mission at *Slate* will be trying to bring cyberspace down to earth."

That kind of prose encouraged a group of New York–based writers to launch a parody of *Slate* that they call *Stale*. Its stated mission, in part, is to have everyone wear comfortable clothing and worship one god. "*Slate* took a supreme attitude, but it didn't do anything original with the content," Krasilovsky said.

Eight months ago, Turner Online launched *Spiv*, an e-zine aimed at 15- to 24-year-olds. The site offers sections titled Zooey, about style, voice and urban culture; Waxed, on sports; Antidote, for music reviews; and Rough Cut, for movie reviews. Most of *Spiv*'s content is developed by its 10 staff members, but it does have tie-ins with Turner's other resources, said Scott Arenson, marketing manager for Turner Online.

For the Rough Cut feature, Turner Network Television provides *Spiv* with regular updates and analysis on box-office winners and losers, star casting, executive shuffles and weekend previews of films. "It's not your typical on-line magazine," Arenson said.

Other e-zines, with names like *Suck*, *Urban Desires* and *FEED*, do not have the deep pockets of a Turner Entertainment Network or Microsoft but still attract readers. They change their content daily, weekly, biweekly, monthly or sporadically. Most do not charge subscription fees but require people to register at the site.

Suck, a daily publication based in San Francisco, describes itself as "an experiment in provocations, mordant deconstructionism and buzz-saw journalism." *Suck*'s by-line contributors include writers who call themselves Corporate Lackey, Strep Throat and Pop.

Scoop, a gay and lesbian weekly magazine with a circulation of 10,000 in Broward and Dade counties, launched its e-zine in January with $300, said Bob Kecskemety, *Scoop*'s editor and webmaster. "The printed version is so expen-

117

sive," Kecskemety said. "We can put features in the on-line version that we didn't have room for in print."

. . . Some popular e-zines such as *HotWired*, the on-line extension of *Wired* magazine, charge up to $10,000 for a banner advertisement. But few e-zines have been able to attract that kind of advertising cash.

Utne Reader spent $500,000 to create its on-line site, *Utne Lens*, with a staff of seven. The site launched on the Internet in mid-July 1995, but by October, the magazine pulled the plug on the project, eliminated five staff members and redesigned the site. *Utne Lens* couldn't attract enough advertisers to support its original content. "Absolutely everybody is trying to do a Web site," said Griff Wigley, manager of *Utne's* on-line division. "But no one can create original content and garner enough advertising dollars to pay for it. You've got to have deep pockets."

Although *Utne's* site attracted 25,000 readers a month, it didn't attract the big advertising dollars necessary to sustain it. The company charged $10,000 a month for an ad on its home page. The only company to sign up was Saturn.

Today, *Utne's* on-line site more closely mirrors its print version with its on-line budget cut to $150,000 for 1996. The site is also attracting more advertisers but instead of fetching $10,000 an ad, the site gets $200 to $400. And *Utne* is charging people $36 to join its Utne Cafe, an on-line community with special perks such as CD giveaways and a subscription to its printed product. "Maybe at some point we will do more publishing of original content on-line," said Wigley, "but right now, it makes the most sense to do minimal amounts of content publishing and major amounts of interaction on-line."

DISCUSSION QUESTIONS

1. Read *Slate* <http://www.slate.com>, *Feed* <http://www.feed.com>, or *Salon* <http://www.salonmag.com>. What do you like or dislike about one of these magazines?
2. Analyze the differences you find between online magazines and printed magazines.
3. Would you pay for online magazines, as you do for printed magazines? Why, or why not?

WHOLEHEARTED
COMMITMENT
DM News

■

Stephanie Stokes Oliver
Birthplace: Seattle
Education: Journalism major at Howard University, Washington.
Career: Fashion and beauty merchandising editor for *Glamour.*
Editor of *Essence.* Joined Rodale last August as editor in chief, *Heart & Soul.*
Family: Married to management consultant. Four daughters.
Leisure time: Classical dance, classical piano and walking (she hits all the parks in northern New Jersey, where she lives).
Favorite composers: Bach, Mozart and Beethoven.
Recent books read: "Saving Our Sons," by Marita Golden, and "Segmenting the Women's Market—Using Niche Marketing to Understand and Meet the Diversities of Today's Most Dynamic Consumer Market," by E. Janice Leeming and Cynthia F. Tripp.

W hen Reginald Ware proposed the idea of a health magazine for African Americans to Rodale Press two years ago, it took only 10 minutes for management to sign on the dotted line and agree to work with his entrepreneurial Ware Communications.

Ware was looking for financial support and publishing expertise to expand *Feelin' Good!*, a magazine about healthy living that he produced and distributed in physicians' offices. But it had outgrown the tender loving care he could provide on his own.

Within the past two years, Ware has been the inspiration and cheerleader for a renamed and fine-tuned magazine aimed at helping African American women maintain a healthy lifestyle. Starting with the current issue, the editorial side is spearheaded by a 20-year veteran of women's lifestyle and black women's magazines. Stephanie Stokes Oliver, who epitomizes what "heart and soul" is all about.

Ware's timing in approaching Rodale was perfect: The Emmaus, PA–based publishing company had already laid out a corporate strategy stating that it wanted to be the health and fitness authority for all Americans, and although the firm published a number of health-oriented magazines, none filled the niche for African Americans.

While making the decision to enter such a venture didn't take Rodale long, carrying out its plans in typical Rodale fashion has meant that the magazine, renamed *Heart & Soul*, is just now expanding beyond the four-times-a-year test phase.

When the deal was consummated, Rodale assigned the project to its special division that handles one-shot magazines and supplements with the idea that they will be pushed as far as possible and sometimes grow into regularly scheduled periodicals. Ware continued as publisher and retained the title of editor, but he was relieved of some editorial duties by Catherine M. Cassidy, who served as managing editor and relied on editorial support from other Rodale staffers and free-lancers.

"The first quarterly issue appeared on newsstands in the summer of 1993 and sold about 60,000 copies," said Reynold McDermott, who became the magazine's first full-time circulation manager last November. One reason for Rodale's enthusiasm has been an overwhelming response to the blow-in and bind-in cards within the magazine, and that encouraged Rodale to test a direct mail package sent to about 250,000 potential customers derived from a variety of lists the following February.

Based on those results, Rodale upped its ante in the venture. Offices were opened in New York for a full-time editor-in-chief and other editorial staff, and the decision was made to publish six times a year. The first mass mailing offering six issues of *Heart & Soul* annually for $16.97 was sent to about 1.2 million potential subscribers last September, and from that *Heart & Soul* has been able to increase its rate base to 200,000 from 125,000.

The current issue—the first under the complete direction of Oliver and her team—inaugurates a new phase: displaying a redesigned logo and new look throughout.

A former editor of *Essence*, where she served in a number of editorial posts during her 16-year tenure, and prior to that, fashion and beauty merchandising editor at *Glamour*, Oliver has always been a big advocate of healthy living. "I never smoked or drank. I have been a vegetarian for over 20 years, and people know that," she says. At both magazines she worked on earlier, there was a big emphasis on health, and *Heart & Soul* has many of the same kinds of sections. The difference is the focus on lifestyle and health issues that are more specific to African Americans and their families.

For example, she says, the top 10 health risks might be a little different for African Americans than for the general population. Take breast cancer. "Black women are diagnosed at a younger age than white women so it's too late to suggest mammograms at 40 or 50," she says. The current issue carries an in-depth feature on breast cancer and its implications for African American women.

One reason for the positive response to the magazine, Oliver believes, is that there is no other magazine specifically aimed at assisting black women with a healthy approach to life. There are women's health magazines, such as *Self* and *Shape*, and there are black women's magazines, but they're not devoted strictly to encouraging a healthy lifestyle. So for now *Heart & Soul* has the market to itself.

"My mission is to not only make *Heart & Soul* a household name, but to position the magazine as a resource for information on fitness, weight loss, exercise, parenting and love relationships edited specifically for the black community," she says.

If all goes as planned, the magazine will progress to a frequency of nine times a year and eventually monthly as it gains in circulation and advertising.

The next steps for McDermott are to continue with direct mail and try to aggressively grow the rate base as quickly as possible. "We have good support from advertisers. Now we have to provide them with the customers," he says. A one-time color page ad costs $10,500.

Another mailing was sent out in March and the next is scheduled for July, each sent to more than one million names. Eventually, he hopes to add TV to the mix, but that won't be for at least a year, he says.

Oliver believes the timing couldn't be better because the country is so focused on health, from the White House to grassroots efforts. "It's an honor to work on a magazine that is discussing such a timely and important subject in our readers' lives," she says.

Despite her busy life, Oliver doesn't neglect the fitness side of the equation for herself either. "I don't get to the gym much," she says. "I'm more of a dancer and walker."

A student of ballet from ages 4 to 22, she performed in her home town of Seattle and studied for a time with Alvin Ailey's company in New York. Now, she's satisfied to dance in her living room on the weekends, and she leaves the performances to her 13-year-old daughter, who is part of the Ailey children's company.

Her recreation and relaxation also involve lots of walking in parks in northern New Jersey, where she lives. "Instead of going out to lunch or for drinks with friends, we go for a walk," she says. And for refreshment afterward? Herbal tea, of course.

DISCUSSION QUESTIONS
1. What personal and professional qualities do you think are necessary for a good editor?
2. Define what is meant by a "niche publication."
3. What niche publications do you read and why?

CHAPTER 9

ADVERTISING

Leslie Savan, *2-OH-OH-OH: The Millennial-Ad Challenge*
Katie Hafner and Jennifer Tanaka, *This Web's for You*
Tim Clark, *Web Advertising*

Most advertisements try to convince you to act: to buy something; vote for someone; save the children. Advertising lets you watch network television for free. Advertising even lets you buy a newspaper for a lot less than you would pay without ads—maybe about $2 for your daily newspaper.

You don't have to thank the advertisers. Just keep in mind that your eyes are important to them, and you get a significant savings even if you choose not to look at a single ad.

Advertisers spend the most on newspaper advertisement—about $30 billion a year. Television gets more than $20 billion, while direct mail, magazines, and radio each earn about $10 billion of the total advertising pie.

Advertising agencies serve their clients with a variety of experts—people whose roles are somewhat similar to those of the experts in print and television. Every person in an ad agency has a role. An agency's copywriters and art directors take their assignments from the account executive. When decisions on content are completed, often after research studies to determine consumer response, the production department prepares the finished ads with the aid of typographers, engravers, printers, and radio- or television-commercial production companies. The media department prepares a plan to use print or broadcast or both.

An advertiser may reach fewer eyes on the Internet, but the computer technology makes it easier to determine who is seeing the ads because people may register on a particular Web site or are lured to give additional information if they click through a digital ad.

As technology progresses, the World Wide Web may drain money away from traditional media, particularly newspapers. The first article, written by Pulitzer Prize finalist Leslie Savan of the *Village Voice*, analyzes the use of advertising campaigns emphasizing the approaching millennium. The second article, from *Newsweek*'s technology expert, Katie Hafner, assesses the effectiveness and cost of advertising on the World Wide Web. The third article, from CNET's Tim Clark, focuses on specific research being done on Web advertising.

2-OH-OH-OH:
THE MILLENNIAL-AD
CHALLENGE

Leslie Savan

∎

Anew MCI slogan promoting the Internet and all its wonders: "Is this a great time, or what? :-)" A new promo for Fox TV's Millennium: "As the millennium approaches, the world as we know it is going mad and getting worse every day."

It was the best of slimes, it was the worst of slimes. Either way, it's time, again, for the millennial-ad challenge: How do corporations best exploit the changing of a few digits by tying it in with all the hope and fear the world has ever known?

As soon as the big Swatch in the sky struck 1997, advertisers started to hit us with the forked future, as legends both sacred and secular would have it, that is supposed to kick in around the year 2000. The Rapture or retribution, the dawn of the New Age or terrible nights of Apocalypse—ready or not, something really really good and/or something really really bad will happen when we hit the big deuce-triple-aught.

This season is hardly the marketers' first attempt to grab those zeros like they were the brass rings of the universe. Back in 1990, all the media predicted that the new decade would be the anti-80s, a social cleansing, a humbling experience, an economic getting-down-to-basics, i.e., a 10-year trudge on a spiritual Stairmaster to prepare us for the final reckoning.

Commercials began to feature more shots of heaven. Jingles went New Age and chanty, using Enya or, more likely than not, imitating the religious score from the movie *The Mission*—for everything from Maxwell House to Security Pacific Bank to AT&T and MCI. Ad after ad dropped the phrases spirit or One World as shots of Earth from outer space became a commercial punctuation point.

But we're a fickle lot. And since our economic Pritikin diet was belied by disgustingly large CEO salaries, a bursting-at-the-seams stock market, and an ever-increasing gap between rich and poor (and because it was hard to fetishize digits from the middle of a decade), the spiritual sell went into remission—until now, as if on cosmic cue.

The ads and promotional schemes are only just starting to dribble in, but Millennial Marketing II is definitely under way, heralded by Clinton's rickety Bridge to the 21st Century—and it will only get worse over the next three or four years. (Frankly, I can't understand why GE, Whirlpool, or some appliance company hasn't launched A Fridge to the 21st Century.) Thus far:

Last month, *Newsweek* inaugurated a weekly, one-page feature, The Millennium Notebook, created the position of a Millennium editor, and announced that it plans special issues on millennial themes.

The music for a new Jaguar spot (called New Breed Reincarnation) is Enya-like Irish celtic, and an onscreen title states that the car is fueled by the spirit of its ancestors.

The new tag line for Time Warner Cable is Working Straight Through the Millennium. Well, aren't we all?

Blockbuster Video's new slogan is One World, One Word, apropos of absolutely nothing else in the ad. (Oh, wait, I get it—they mean the big, expensive, stupid adventure movies that Hollywood keeps making because pictures high on moving objects and low on lingo are the easiest to export the world over. By squeezing out wordier, more-subtle movies and further dumbing us Americans down, the well-to-do few, like studio and Blockbuster execs, can make more disgustingly large salaries.)

The last millennium had religion—the fear of the End Days, the hope of salvation—to give their people some triple-0 pop, but we have technology. On one hand, living in a technological society, we may feel rather blasé about 2000—the biggest threat may be those computer calendars, because if they aren't somehow recalibrated to reflect the 2 in 2000, it could screw up e-mail, not to mention the whole world! On the other hand, digital technology actually may chance the dualistic nature of millennial expectations by encouraging us to think, if that's the word, in binary, either/orisms. Either we'll suffer Independence Day–style, worldwide destruction, or we'll end world hunger and all have great sex til age 110. Click the mouse either once or twice.

You might figure that we would no longer buy such melodramatics, especially since we're supposedly so cynical about the possibilities of real political and economic change. And maybe most of us now do understand that our passage through 2000 will be more like a Clintonian muddling and middling, nipping and tucking, than a matter of facing down fire and brimstone or the cast of *Hair*.

Squishy middle roads, however, aren't profitable to techy corporations. They prefer to portray a fearsome future without them. It began with Apple's classic 1984 spot, in which an IBM-only world was portrayed as tantamount to rule by Big Brother. Today, there's a Packard Bell spot that shows life sans their computer as a bureaucratic purgatory in black and white, where young women age into wrinkled hags while waiting in lines—but a Packard Bell–generated future is shown as a fun, efficient, suburban arcadia colored in cartoon-bright hues and constructed from blemish-free geometric solids, just like in *Toy Story*.

But no commercial scales the upside of the millennial mountain as boldly as the anthem spot for MCI Internet network, which broke, appropriately, January 1. In a series of very fast-cut vignettes that veer from B&W to rainbow color, a deaf girl signs, a wheelchair-bound boy testifies, an older black man states, and children everywhere reiterate this manifesto of diversity, fairness, and hope:

"People can communicate mind to mind. Not black to white. There are no genders. Not man to woman. There is no age. Not young to old. There are no infirmities. Not short to tall. Or handsome to homely. Just thought to thought. Idea to idea. Uninfluenced by the rest of it. There are only minds to minds. Only minds . . . What is this place? Utopia? No. No. The Internet. The Internet. The Internet. It's a nice place, this place called the Internet." After warm scenes of children drawing rainbows comes the line we'll be seeing a lot of for a while: "Is this a great time, or what? :-)," emoticon and all.

It's hard not to be moved when the boy in the wheelchair arrives at this nice place. If the Internet can make the lame walk, then maybe it is the closest we'll ever come to utopia—a thought MCI firmly seeds by first raising and then denying the possibility that the Net is the Promised Land.

These are noble aspirations, this color-, age-, gender-, ableness-, and looks-blindness, but how is MCI so sure it exists? It's not based on research, admits Gretchen Gehrett, MCI's executive director of advertising and communications, but on the experience of the campaign's creative director and art director. Working together via the Net from two different places, they had never met in person. They finally met at the agency, says Gehrett, and one was black and one was white, and neither knew that was the case, and it made no difference, and that was inspirational. The point of the anthem, she adds, is to show how by embracing technology we can improve our lives and our work, and how by embracing the Internet we can bring down barriers.

It's so ridiculous, says a young woman who just quit AOL, not because of its massive gridlock, but in part because it was usually less about mind to mind than asinine comment to bad pickup line.

In chat rooms people are definitely interested in representing what they are. Even if they're lying, they're trying to be something. It's unavoidable. People like their labels. I can't tell you how many perverted men there are out there. Their first question is, "What do you look like?" When I'd tell them to get lost, I'd get hate letters. It's really kind of creepy.

And though MCI's land of milkin' money is full of people of color and wizened old people of both genders (as, come to think of it, was Microsoft's anthem ad two years before), and there's nary a white mid-aged guy among them, the majority of actual Internet users are still white males, according to various sources. Sure, the Internet can be used to do a lot of good, even some of the good that MCI claims. But what MCI is really selling here is the capacity for the Net to lie.

The Intel ads starring *Seinfeld's* Jason Alexander, while not quite up to George Costanza standards, are at least honest about this ability to lie and the irresistible urge to use the Net to escape your physical self. Alexander plays a jerk named Bob who uses e-mail to set up online video dates. One woman sees through the ruse that his apartment has an incredible view when the huge poster of a magnificent skyline he has positioned in front of the monitor crashes to the floor behind him. Another telegal spurns him because he forgets to give himself a virtual toupee.

At least Intel's not doing a rapping with the Rapture bit—yet. For better or worse, the marketed millennium is the only one we'll have. As the millennium approaches, the world as we know it is going ad, and getting worse every day. :-(.

DISCUSSION QUESTIONS

1. Find an advertising campaign that emphasizes the future—the next millennium. How does the ad portray that future?
2. Discuss whether the content of the millenium ad is persuasive.
3. Do you think using the approach of the millennium is a good way to design an advertising campaign? Why, or why not?

THIS WEB'S FOR YOU

Katie Hafner and
Jennifer Tanaka

∎

P rime-time handyman Tim Allen is on the cover of a magazine. This time it's *A Man's Life*, a new title that makes for perfect couch-potato reading: redo your budget; fix your wardrobe; jump-start your sex life. But you probably won't take this magazine to bed with you—unless you sleep with a computer. *A Man's Life* appears on the World Wide Web, the Internet's most user-friendly area. And the publisher isn't Condé Nast, Hearst or Hachette. It's Toyota.

This is the state-of-the-art of advertising on the Internet—a soft sell to a niche market. The Web is still tiny compared with newspapers, magazines and TV, but that hasn't stopped dozens of ad agencies from creating "new media" divisions to explore its potential. Scores of start-up companies do nothing but create Web advertising. Many, like Organic Online in San Francisco, are a motley collection of defectors from advertising, publishing and technology firms. Organic has developed sites for companies like Levi Strauss Co., Saturn Corp. and Colgate-Palmolive.

That's a lot of activity for a medium that has yet to prove an effective marketing tool. By all indications, advertisers are coming onto the Web slowly. According to Forrester Research, Inc., a high-tech research firm, in 1995 U.S. companies spent about $837 million on advertising on the Web—a minuscule fraction of the $860 billion that American corporations spent last year on advertising. "For AT&T, the Web budget is a rounding error," says Josh Bernoff, a senior analyst at Forrester.

Web-based pitches come in two forms: A company can set up its own Web site (those clunky Internet addresses that start with http://www) or buy an ad on someone else's. Online publications, for instance, carry ads just as their print counterparts do. But the real marketing potential is in the more elaborate corporate Web sites' multipage electronic brochures. Since May of last year, more than 500 corporations have put up Web sites to promote their products, according to WebTrack, an Internet research firm in New York. Most traditional advertising—like television or freeway billboards—is in broadcast mode. What happens on the Net is narrowcasting: one-on-one, highly targeted marketing. And on the Web, it's even interactive—click on a picture of a car, and a more detailed description appears.

. . . Many companies are finding that a good place to start is with a $15,000 or so investment in an ad banner—a graphical link to the advertiser's Web site—posted on a more popular site. Luxury automaker Lexus has found that the biggest source of visitors to its Web location is its ad banner on Yahoo!

Dollar for dollar, Web advertising is expensive. Compared with television, magazines and newspapers, an ad on the Web costs more per thousand consumers. But the ultra-niche nature of the Web is what has companies intrigued. Web users tend to be either students, or highly educated white males in their late 30s with median incomes of about $55,000. The most successful sites offer customers reasons to keep coming back, without seeming too commercial. Molson Breweries' Web advertising begins on its bottles: The label lists the company's Web address. But click on the site and you get a National Hockey League betting pool and an online magazine about the art of brewing. "Ninety-nine percent of our site is not about our beer," says Brian Flanagan, Molson's supervisor of Internet Projects. "We provide something so somewhere down the line maybe you feel compelled to buy a case of Canadian."

As part of the effort to create a place people will return to, some advertisers are becoming their own publishers. The Toyota site, for example, features The Hub, a group of six different electronic magazines put out by eight full-time staffers and two dozen contributing editors. The Levi's Web site has a magazine about deejays, clubs and other cool Web sites. Selling blue jeans seems beside the point. L. L. Bean offers a database of national parks. Black & Decker's site offers home improvement tips.

Gathering hard demographic data on Web users is difficult. It's possible to count the number of times a Web page has been accessed, but that tells you nothing about who stopped there and for how long. PC-Meter Service of Port Washington, N.Y., one of several new companies tracking Web use, enlists households as volunteers to allow software to track every user's "click stream," including the number of minutes they spend on each Web page.

Information gathering doesn't need to be intrusive. The Gate, the online service of the *San Francisco Chronicle* and *Examiner* newspapers, runs a monthly raffle where entrants fill in questionnaires. "We're working to know as much as we can about our readers and who they are without violating their sense of privacy," says John Coate, manager of The Gate. One thing is certain: the technology will grow up. In a few years, the Web could turn into a big hit for Madison Avenue—or, just another intrusive distraction for us.

How Much Bang for the Buck?

Compared with TV and print, Web ads are pricey. But for some companies the ultra-niche targeting is worth it.

	Cost	Audience	Cost Per 1,000 Consumers
Television			
30-second spot, network news	$65,000	12,000,000	$5.42
Magazine			
Full-page color ad, national weekly	$135,000	3,100,000	$43.55
Newspaper			
Full-page ad, midsize city	$31,000	514,000	$60.31
World Wide Web			
Online magazine, one-month placement	$15,000	200,000	$75.00

Source: Forrester Research, Inc.

DISCUSSION QUESTIONS

1. Analyze the graphics and information in an advertising campaign on the World Wide Web.
2. Would you buy a product based solely on its advertising campaign? Why, or why not?
3. How effective is Web advertising in convincing you to buy something, or at least to take a closer look at what is being promoted?

WEB ADVERTISING
Tim Clark

■

Want to run a banner ad on a Web page? Be wary of Mondays. That's the one day of the week Netizens are least likely to click on the ad, according to a study that, ironically, is being released today. Internet Profiles (I/Pro), the largest Net service that counts ad-supported Web site visitors and DoubleClick Network, which works with advertisers in targeting specific demographic groups, crunched the numbers from more than 100 million ad views.

The results are being released in their study, entitled "A Comprehensive Analysis of Ad Response." Nuggets in the study range from which day of the week gets the best results for clicking on banner ads to effective phrasing to snare customers. Netizens click on 2.11 percent of all ad banners displayed, while direct mail typically generates a 1 percent to 2 percent response rate and print ads .5 percent to .75 percent, the study states.

And what about advertising on the best day? Saturdays got the best response with 2.28 percent, followed by Sundays with 2.20 percent. But Web usage is about 25 percent lower on weekends than during the work week, Bob Ivins, I/Pro's vice president of research, told *CNET*. Mondays generated the lowest response rate of 2.01 percent.

Outside of choosing a date to run the ad, a number of other details need to be considered. Here are a few tips offered in the study:

—Animated ads work best. Adding animation to a simple image or GIF boosts response rates 25 percent.

—Cryptic messages ("Click here"), unaccompanied by any other text, increase the response rate 18 percent over the average.

—Questions ("Too many passwords to remember?") elicit a 16 percent higher click-through than the average.

131

—Calls to action ("See us now") improve response rates by 15 percent.

—Free stuff doesn't always work; it depends on the stuff. Offers of free hardware or software shot response rates up 35 percent above the average. But free travel offers produced a 10 percent lower click rate, while money offers were 6 percent less effective than the average.

—Bright colors (blue, green, yellow) work best, while red, white, and black are less effective.

—Don't rush people. "Limited time only," "one more week remaining," and similarly urgent offers generally performed below average.

"Advertisers have to know what their objectives are," Ivins said. "If you want to do an awareness campaign, you can treat the Web like a billboard and get low response rates. If you want to get responses, use questions."

The study divided the data into even more specific chunks based on user demographics. For example, users from a ".net" domain produced 20 percent higher click-through than those from ".com" addresses.

Visitors from non-Western countries such as Asian nations generated much higher response rates than U.S. users. Click rates from Taiwan drew 4.3 percent and Korea a 4.2 percent rate. U.S.-based visitors, on the other hand, had a 1.9 percent click rate.

"One theory is that the countries in the early stages of Web development are still enjoying the novelty of it," Ivins said.

Discussion Questions

1. How often do you actually click on an advertisement on the Web?
2. What types of advertisements are you most likely to explore?
3. Do color, the day of week, giveaways, or the style of the advertisement affect whether you read an online ad? Why, or why not?

CHAPTER 10

PUBLIC RELATIONS

Julie McHenry, *Take Your PR Out of Box: Clients Are Demanding Creative Thinking*

O'Dwyer's PR Services Report, *Internet Boom to Revamp Way PR Pros Deal with Reporters*

Robert Steyer, *Firms Advised to Respond Quickly in Time of Crisis*

E dward Bernays, the father of public relations, died in March 1995 at the age of 103. Bernays was one of the first people to expand what had been a narrow concept of press agentry, or working to influence government policy, into a far more ambitious and controversial realm of seeking to influence and change public opinion and behavior.

Bernays, a nephew of Sigmund Freud, was born in Vienna and grew up in New York. After World War I, women started to discard hairnets, much to the dismay of Venida, the leading producer of the product. Bernays launched one of his early public relations campaigns when Venida called upon him to reverse their sagging sales.

Among other elements in his strategy, Bernays got artists to praise the "Greek-coiffure" look that hairnets gave their wearers. He convinced a labor expert to urge government officials around the country to insist that women working with or near machines wear hairnets for their own safety. Even without mentioning Venida's name in the public relations campaign, the company's sales soared. Later, Bernays set up a national panel that for years oversaw soap-carving competitions to promote Ivory soap and make bathing more popular with children.

"Public relations, effectively used, helps validate an underlying principle of our society—competition in the market place of ideas and things," he wrote.

But in an interview he gave in 1991 when he turned 100, Bernays said: "Public relations today is horrible. Any dope, any nitwit, any idiot can call him or herself a public relations practitioner." These days, spin doctors are identified more than public relations practitioners as those who try to influence the media and the public.

The first reading allows that the godfather of public relations may be right about the state of modern public relations. Like all media professionals in the new age, public relations experts must think differently about the task at hand. The second reading looks at how these experts can use new technology, while the third article urges public relations professionals to observe old values: Tell the truth in times of crisis.

TAKE YOUR PR OUT OF BOX: CLIENTS ARE DEMANDING CREATIVE THINKING

Julie McHenry

■

Ah, the never-ending quest for public relations creativity. How do you spice up that press release information to make it really grab the editor by the throat? How do you break through the clutter of noise that journalists are dealing with at every level—print, online and broadcast? Most important, how do you present technology to the consumer in a way that is personal, compelling and exciting?

As public relations professionals, we get bogged down in the day-to-day minutiae of servicing the client—attending meetings, counseling on timing of product launch scenarios, educating on positioning, fighting fires, getting work out the door and pitching stories. It is a challenge to step back and take the time to think and be creative.

But in today's competitive world, clients are demanding creativity or "out of box" thinking. Our new reality of "Internet time," where markets move faster than the speed of light, demands a new level of creativity from all of us. It's relatively easy to sit at a word processor and write that we need a new level of creativity, but it begs the question of "how?" How can we build in a process to be as creative as possible in solving the needs of our clients, and in bringing information to the media? Here are some simple ideas for rekindling the creative juices.

IDEA 1

Integrate your public relations more closely with other marketing activities. Get you and your team involved in brainstorming meetings with professionals on the marketing team from the related disciplines, such as advertising, direct mail and promotions. Oftentimes these service groups are reaching for the same objective but will be approaching the problem in different ways. This difference will lead to some OOB thinking for everyone. The shared thinking in these kinds of brainstorming sessions usually results in a higher quality marketing plan for everyone, with messages that are more consistent and more innovative creative tactics. Consider executing the advertising and collateral creative [campaign] into the "look and feel" of your press materials. If your client or your company is investing in some exciting consumer marketing promotions, tie a pure publicity campaign around them. This is one way to kick start your consumer branding work with the media.

Idea 2

Read and learn from marketing and public relations activities from outside our industry. In order to think outside the box, sometimes you literally need to get outside of the box! Pick up trade publications from other industries and learn about new and exciting promotions and campaigns that might be applied to your business and segment. Use one of the Internet search engines to look for interesting public relations cases and examples that are from other industries but will give you new and different ideas to apply to your business. One of my close friends, who is a high-level marketing communications manager at a workstation company, told me that she often gets her best ideas on trade show exhibits and creative [campaigns] by attending trade shows outside the computer industry. Her favorite is the National Sporting Goods Show, which attracts consumer brand experts such as Nike, Reebok and Adidas. By watching the new and exciting ways they manage their trade show exhibits, product launches and creative [campaigns], she picks up valuable new ideas to guide her own thinking. If you are feeling stale, it's time to hit the road and find some new ways of thinking.

Idea 3

Use the Internet to do some online brainstorming. Yes, a lot of surfing can be called wasted time. I don't necessarily advocate aimlessly wandering around the Web. But, again, if you take the time to visit a few sites of master marketers, you are very likely to pick up new ideas and thoughts that can be applied to your business. For specific public relations ideas, take a look at the way various companies are organizing and presenting their press materials via their Internet sites. Again, don't just visit the big-name companies in your market segment (this assumes you have already checked out the sites of your competition!) but visit the startup and emerging growth company sites. Young companies are sometimes more innovative. Take a look at some of the more innovative marketing sites such as

www.cadillac.com
www.washingtonpost.com

IDEA 4

Let's not forget the "old" way of brainstorming, the in-person, gather-around-the-table-and-throw-your-ideas-out kind of brainstorming. Regardless of how busy we are and how enamored we are of technology, old-fashioned, face-to-face brainstorming is still going to get the best results. You have probably heard the No. 1 rule for brainstorming: "Every idea is a good idea." The secret is to have all participants open up their thinking and really stretch their imagination for some great ideas.

To promote innovative thinking, we brainstorm in a large room—not the normal conference room. A change of scenery is good for everyone. Also, don't include the same team members that you have had at your last several brainstorming sessions. Unfortunately, we all get into our familiar roles, which doesn't promote creativity. Invite new participants. Get some outside thinking to pull the rest of you outside the box. Bring in some thinkers from outside the organization, a facilitator or a friend of the company. If you are discussing a "top secret" product launch strategy, have them sign a non-disclosure agreement so everyone can be open and honest. You'll need some innovative thinking to get you through one more high-volume fall product launch cycle.

DISCUSSION QUESTIONS
1. In Idea 1, the author talks about public relations and marketing teams. What do you think is the difference between public relations and marketing?
2. As suggested in Idea 2, find and analyze an interesting use of public relations on the World Wide Web.
3. In Idea 4, the author argues that in a brainstorming session "every idea is a good idea." What do you think about that concept?

INTERNET BOOM TO REVAMP WAY PR PROS DEAL WITH REPORTERS

O'Dwyer's PR Services Report

•

The growing acceptance of the Internet as a way to communicate information has high-tech PR pros predicting that the 'Net will reshape media relations over the next few years. They realize, of course, the 'Net will never replace the importance of one-on-one personal contact with reporters, a relationship that is the hallmark of good press relations.

PR people do believe, however, that the use of cyberspace will enable them to cast a wider net when looking for placements as more reporters log onto the Internet. In the near future, websites that are packed with information will be the "hook" used by PR firms to hike media interest in a client.

Larry Weber, CEO of The Weber Group, is among those bullish on the prospects of cyberspace as a media relations tool. The Web, he said, "will change PR forever during the next ten years and will serve as the core of media relations."

Websites will have customized icons for reporters that could be updated on an as-needed basis by a company or its PR firm, said Weber whose shop ranked as 1995's No. 1 high-tech specialist, according to "O'Dwyer's Directory of PR Firms." Weber's confident that Web-based media relations will enable PR firms to better serve their clients. "Senior people attached to the smartest desktops" will handle media relations in a Web-based PR environment, he said. That's a far cry from having junior staffers pitch reporters, a practice that is common in most PR firms.

To position for the Web-dominated future, TWG has set up a unit called Thunder House to develop and market websites for clients and to serve as its laboratory to test the Web's impact on public relations.

There's been a surge, especially in recent months, in the use of the 'Net to promote products and services. Tom Tardio, Co-Chairman and Managing

138

Director of Rogers & Cowan, a Shandwick company in Los Angeles, said Internet business is running 50 percent ahead of last year, and now accounts for 15 percent of billings. R&C's Los Angeles office had overall fee income of more than $10 million in 1995.

Tardio's firm, which has been promoting TV programs and entertainment for many years, is using that experience to promote client Web sites. He said there's a convergence among entertainment, consumer marketing and technology that bodes well for the future of Web-based communications.

Weber, whose firm handles America Online and the World Wide Web Consortium, said 25 percent of TWG's new business is Internet-related.

Edelman PR Worldwide is another firm that is actively involved in Internet communications. Its Edelman Interactive Services unit designs home pages for clients, explained Paul Bergevin, Executive VP and Managing Director of Global Technology. In its first year, the new service went from "zero to a couple of million dollars," Bergevin said. Edelman is using the Internet both as a profit center and a new marketing vehicle. It's also a new communications medium, Bergevin said, because unlike the TV viewer and newspaper reader "your interlocutor can talk back . . . we're just now beginning to define the rules of how you behave on the Internet."

PR executives are closely monitoring MSNBC, the joint cable TV and Internet venture between NBC and Microsoft, to see if a traditional broadcaster can adapt to the free-wheeling spirit of cyberspace. The operation is an attempt to use the 'Net to add more information about headline news and get viewer feedback.

MSNBC Internet Correspondent Mary Kathleen Flynn and her producer Warren Lewis and their staff in Fort Lee, N.J., comb the Web for items that would take the day's headline stories a step further. Sometimes, Flynn said, those stories are about the phenomenon of the Internet itself such as gangs using the 'Net to recruit members and the CIA's page being vandalized. Flynn, a former *U.S. News & World Report* Senior Editor, is MSNBC's only full-time, on-air correspondent. The venture uses six daytime anchors or hosts, who usually interview regular NBC correspondents covering the day's breaking stories.

Flynn has a website column in which she "shares with Internet users what I've talked about on television and also to provide links to those websites." She described her Web column as "the intersection between the Internet and headline news."

'Net users can access her column by clicking on her picture on the MSNBC home page. But the Internet correspondent said PR people should never phone her. Instead, they should send info via E-mail. She complains about PR people trying to pitch her technology stories. "I don't care about technology unless there is a content reason to care about it," she said. For example, she said, a new development in audio sound on the Web would not be of interest in and of itself. "It's interesting to me when a website that has newsworthy content is using it," she added.

MSNBC currently employs 400, with 100 in Redmond, Wash., and 300 in Fort Lee, N.J. The Redmond staffers do stories for the network's online Internet service. Of the 300 in Fort Lee, 25 are working on Internet-related stories.

MSNBC is currently carried by 25 million cable homes compared with 22 million at the time of its July 15 launch. Contracts are in place to have the service carried in 50 million homes by the year 2000.

Andrew Goldstein, an Associate Producer on NBC's "Today" show specializing in technology, said he has been using the Internet at home to check out claims made in PR pitch letters. "I will get a letter from someone in PR and I'll check out their company's site before calling back," he said. "I'll also try to look at other things similar to it so that when I call them I'm not going in uninformed. I have an idea what's out there in their particular area."

Goldstein said most of his checking until now has been done at home but NBC is in the process of giving all its news people access to the Internet. He's interested in stories that tell the consumer how to get the most out of his or her computer at home. The emphasis is on "her" since women are the fastest growing group using the computer, he added.

The "Today" show rarely airs a story based on a single product, Goldstein said, and that is why the Internet is an invaluable tool in checking out what similar products exist for a market story. "That would become a segment," the producer said.

Goldstein cautioned PR people that the "Today" show is focused on "news that you can use." Examples would be educational software or checkbook writing programs. He said: "There are occasions we've pitched a story that's interesting but it's only interesting to the industry."

. . . Some reporters have complaints about the way PR people use cyberspace. . . . "PR people don't use the Web properly," said Dan Gillmor, Computer and High-Tech Editor of the *San Jose Mercury News*. "The Web ought to be the first place reporters look for information. PR people need to work with clients on making websites more useful. . . . There's plenty that can be done."

Gillmor moaned that some companies appear to be using the 'Net to keep reporters and others from calling them by not including the names and phone numbers of press contacts. "If I can't find the phone number on the website, the company doesn't want me to call," he said. He mentioned Microsoft, Intel and the Claris subsidiary of Apple Computer as examples of companies placing some of the better sites on the Web complete with press contacts and phone numbers. "Believe it or not, that's rare. . . . The major motivation of many companies seems to be to use the website to keep companies from phoning," he said. A website's first screen also "should tell me why I should keep reading it," Gillmor said.

Other reporters say stuff on the Web does not interest them. Ron Rosenberg, who covers biotechnology and emerging companies for the *Boston Globe*, said putting out screen after screen of data on the Internet is not the way to go as far as he is concerned. He also complained that PR firm staffers are too young and don't know enough about the product and company they're pitching. "I ask questions and I don't get answers. I find this frustrating," he said.

Rosenberg said: "PR people are loathe to put things in context and admit their client has competition. It drives me nuts. The top executives of a company admit they have competition, why can't the PR people?" In addition, Rosenberg lamented "mammoth press kits that don't give much information," adding that the better PR people will include a market research report giving a quick read on the market their client is in. "Lack of information is the biggest problem," he concluded.

Discussion Questions

1. Find the Web site of one of the companies mentioned in this reading: Microsoft, Intel, and Claris. Can you find the names and telephone numbers of the public relations people?
2. If you were reporting a story about one of these companies, how helpful would the information on the Web site be?
3. How much can you trust the information on these Web sites? How much information can you trust from Web sites, user groups, and the Internet in general?

FIRMS ADVISED TO RESPOND QUICKLY IN TIME OF CRISIS

Robert Steyer

■

W hen a bacterial infection was linked to hamburgers at several Jack in the Box outlets, the first casualties were a boy who died and several hundred people who were sickened from eating the meat. The second casualty was the fast-food firm's sales and the stock price of its parent, Foodmaker Inc., of San Diego. The stock is down by about 33 percent since mid-January when the food contamination was detected. The third casualty was Fleishman-Hillard Inc., the St. Louis–based public relations firm which counseled Foodmaker on managing the bad news. The companies said recently that they parted by mutual consent. Whether the next casualty is the fast-food chain's reputation depends on how well it acts to regain the public's trust.

The chairman of Jack in the Box's parent company took to the airwaves, explaining how the problem occurred and how his company would ensure safety. But some critics said the response was too little too late.

Public relations experts say there is no magic formula to repair a corporate image because each crisis is different.

Exxon Corp. got bad marks for handling the Exxon Valdez oil spill in Alaska, but it's doubtful people stopped buying Exxon gasoline. Johnson & Johnson won praise for handling the Tylenol capsule poisonings 11 years ago, but it took 18 months for J & J to recapture its painkiller business even though the company was blameless.

Although no one can predict the long-lasting effects of a crisis, corporations can follow some simple procedures to make the best of a bad situation. "You have to respond quickly with authority," said Dan Bishop, director of corporate communications for Monsanto Co. "Otherwise, the vacuum is filled quickly with your adversaries, and then you'll always be on the defensive," he said. "You've got to tell the truth in a no-nonsense way."

Dana Spitzer, who counsels companies on crisis management, said the company must tell the public quickly that it is addressing a problem. "Saying 'No comment' implies guilt even if you don't know everything," said Spitzer, a vice president in the St. Louis office of Hill and Knowlton Inc., a public relations company.

"We advise clients to comment even if they don't have all the facts," Spitzer said. "If you don't comment, then the media will get comments from the fire department or police department. You must take charge."

Spitzer recalled the case of a local company that wasn't prepared for the onslaught of press coverage. After a late-night explosion at a plant, two TV crews, which had been monitoring police radios, rushed to the plant's gate. They were met by a guard who wouldn't respond to their questions. "The company had no plan," Spitzer said. "The next day's paper quoted a fire chief and the company's 'no comment.' Employees read about it and got concerned."

The company could have saved itself considerable grief if it had a designated team of executives who could quickly respond to the media, health agencies, government agencies and local politicians, Spitzer said. "You need a credible spokesman," he said. "A plant manager may speak in very technical terms. You have to choose someone ahead of time."

Monsanto has two crisis teams—a primary and a back-up. Each team consists of a lawyer, finance expert, communications executive, security official and a member of top management.

Because Monsanto has many products and many divisions, it must remain flexible. A response involving a prescription drug will be different than a response involving a chemical used in making plastics. So a crisis team enlists experts at each division to address a specific crisis. Each team conducts at least one trial run a year, Bishop said. He added that companies shouldn't overreact by placing their chairmen in front of television cameras after every problem, accident or setback.

In recent years, Monsanto has been embroiled in controversies involving its Lasso herbicide, the CU-7 intrauterine device and the artificial sweetener NutraSweet. Each dispute merited a swift response—in the press, before regulatory agencies or in court. But none was considered a crisis, Bishop said.

The Doe Run Co.'s business—lead mining—has a built-in potential for bad publicity. So the company has a crisis plan that gets tested through trial runs every year, said James E. Stack, vice president for human resources. Doe Run assigns senior managers to contact government officials, health agencies and the press in case of an accident at the company's headquarters or three operating divisions. Managers are instructed in safety procedures. Doe Run also hires a consultant to conduct a course called "TV Without Terror"—a guide to dealing with the media.

Each year, the company conducts a "walk-through" for managing a crisis, videotapes managers' responses and critiques their efforts, Stack said. Doe Run also creates a surprise mock disaster at each division each year. For example, it might fabricate a mine fire. "We do this because we have all the potential of significant negative exposure," Stack said.

Ironically, the company that virtually wrote the book on crisis management didn't have a crisis plan. "We were quite unprepared," said Robert Kniffin, vice president for external communications at Johnson & Johnson. "We had to invent things as we went along."

Seven people died in the Chicago area in 1982 after taking cyanide-laced Tylenol capsules. J & J quickly removed all capsules, first from Chicago-area stores and then from all U.S. stores. The recall cost J & J $100 million. Tests showed a few other samples of tainted Tylenol in the Chicago area. Seven weeks after the recall, J & J said it would bring Tylenol capsules back in protective containers. The announcement was made by J & J Chairman James Burke.

During the crisis, J & J responded "promptly" to press inquiries, Kniffin said. But Burke didn't make a televised announcement until the product was restored.

The experience remains vivid in Kniffin's memory. The press was pressing him and other officers to speculate about the poisonings and about the fate of Tylenol. Even when it was clear that the company didn't cause the problem, it took awhile to disabuse people of rumors that the poisonings were caused by a manufacturing failure or by a crazed employee. "Any time anybody got sick in America, it was ascribed to Tylenol capsules," Kniffin said. "Experts said they thought the product was dead."

DISCUSSION QUESTIONS

1. One expert quoted in the article maintained: "Saying 'No comment' implies guilt even if you don't know everything." Do you agree with that statement? Why, or why not?
2. Are you skeptical or not about a company's comments during a crisis such as those with Tylenol or the Exxon Valdez? Why?
3. Do agree that a quick response in a crisis is important? Why, or why not?

CHAPTER 11

THE CULTURE
OF NEWS

Carl Hausman, *The Medium versus the Message*

Carole Rich, *The Thrill Is Alive*

Edwin Diamond and Gregg Geller, *Idiots with Email: The Dangers of Internet Journalism*

Jimmie Reeves and Richard Campbell, *Coloring the Crack Crisis*

D iscussing ethics in the media has always been difficult for me. My basic standard comes from religion: "Do unto others as you would want done to you." Treat individuals with respect. There is only one stupid question in the journalistic vernacular. That's going up to a mother who has just lost her children in a disaster and asking: "How do you feel?"

There is another touchstone I teach my students from the movie *Broadcast News.* The anchorman, played by William Hurt, is confronted by the news director with proof that he faked tears when interviewing a source. "You crossed the line," the news editor claims. "The problem with the line," the anchorman retorts, "is they keep moving the little sucker." There are important ethical questions posed by those who use and work in journalism. What is most important, however, is to develop one's own moral compass.

Ethical questions can be discussed at length in a classroom, but more often than not an individual has to make a decision about ethics quite quickly. The evaluation in the classroom does serve a useful function, but what would you do if given the chance to steal a photograph from Madonna's mantelpiece, or to present to your editor the murder weapon that the police left behind at the scene of the crime? How do you evaluate the role of a reporter who provides a distorted view of a story?

This chapter contains four different readings about the culture of communication. One deals with the medium of journalism, and one deals with the nature of the newsroom. The other two readings deal with how the world of journalism works and the sometimes improper ethical judgments that are made in it.

THE MEDIUM VERSUS THE MESSAGE

Carl Hausman

∎

P ossibly the most recognizable words in journalism are not from Edward R. Murrow or Walter Cronkite, although "This is London . . ." and "That's the way it is" will always hold a place in most of our memories.

But *every* journalist recognizes these words:

> Jimmy is eight years old and a third-generation heroin addict, a precocious little boy with sandy hair, velvety brown eyes and needle marks freckling the baby-smooth skin of his thin brown arms.

Those words appeared on September 28, 1980, a black day in the annals of the *Washington Post.* The lead above belonged to a page-one story called "Jimmy's World," a story written by Janet Cooke, an ambitious reporter who won a Pulitzer Prize, but had to give it back.

Because she was a pipe artist.

A pipe artist, in the journalists' lexicon, is someone who makes up quotes and stories. Cooke, when the dam first began to leak, initially claimed that Jimmy was a "composite character," an individual conveniently created by melding the quotes and actions from several characters into one, a dubious practice but not necessarily a mortal sin in some journalistic circles. But under ever closer scrutiny from the Pulitzer board and her own editors, Janet Cooke finally admitted that she just made the whole thing up.

The Cooke affair was one of the most traumatic blows ever to the collective integrity of journalism. Many explanatory theories were concocted, among them the hypothesis that there is simply too much pressure put on reporters when they compete for good stories and good exposure. Perhaps there is some truth in that, but the argument does not change the fact that Janet Cooke will always be remembered as the craft's premier pipe artist.

147

What further inflamed the situation was open speculation by critics and journalists that there is a little of the pipe artist in most reporters. When Tom Goldstein was testifying as an expert witness in the *New York Daily News* libel trial, he was asked by a lawyer: "Is it perfectly acceptable journalism to report as if you are an eyewitness to an event when in fact you are not an eyewitness?"

His answer: "Absolutely. It happens all the time."

The lawyer then read aloud the lead of the story in question:

"A cold wind was ripping up 125th St., and the man in the full-length leather coat dug his hands deep into his pockets as he stepped from the black BMW.

" 'Yo,' one of the teenagers standing in front of the Oasis Sandwich shop just off Park Avenue shouted when he spotted the man crossing the sidewalk. Scattering like pigeons, the teenagers crossed to the other side of the street."

Goldstein reports that the lawyer was incredulous that despite the specific detail, neither reporter involved in the case had been at the scene. Goldstein testified that this kind of reconstruction was "common practice." "Since reporters cannot be everywhere all the time," he said, "it is necessary sometimes to reconstruct scenes after the fact."

Was the scene on the Harlem street re-created in too much detail? In retrospect, Goldstein now admits that with the benefit of hindsight, perhaps the depth of detail in this particular case was overly misleading; but the point is that reconstruction of events was and is accepted practice.

How extensive a practice is it? Before writing this paragraph I grabbed, at random, a sheaf of clippings from my file. The very first story in the pile is titled "The Making of a Doctor," and follows several students through a week of medical school. One particularly cloying reference describes a medical student who looks tired because he spent a long, restless, "burning eye" night cramming for a final.

The reference is stated as fact. But the fact is, I personally did not know then and do not know now if the student was tired from studying all night or from dancing the flamenco. He *told* me about his restless night, the cups of coffee, the burning eyes, and so forth. I believed him. But I didn't spend the night with him.

What I did was relatively harmless, I think. What Janet Cooke did was quite damaging. And according to the judge, what the reporters did in the *Daily News* case in which Goldstein testified was legal (not libelous), but disturbing, anyway.

The problem here, of course, is where we draw the line in this particular continuum. How closely must a reporter stick to reality in *portraying* reality? There is a difference. No reporter *repeats* reality; only stenographers do that, and even a stenographer cannot re-create all of the gestures and nuances that are part of reality. Even the "neutral" TV camera is more than an observer. As Mike Wallace pointed out, a medium-long shot allows the guest an air of decorum, while a tight close-up shows the "tics and perspiration." That camera—which is capable of producing either shot—is hardly a neutral tool.

This reading continues, to an extent, the discussion of whether ends justify means, but examines an ethical dilemma specific to the mass media: The fact that a medium "creates" its own reality. When this happens, the medium and the message—or, stated another way, the drama and the reality—come into conflict.

The fact that cameras, microphones, and notebooks are not always neutral instruments of observation raises a question about just who qualifies as a pipe artist, and to what degree we practice our artistry. And to pose a broader question, what exactly is reality, anyway?

The reality issue is a question which we cannot hope to answer, at least not here. Generations of scholars—philosophers, scientists, sociologists, literary experts, the list goes on—have posed that question, and have not yet produced a definitive answer.

Within the narrow confines of journalism, though, we can at least scratch the surface of the media-created reality issue, and examine whether that media-created image distorts reality. For example, Judy Vanslyke Turk, writing in *Journalism Monographs* of December 1986 (p. 3), made this observation about research in journalistic agenda setting:

> The media present a pseudo-environment, a self-conceived perception of the world which is not necessarily the same as the world that is "really" there. But this pseudo-environment is not entirely of the media's own making. While individuals working for media organizations make decisions as to what does or doesn't get on the agenda of salient, important "news" which is presented as media content, it can be argued that the sources of information upon which journalists rely ultimately have more to do with media content than the selection processes of journalists themselves. News is not necessarily what happens but what the news source *says* has happened because news doesn't "happen" until there is an exchange of information between newsmen [presumably she includes women, too] and the sources.

In other words, we rely on others to create the admixture of words, ideas, and images we use to represent reality. (As I relied on my medical student's report of his "burning eye night.") Sometimes, the people who furnish those words, ideas, and images do so with their own interests in mind, so another layer of distortion is added. In other words, the information is skewed in the first place—say, by a political candidate staging a rally—and then further distorted by our efforts to transplant the information via a mass medium. The situation is likened to a "reality trap" by media analyst W. Lance Bennett in his book *News: The Politics of Illusion* (p. 128):

> Although the goals of documentary ["documentary" meaning, in this case, reporting which relies on eyewitness accounts or accounts from reliable sources] reporting are hard to fault, the practice of the documentary method creates a trap for journalists confronted with staged political performances. Only in rare cases when the performances are flawed, or when

the behind the scenes staging is revealed, can reporters document in good professional fashion what they know otherwise to be the case: The news event in question was staged for professional purposes. Since, as [historian Daniel J.] Boorstin pointed out, pseudo-events contain their own self-supporting and self-fulfilling documentation, the documentary method highlights the very aspects of news that were designed to legitimize them and blur the underlying reality of the situation.

The "underlying reality" is frequently difficult to pin down because of the problems inherent in reproducing a fair representation of reality. Media mechanics, at the most basic level—like Mike Wallace's tic- and perspiration-seeking camera—can distort reality, whatever that really is.

Consider these examples of how the medium intrudes on the message:

- A television reporter covering an acrimonious city council meeting uses up most of the allotted time for the news package with tape of a shouting match between two councilors. The confrontation makes compelling video, but the rest of the items acted upon get little or no coverage.

    This actually is quite a common scenario, and a typical complaint lodged against television news departments. ("We passed a million dollars' worth of appropriations and all you showed was that loudmouth from the Fifth Ward!")
- A newspaper writer interviews two spokespersons representing opposing viewpoints on an issue. Spokesperson A is colorful and provides pithy, eminently quotable replies. Spokesperson B is softspoken, not very experienced with the media, and while providing reasonably clear responses produces nothing quotable. The reporter leads and closes with anecdotes and quotes from Spokesperson A; while the amount of *space* is balanced in the story, the impression may not be. Spokesperson A clearly comes out the winner in the battle of the pithy quote. (Journalists do debate the ethics of this type of situation. Many reporters feel they must be on guard against a facile, experienced spokesperson, or a slickly staged event, because news that comes to them in a convenient package may not be particularly fair.)

In sum, "balancing" an issue in order to give a fair representation of reality is not always a simple matter of "reporting the facts." Requirements of the medium—including the difficulty of covering a very complex story in a limited amount of time or space, the problems of using compelling video in place of the more routine activities connected with a news event, and avoiding having coverage manipulated by interested parties who have mastered the art of making the journalist's job easier—do intrude on the message, giving new light to Marshall McLuhan's aphorism that the medium *is* the message.

Humans seem to have an innate need for drama, a fact not lost on ancient Greeks, Elizabethans, and every other group of people who have sought to understand the human condition, or at least make themselves feel better, cathartically, by watching someone else struggle with the human condition. That fact—our need for drama—appears in many aspects of everyday life. Clifford Geertz, professor of social science at the Institute for Advanced Study at Princeton, noted (1980, p. 173) that an emerging school of thought tracks drama at all levels of social organizations. Those dramas, he says:

> . . . arise out of conflict situation—a village falls into factions, a husband beats a wife, a region rises against the state—and proceed to their denouements through publicly performed conventionalized behavior. As the conflict swells to crisis and the excited fluidity of heightened emotion, where people feel at once more enclosed in a common mood and loosened from their social moorings, ritualized forms of authority—litigation, feud, sacrifice, prayer—are invoked to contain it and render it orderly.

Such telling and retelling of the human experience is as much a staple of the news story as any other form of drama; anyone in doubt can attempt to locate a news story without the essential element of drama—conflict. Be forewarned that such stories are few and far between.

Conflict, crisis, and denouement (those elements of drama with which we are so accustomed) contribute to our perception of reality, that "collective hunch" about what is going on. In fact, historian Arthur Schlesinger Sr. maintained that we *have* to interpret this drama as a mirror and as an integral part of reality. In his autobiography, Schlesinger wrote (1963, p. 106):

> [In an article, I] argued the need for studying literature as a direct or indirect expression of social and economic conditions rather than as something which had developed "in a vacuum, without relation to anything but itself"; and the essay further urged that researches extend beyond belles-lettres to the reading matter of the masses, which in a democratic country offers the only true picture of the national level of taste and interest.

To rephrase, when Schlesinger contends that the material "of the masses" is the only "true picture" of the national level of taste and interest, isn't he implying, too, that the medium is the message?

Saying that the medium is the message and that the medium sometimes fights the message is really saying the same thing: Since there is no perfect way of conveying reality, we rely on media, which—because of their mechanics and requirements—distort the message, but that distorted message in turn becomes reality.

In many cases, we're hard-pressed to determine what is "real" and what is not. For example, as cited above by Bennett, a political rally is often an event specifically staged for the media; the media, in effect, *create* the event and then *report* on their own creation. Seasoned public relations professionals know, of course, what will "play" in the media and go to great lengths to create usable material, material which reporters can witness and attribute to reliable public figures.

For example, while working as a television reporter I once covered a political "rally" where no one—literally *no one*—was rallying. But there was music (taped) and balloons, and a politician on a dais, and a small hall full of no one but reporters. When I had the camera operator pan the near-empty hall, a campaign manager accused me of taking a "cheap shot" at the candidate.

Was it a low blow? Maybe. It has never been standard practice, as far as I know, for any television station routinely to report crowd sizes at events of this type, so I was departing from standard practice by taking the pan of the near-empty hall. Also, anyone who covers politics knows that the long and grinding obligatory schedule of campaign appearances precludes huge attendance at each and every function, especially for local and statewide races. But on the other hand, is it a fair representation of reality to show a politician who appears to be speaking to an audience when there *is* no audience? Such is the problem of Boorstin's "pseudo-event."

Another closely related factor in the tug-of-war between the medium and the message is the *bureaucracy* of news reporting. Just as Schlesinger's dramas do not spring from a vacuum, neither do our news reports. News is produced within an organization, and reporters must produce material which "sells" to an audience and, in addition, "sells" to the editor. (The point being that reporters compete for space or airtime, and by pleasing an editor—supplying him or her with stories the editor is likely to regard with favor—the relationship of news to reality is skewed by the reporter's natural desire to please a boss.)

In addition, the news process involves many methods of obtaining information; a particular aspect of this news bureaucracy is what Mark Fishman, in his book *Manufacturing the News*, calls "accounting."

> The entire news production process occurs in several successive "levels," stretching from the earliest formulated account of something on up to the reporter's written news story. For example, the accounting process which underlies any one crime story can be traced through successive levels of accounts. Only the top level consists of the police reporter's work of detecting, interpreting, investigating and formulating the story. Behind the news story, inside the agency through which the reporter first sees the story, are the bureaucratically produced accounts upon which the news will be based.

Many who have worked as reporters recognize the problems associated with bureaucratic reconstructions of news. The police reporter, for example, has little alternative but to accept police accounts of arrests as prima facie truths. After all, reporters typically do not witness arrests and interrogations, and often have virtually no access to a person charged with a crime.

The "accounting" which Fishman cites takes place within the news organization, too. Most news organizations maintain a library of sorts, and archival material from that library often comprises the building blocks of future stories (Hansen, Ward, & McLeod, 1987). The material is retrieved for reference purposes—with the practical result that the first account of a situation may indeed provide the "boilerplate" copy, used again and again in recounting following versions of the story. That type of overreliance was what we found in the analysis of the Brown and Sharpe strike stories.

One reason for overreliance on boilerplate copy is the fact that reporters handle a wide variety of assignments; they are not, and cannot be, experts in all areas. The library or other repository of archival material becomes an important part of their method or story (and "reality") construction.

Ironically, the bureaucracy of reporting plays a similar role when journalists become excessively close to a story. When we cover a story day in, day out, we tend to leave out details. We take it for granted that the reader, listener, or viewer knows these facts that have become so familiar to us.

Sometimes, we (as reporters) leave out information *because we don't understand it ourselves.* Most reporters will admit that there are many subjects which baffle them, and they simply do the best they can, reporting incomplete information. For example, the first important news assignment of this author was covering a murder trial. While murder trials are completely understandable in TV dramas, some of the real-life aspects of the proceedings can be virtually incomprehensible to the layperson. The vocabulary is arcane, the scheduling and motioning process is mysterious, and sometimes a spectator cannot even clearly hear what is happening. My report may have been fairly accurate—I know I got the verdict correct, anyway—but beyond that, I am not sure.

Many of the effects of this news bureaucracy go unnoticed by the public. Consumers of news are conditioned to accepting incomplete information, and in some cases for good reason. Every story dealing with Middle East conflicts, for example, cannot recount the entire history of the conflict—although occasional stories taking such an approach would certainly be welcomed by many news consumers.

So, try as we might, the battle of the medium versus the message puts a little of the pipe artist in every reporter. This certainly does not imply that reporters cannot be relatively fair, or reasonably objective, or as accurate as possible; only that these qualities are elusive because reality—whatever that is—cannot be picked up and transplanted without *some* alteration in what we see as "real."

There are many theorists from all disciplines who describe this effect in great detail. The best summary comes from one Pogo Possum, who postulated: "We have met the enemy, and he is us."

DISCUSSION QUESTIONS
1. What does "objective journalism" mean to you?
2. Do you believe there is a difference between objective and fair reporting?
3. Do you think that journalists can accurately describe an event if they are not present at that event? Why, or why not?

THE THRILL IS ALIVE

Carole Rich

■

Consider these articles published in the past 18 months:

"Battle Weary: Fighting the Bottom Line Takes Its Toll," *Quill.*
"Kissing the Newsroom Goodbye," *American Journalism Review.*
"The Media as Monsters," a series of six articles in the *American Editor.*
"A Generation of Vipers: Journalists and the New Cynicism," *Columbia Journalism Review.*
"The Thrill Is Gone," *American Journalism Review.*

The list could go on. And in a major study of journalists, David H. Weaver and G. Cleveland Wilhoit report that job satisfaction at newspapers is declining. In their book *The American Journalist in the 1990s: U.S. News People at the End of an Era*, they write that only 27 percent of journalists were satisfied with their jobs in 1992 compared to 40 percent in 1982 and 49 percent in 1971.

Although I usually bemoan the fact that my students don't read enough, sometimes I long for a print V-chip to shield them from negative news about the industry.

But the studies and articles accurately reflect industry problems: declining circulation, the public's distrust of the media, perpetually low starting salaries for journalists, and corporate emphasis on business profits versus editorial demands to improve the product. Now comes a new threat—the Internet.

A recent "State of the Newspaper Industry" study found that 45 percent of U.S. newspaper publishers, editors and advertising directors said the Internet would be newspapers' biggest competitor in the next 10 years. Although online publishing offers the promise of new opportunities, many print journalists fear it is the Armageddon that will make newspapers as passé as Gutenberg's printing press.

It's enough to inspire a journalist or a journalism student to seek another career. But what a rewarding career they would miss! The thrill of it endures for the journalists who thread through my life—newspaper colleagues, journalism professors and former students. They echo a common theme: Journalists can make a difference in people's lives.

The day begins shortly before 6 A.M. for John Bodette, managing editor of the *St. Cloud Times* in Minnesota, where he has worked for 22 years. The 46-year-old Bodette sprints around the newsroom to consult with editors and reporters, then lands at a computer terminal to edit and lay out the news pages. "I still do a copy editor shift every day," he says. "It surprises people that the managing editor gets his hands dirty. I love the idea of helping in the newsroom."

Except for three years in the early '80s when he worked on the prototype of *USA Today* and helped redesign a few other Gannett newspapers, Bodette has never wanted to leave this afternoon newspaper with a circulation of 28,422 daily and 38,342 on Sundays. "I know I'm unusual being in one place," he says. "I guess I made the commitment to be here. A small paper like this is an awful lot of fun. It's like driving a sports car most of the time. You can make changes. It's not like turning around a battleship."

When Bodette began working at the *St. Cloud Times* as a wire editor, he had a liberal arts degree from St. John's University in Minnesota and a year of graduate school, but no journalism training. "I came out of a background where you teach yourself. Every night after work I would go to the St. Cloud State University library and read everything I could about newspapers and newspaper design."

In 1980 he met world-famous newspaper designer Mario R. Garcia at an American Press Institute seminar, and the two of them returned to St. Cloud to redesign the newspaper. Since then, Bodette has become a design expert in his own right, conducting seminars on the subject throughout the country. "I travel a lot to speak to groups," he says, "but it's always fun to come back to this newspaper."

On this day Bodette is having more fun than usual. A good news story broke overnight. Police ticketed 150 students for underage drinking at a fraternity house at St. Cloud State University. "Not a huge story," he says, "but it makes coming to work today interesting."

By early evening, it's time for Bodette's daily run of five to 12 miles (weather permitting) while he unwinds and thinks about the next day's paper. Despite the spate of negative reports, Bodette is optimistic about the future of newspapers. "We are doing a good job of beating ourselves up," he says. "We want to improve so much that we overwhelm ourselves. I absolutely think there is a great future in newspapers. It's too terrific a life to think it's not going to be here five or 10 years from now. I can't think of any way to have more fun."

Some days Lara Weber spends hours gathering statistics and other facts for a graphic in the *Chicago Tribune*. But one graphic idea she delights in came to her in an instant.

A woman had filed a suit against her condominium board because it wanted to reduce her parking space at the complex by 18 inches. "I had this idea we should show people what 18 inches is, so we just ran an 18-inch ruler along the edge of the story," Weber says. "It's nice when you can have a fun idea and see it show up in the paper."

As an assistant graphics editor at the *Tribune*, the 29-year-old Weber doesn't draw the graphics; she helps conceive the ideas and often gathers information for them. Not long ago Weber, then assigned to the business desk, gathered hundreds of statistics for graphics for a series about the global economy.

"Our job was to make it interesting to the reader," she says. "So we brought these giant figures to an understandable level by comparing prices in different parts of the world. It turned out to be a real challenge to find comparable information, like the price of a haircut, a bag of apples or a gallon of milk."

Weber, now working with the national desk, says her job combines everything she enjoys about journalism. "I love the excitement of a newsroom," she says. "I feed off that energy. I work with all these different areas—artists, page designers, reporters and editors. It's exciting to see all these people coming together and putting out a product every day."

She also thrives on learning something new every day. "It's almost like being in school," she says.

When she graduated from the University of Kansas with a degree in journalism in 1989, she couldn't decide whether to be a reporter or a copy editor. The newspaper industry decided for her. Jobs for reporters were scarce, so she took a position as a copy editor at the *Rockford Register Star* in Illinois.

"I don't think anybody grows up thinking, 'Wow, I want to be a copy editor,' " Weber says. But she enjoyed the work, especially layout.

After 18 months in Rockford, an editing job at an Indiana women's business magazine that folded, and a stint at the *Times* in Munster, Indiana, she joined the *Chicago Tribune* as a copy editor in 1993. She became a graphics editor about 18 months ago.

"I think my job is a good example of the potential for journalism," Weber says. "Newspapers are changing and maybe newspapers are not always going to be around in exactly the same form as they are now. But there are ways to look at the news that are exciting, whether it's writing or editing or using the Internet. Finding new ways to throw it up there is a lot of fun."

Recently she was discussing her job with a reporter who is also her best friend. "We were talking about what we would do if we weren't working for a newspaper, and we were dumbfounded," Weber says. "We couldn't think of anything that would excite us as much."

DISCUSSION QUESTIONS
1. Why do you think many journalists claim to be dissatisfied with the work they do?
2. Do you think that journalists are too cynical about the world? Why, or why not?
3. How would you describe John Bodette or Lara Weber—as naive, self-satisfied, or with some other word?

IDIOTS WITH EMAIL: THE DANGERS OF INTERNET JOURNALISM

Edwin Diamond and Gregg Geller

■

W hite House Press Secretary in the Kennedy years, U.S. senator from California, *ABC News* foreign correspondent, author, bon vivant, celebrity . . . and now, Internet nitwit? After a distinguished 40-year career in bigtime journalism and politics, Pierre Salinger appears about to exit public life vaudeville style, cigar exploding in his face, baggy pants around his ankles.

Salinger, as an alternately astonished and angered public now knows, loaned his name and fading prestige to one of the more outrageous pieces of misinformation that routinely bounce around the Internet: an anonymous post dated August 22, 1996 alleging that TWA Flight 800 was shot out of the skies off Long Island as a result of a U.S. Navy missile test gone awry. The August "friendly fire" posting could easily be lumped with the mountains of malicious malarkey on the 'net—generally the work of idiots with email accounts and pieces of cheap cyberturf included in their $19.95 monthly account. But a few puzzles are still left unsolved: What motivated Salinger? Wherein lies the staying power of paranoid, politically-loaded conspiracy theorists? Will the 'net itself get knocked out of the sky by friendly fire from cyber psychos?

Salinger's former colleagues at ABC think they know the answer to the first question. "Of course, it's bizarre," says one *ABC News* reporter, speaking only on condition that his name and title not be used. "Any careful journalist would recognize there's not a shred of truth to the missile story." Another former co-worker confirms that Salinger does have good sources from his days with ABC in Paris—about 15 years ago.

That may be the problem. Salinger made major news back in 1980–81 with a story about the secret negotiations that freed the American hostages in

Teheran. In his fellow journalists' opinion, his subsequent efforts to match that Big Story invariably fell flat. During the Gulf War, one reporter recalls, Salinger pushed ABC to do a story about the "massing" of Iranian troops along the Iraq border, to fight alongside Saddam Hussein's forces. "We're still waiting for those 'masses' to cross over," says this reporter dryly.

If Salinger was seeking to stay in the public eye, it wouldn't be the first or last time a onetime high-profile figure resisted disappearing off stage.

Two elements gave the old gossip new momentum. First of all, the U.S. government has attempted cover-ups. You don't have to believe in UFO landings in Roswell, N.M., to realize that something really bad went down, say, in the Tuskegee syphilis experiments. (And yes, accounts of the "UFO sightings" in New Mexico are also floating in cyberspace: The Crash Site in 1947 is one site dedicated to the subject—complete with Alien Gift Shop.)

Second, there's the cyber connection. Put the word "Internet" in any story and it sounds hip, cool, with it. The 'net is the great equalizer: The Web pages of Conspiracy Joe and Calamity Jane exist right alongside the pages of the old-media titans (the networks, the dailies, the news magazines). And, as it turns out, the unedited stuff is so much . . . livelier. No fussy fact checkers, no accountability.

It wasn't just Salinger who bit, picking up and re-broadcasting the cyber gossip. A number of establishment media outlets, such as the *Chicago Tribune*, gave it more legs online, in print and on air. To be sure, the *Tribune* did a thorough analysis of the "flood of falsehoods" on the 'net—but in the process reposted, in full, the discredited TWA 800 missile material. Moreover, the *Tribune* offered a message board for Flight 800 theories. The *Trib*'s links to other conspiracy sites carried the headline, naturally, "Plotting Your Way."

So can anything be done to separate the real stuff from the fake? In the last year you could pick up on the Web the "breaking news" that Microsoft had purchased the Catholic Church, Courtney Love ordered the murder of Kurt Cobain, Lexis-Nexis was selling your credit-card data, Vincent Foster died for unrequited love . . . you get the idea. During the '96 campaign, people who clicked on hyper-text links enough times "learned" that voting machines had been rigged all over the country (Votegate?). A search using AltaVista found some 41,316 online references to "conspiracy."

This column, we realize, can be regarded as merely number 41,317—part of the problem rather than the solution. In fact, the Web is a virtual newsstand with 10 million or so publications, each vying for the attention of passersby. The old media no longer have a monopoly on all the eyeballs out there. Still, they do have something going for them: the old, dull, plodding techniques of reporting, fact-checking, editing. In short: laborious news gathering. In contrast, new media can operate at the speed of light—imagination to keyboard to audience in nanoseconds.

No wonder it sometimes plays like bad vaudeville.

DISCUSSION QUESTIONS

1. Do you believe Pierre Salinger got the TWA 800 story right or wrong? Why?
2. What, if anything, would you have done differently from Salinger if you had reported the TWA 800 story?
3. How do journalism reporting styles on the Internet differ from those of traditional journalism?

COLORING THE CRACK CRISIS

Jimmie Reeves
and Richard Campbell

■

T echnically speaking, cocaine is the principal psychoactive alkaloid of the coca leaf. Culturally speaking, however, the meaning of cocaine has undergone many revisions since the 1860s, when organic chemists first isolated the substance in the laboratory. In an age when cocaine has become condemned as a toxic contaminant—the killer of mighty athletes, the corrupter of admired politicians and the catalyst of frantic moral crusades—it is instructive to remember that in the 1870s and 1890s the substance was hailed as a wonder drug. Sigmund Freud, for instance, argued that cocaine, like caffeine, was helpful in the treatment of fatigue and nervousness—and even valuable as a cure for morphine addiction and alcoholism. During this period, Vin Mariani, a coca preparation marketed as a proprietary medicine, received enthusiastic endorsements from such figures as Thomas Edison, Pope Leo XIII, the Czar of Russia, Jules Verne, Emile Zola, Henrik Ibsen and the Prince of Wales.

Around the turn of the century, though, cocaine use increasingly became associated with an especially menacing form of modern deviant: the "dope fiend." But initial campaigns to make cocaine illegal were tainted by racism. For instance, in a 1903 report to the American Pharmacological Association, a committee on the Acquirement of the Drug Habit concluded that "the negroes, the lower and criminal classes are naturally most readily influenced" by cocaine. In keeping with contemporary trends in reporting, the press of yore contributed to the climate of racist hysteria surrounding the early regulation of cocaine, often using cocaine as a chemical scapegoat for the murder and mayhem that attended urban poverty in the early 1900s.

In the realm of the cultural, though, cocaine made something of a comeback in the late 1970s in terms of how the media portrayed the drug. Snorting the white powder form of cocaine became a rather naughty but generally socially acceptable display of conspicuous consumption that was as much a part of the mythical "Yuppie Way" as driving a silver BMW or sipping chilled Perrier. Over the course of the 1980s, however, the social meaning of cocaine again underwent radical shifts. Between 1981 and 1985, for instance, cocaine became increasingly known in the press and elsewhere as the drug of choice of the middle class, a mood-enhancing accessory of life in the fast lane. But in 1986, as drug experts and journalists discovered that small vials of crack priced within the means of the poor were becoming increasingly available in America's major metropolitan areas—New York, Los Angeles, Miami, and Oakland, among others—these meanings would be almost completely inverted. As a packaging and merchandising innovation, crack secured a vastly expanded market for the legendary pleasures of cocaine—and as a spectacular news story of 1986, the crack legend would transform the meaning of cocaine from its status as the recreational drug of America's elite into the "desperational" drug of America's destitute.

In *Cracked Coverage*, our book-length study of 270 network television news reports broadcast between 1981 and 1988, we examine this latest struggle over the meaning of cocaine. The volume of cocaine stories rose dramatically during the decade before peaking in 1986. In 1987, TV news coverage dwindled a bit, only to rise again in the following presidential election year. Collectively, these reports form a kind of grand mosaic that may appropriately be called "The Reagan Era Cocaine Narrative." Like other major social and cultural controversies such as AIDS, abortion rights, television evangelism and environmental protection, the media's cocaine narrative at various moments expressed many of the prominent themes and antagonisms of the Reagan years: the meaning of cocaine would be inflected by class issues, take on racial overtones and would even animate myths about the sanctity of small-town life in Middle America.

Perhaps the chief finding of the larger study is our documentation of a disturbing disparity in the journalistic treatment of white "offenders" and black "delinquents" that jibes with racial politics of the Reagan coalition. In the early 1980s, when cocaine was seen as recreational and primarily associated with white "offenders," the approved purifying solution for the cocaine problem was therapeutic intervention. Most of the authorities on whom the media depended for sound bites in drug stories and to define the problem during this period were treatment experts working at private rehabilitation centers (e.g., psychologist Richard Miller of COKENDERS) or drug hotlines (e.g., Mark Gold and Arnold Washton of 800-COCAINE). The signature image of this coverage was of white, middle-class male cocaine "victims" in their late 20s, voicing the clichés of a cleansing confession during a group substance abuse therapy session ("I lost my home, I lost my wife, I lost my family, I lost my job," etc.). Like the rebirth rhetoric of Reaganism, then, the drug news of the early

1980s was heavily informed by the desire for recovery and the hope of rehabilitation. As Joanne Morreale, a campaign media analyst, puts it, "Reagan's rebirth rhetoric offered secular salvation, a symbolic resolution of personal and
public crises."

Journalism's discovery of crack in late 1985 signalled the beginning of a period
of frenzied coverage in which the race and class contours of the cocaine problem established in the early 1980s would be almost completely reconfigured:
What was once defined as a glamour drug and decadent white transgression
became increasingly associated with pathology and poor people of color isolated in America's inner cities—the so-called urban underclass. During this crisis period, the approved journalistic solution to the drug problem was no
longer therapeutic intervention devoted to individual rehabilitation and recovery. Instead, crack coverage favored modes of exclusion enforced by the
three P's of the hard sector of the drug control establishment—police, prosecution and prison. While most of the primary definers of coverage in the early
1980s had been treatment experts, once the crack crisis broke, crusading politicians (such as President Ronald Reagan and U.S. Rep. Charles Rangel, D-NY)
and aggressive law enforcement officials (including DEA agent Robert Stutman, Maryland State Prosecutor Arthur Marshall and New York Police Com-
missioner Benjamin Ward) assumed much more prominent roles in framing
the crisis. Instead of the compassionate tone laced with the hope of recovery
that had typified response to cocaine in the early part of the decade, the crack
crisis helped promote a new racist backlash that justified the symbolic crimi-
nalization of a generation of black youth.

One of the most important developments that facilitated this coloring of
the news framing of cocaine coverage in 1986 was the journalistic discovery
and demonization of a deviant setting that became depicted as nothing less
than a locus of evil in our culture and our neighborhoods—the crack house. A
threatening place of assembly and enterprise, the crack house was often depicted as territory in which the entrepreneurial spirit and the ideology of consumerism (that are so central to Reaganomics) are pushed beyond the limits of
decency, good taste and social and moral control. Indeed, the characters who
frequented the crack house were often described, even in their own public
confessions, as "out of control." But perhaps the most damning thing about the
crack house is its association with an underground economy, a "black market"
that embraces the central principles of capitalism, most notably the profit mo-
tive, while also undermining the legitimate economy's longstanding efforts to
discipline its work force. As sociologist Todd Gitlin observes, America is a
drug culture:

> Through its normal routines it promotes not only the high-intensity con-
> sumption of commodities but also the idea that the self is realized through
> consumption. It is addicted to acquisition. It cultivates the pursuit of
> thrills; it elevates the pursuit of pleasure to high standing; and, as part of

this ensemble, it promotes the use of licit chemicals for stimulation, intox-
ication, and fast relief. The widespread use of licit drugs in America can be
understood as part of this larger set of values and activities.

In a round-about way, by giving concrete form to the limits and the contradictions of "this larger set of values and activities," the crack house plays an
important role in the maintenance of contemporary mainstream institutions
and manners. In the crack house setting, we see the despair, the exploitation
and the perversity of capitalism writ large: consumerism over the edge.

Or Reaganomics out of control.

Journalism's obsession with the site of the crack house as abnormal or deviant space, then, masks the actual ways the crack house mimics the normal and
routine business workings of capitalist enterprise.

The vilification of the crack house as a sinister place of assembly has, of
course, justified the most brutal and excessive of armed responses by the forces
of decency and control. In these purifying expeditions into the chaos and filth
of the crack house, the network news frequently has encouraged strong audience identification with the crusading police. In such "reality-based" reports,
the journalist often literally adopts the outlook of the police—a perspective
that, in the context of the inner city, is perhaps best described as the colonizer's
point of view on the colonized.

This angle of journalistic identification often features the use of the clandestine camera. In television news, the use of a clandestine camera is almost always associated with stigmatization—the John DeLorean sting or the arrest of
Washington Mayor Marion Barry on drug charges, for example. The clandestine camera marks the transgressor under surveillance as an alien "Other"
who does not have the same rights to privacy accorded ordinary citizens. In our
book, we distinguish between two types of clandestine footage—"independent"
and "implicated." The former is footage gathered by news organizations without the cooperation of policing authorities: Footage that uses a hidden camera to record open drug transactions on the mean streets of large U.S. cities,
for example. Implicated footage, on the other hand, is material that can be
gathered only with the cooperation of law enforcement organizations. In some
cases, this footage involves journalists taking cameras along on police sting operations and recording the action; in others, the footage may actually be generated by government surveillance cameras and then incorporated into the reporter's news package, such as the prosecution's footage of Marion Barry in
that Washington hotel room.

The percentage of cocaine stories featuring clandestine footage rises over the
course of the 1980s. In our video sample of coverage between 1981 and 1985,
only about one story in four (11 out of 42) would feature such footage—but in
1987 and 1988, such footage appears in over half the cocaine stories (27 of 48)
we analyzed. But the most striking development in stigmatizing camera work
occurred during the 1986 crack crisis coverage—the emergence of the raiding

footage of a hand-held camera accompanying police forces during the invasion of a crack house. This raiding footage does not appear at all in cocaine coverage of the early 1980s (when cocaine was treated as a "white" problem). But beginning with an ABC news report on July 28, 1986, it became a titillating feature of several TV network drug crisis updates. As DEA agent Stutman observed, it was easy to enlist journalists in the war on drugs because crack was "the hottest combat-reporting story to come along since the end of the Vietnam War." In the post-crisis coverage, as raiding footage became incorporated into the "image bank" available for recycling in any network news story about cocaine, it became something of a visual cliché, appearing in about one out of every four stories in our video sample.

For us, raiding footage represents nothing less than the convergence of the reportorial outlook with the policing point of view. In this convergence, we observe a shift to a proactive strategy in press/police relations, a strategy that would pay off during the 1980s war on drugs in favorable coverage of high-profile drug campaigns choreographed for the television cameras by police organizations in San Francisco on CBS in August 1981, in San Diego on ABC in March 1984, in New York City on CBS in August 1986 and March 1988, in Miami on ABC in July 1986, in Miami on NBC in August 1986 and November 1987, and in New Jersey on CBS in September 1986.

In its coverage of drugs and inner-city America during the Reagan era, conventional journalism provided plenty of description, information, cautionary tales and horror stories. But the public debates over the racial and class dimensions of drugs, over legalization and, especially, over the costs of supporting the expanding police state remained suppressed by media hysteria that succeeded only in manufacturing an apparent national consensus on drug matters: "Just say no." (For the record, for every cocaine- or crack-related death in the United States, there are approximately 300 deaths associated with nicotine and 100 with alcohol.)

Given such crusading journalists, operating under the auspices of professional neutrality and leading consensus-building, it was no great surprise when on April 29, 1992, the four Los Angeles police officers were acquitted in the Rodney King beating case; as one of the lawyers for the four officers told the *New York Times*, he had been able "to put the jurors in the shoes of the police officers." Indeed, with the surge of stories about crack cocaine in inner-city America, TV news since late 1985 had been doing much the same thing as that L.A. defense lawyer—putting mainstream America into the shoes of the police. In the routine, ritualized visual imagery of TV crack coverage—the unstable, hand-held camera bounding from the back of police vans following gun-toting authorities as they break down the door of yet another crack house—journalism became an agent of the police, putting Americans, sitting in the comfort of their living rooms, into "the shoes of the police."

Ultimately, our larger study concludes that, in authorizing and advocating the New Right's anti-drug activism, drug experts and network journalists operated as moral entrepreneurs in the political economy of Ronald Reagan's America—entrepreneurs who benefited personally and professionally from co-producing a series of moral panics that centered around controlling this stuff called cocaine and disciplining the people who used it. By adopting a "support the troops" mentality in their promotion of the war on drugs, drug experts and journalists were not simply involved in disseminating the disciplinary wisdom of "just saying no." Instead, they were also deeply implicated in advancing, even mainstreaming, the reactionary backlash politics of the New Right in a way that helped mask the economic devastation of deindustrialization, aggravated white-black tensions and, ultimately, helped solidify middle-class support for policies that favored the rich over the poor.

While we do not expect that these conclusions will be at all convincing to drug warriors, we do think they are compelling enough to make most thoughtful readers re-evaluate journalistic performance in the area of coverage of drugs and, more broadly, race during the 1980s. But, perhaps even more importantly, we hope our findings are persuasive enough to force thoughtful journalists to reconsider: 1) how reporters deal with government officials and enterprising experts who have vested interests in cultivating drug hysteria; and 2) how reporters routinely mark off certain segments of the population as deviants who are beyond rehabilitation.

DISCUSSION QUESTIONS

1. Research the *San Jose Mercury News* article on crack cocaine and the CIA. What important issues are raised?
2. What do you think about the newspaper's reporting and its aftermath?
3. Do you believe the media coverage of cocaine is a case in which African Americans are seen in a negative light and white Americans are seen in a neutral light? Why, or why not?

CHAPTER 12

ETHICS AND THE LAW

Christopher Harper, *The Dark Side of the Internet*
Marc Gunther, *The Lion's Share*
Carl Hausman, *Information Age Ethics: Privacy Ground Rules for Navigating in Cyberspace*

I t's only 45 words, but it may be the most important sentence ever written—the First Amendment of the U.S. Constitution:

> Congress shall make no law respecting an establishment of religion, or prohibiting the free exercise thereof; or abridging the freedom of speech, or of the press; or the right of the people peaceably to assemble, and to petition the Government for a redress of grievances.

For the media, the First Amendment is a mantra even though few journalists can repeat the exact words. All kinds of deeds and misdeeds are supposed to be forgiven under the First Amendment.

Practitioners of almost every other craft or profession, from plumbers to doctors, need to pass a test or have accreditation. The press does not. Nevertheless, there are a number of roles the media are expected, if not required by law, to play. A traditional view is that the media are supposed to comfort the afflicted and afflict the comfortable. In addition, the media are often called "the fourth estate." In effect, this term implies that the media are supposed to place a microscope on the three branches of government—those who govern in the executive branch, those who make laws in the legislative branch, and those who analyze the laws in the judicial branch.

The first reading in this chapter deals with the legislative and judicial issue of pornography in a digital age. The second selection analyzes the role of television and investigative journalism. The third reading focuses on the issue of privacy in cyberspace.

THE DARK SIDE
OF THE INTERNET

Christopher Harper

■

In one section of a major computer magazine, there are the usual pitches for printers, laptops and a variety of paraphernalia. There's a new pitch, too, for pornography on the Internet.

"Your computer has never done this before! You control the Action, as a hot live nude stripper obeys your every command! Live on your PC!" the ad promises.

"Choose from a menu of Fantasy girls and pick the ones you wish to interact with."

"Gay Men!"

"Love View."

"The Lace Network."

Each ad has an address on the World Wide Web. When a user gets to the Web page, there are usually two choices: click if you are over 18 years old or click if you are under 18 years old. There are easily accessible sites on mutilation, and even one that shows video clips of people being killed. More than 400 Internet news groups discuss issues from bondage to illicit drug use to advocating violence.

Should these sites be protected under the First Amendment to the U.S. Constitution? Will they be protected? Right now, most experts refer to the Internet as the "Wild West" of publishing because there are few legal restrictions on what content can be offered. The Clinton Administration tried to restrict content, but the Communications Decency Act was found to be unconstitutional because it restricted freedom of expression.

169

It is difficult to determine how, and if, the Internet can be regulated. Is the Internet similar to a newspaper, a broadcast network or something entirely different? If the Internet is like a newspaper, there are few restrictions on what can be published. If the owner of a porno bookstore, however, sold a magazine to a minor, he or she would be violating the law. So far, that's not the case on the Internet. Broadcast television, however, is restricted in what types of content can be offered and at what times. Cable television stations have more flexibility in offering pornographic material.

Simply put, there are few laws that limit Internet content, says New York University Professor Stephen Solomon, a lawyer in the department of journalism. Existing law centers on what is designated as "obscene" rather than "pornographic," he says. In order to be considered obscene under the law, Solomon says, the content must depict sexual acts, masturbation, bestiality or other active promiscuity rather than material that sexually excites the reader or viewer. He adds that the "escape clause" in the courts makes material legal if it has literary, political or scientific value. For radio and television, however, the restrictions are tighter. Because radio and television can be immediately available to children, the courts have determined that offensive material must be broadcast during late hours when children are unlikely to be listening or watching.

"No one is forcing any of us to be in this marketplace of ideas. But once we inject ourselves into it, we must be prepared to encounter ideas we find objectionable—just as someone might find our ideas objectionable," argues Eric Meyer, a consultant on online issues who also teaches cyberjournalism at the University of Illinois. The sites "are in very poor taste or downright objectionable. But they are not illegal. Nor should they be. The fact that you or I don't like them is irrelevant. That is precisely the type of expression that needs protection."

Child pornography is banned, and traffickers have been arrested for putting such material on the Internet. In Virginia, a new law forbids state employees from using computers at work to visit sexually explicit sites on line. In New York, posting indecent material in cyberspace to anyone under 17 years old has become a crime. These laws, like many others, are being challenged.

What about protecting children from pornography and other dark sides of the Internet? America Online provides a way for parents to limit children's access to the racier sections of its service, but other protective devices called "filters" are needed to shut off undesirable sites. Working in conjunction with a user's Web browser, these filters block out access to sites before a user can view them. One service, Surfwatch, offers continuing software updates for new sites deemed offensive. So far, the company has isolated 10,000 Internet sites that it monitors on violence, hate crimes, drugs, alcohol and sex. The system allows parents to add sites they find objectionable for their children.

Only a few days ago, I turned on my Macintosh before my young daughter did and found an unsolicited electronic mail for a "virtual" girlfriend or a "virtual" boyfriend. Described as "one of the most realistic, sexually stimulating computer games available," the program was "designed for both hetero-sexuals and homosexuals."

The seller had gotten my email address from a discussion group about journalism and even sent the same mailing to others on the list. Neil Budde, the editor of the *Wall Street Journal*'s interactive edition, warns: "The more you want from the Internet, the more you give up privacy." Ultimately, the only effective way to protect yourself and your children from all objectionable materials is to shut the computer off. But is that really a solution?

DISCUSSION QUESTIONS

1. How concerned are you about the existence of pornography on the Internet?
2. In your opinion, should pornography be banned or regulated on the Internet? Why, or why not?
3. Should you be able to protect your privacy from sexual solicitations on the Internet? Why, or why not?

THE LION'S SHARE

Marc Gunther

∎

T he reaction was all too predictable.

When a Greensboro, North Carolina, jury found that *ABC News'*
"PrimeTime Live" had broken the law in its hidden-camera investigation of
the Food Lion supermarket chain, journalists, media lawyers and defenders of
the First Amendment denounced the verdict. There were dire predictions
about the "chilling effect" of the jury's decision and its subsequent $5.5 million
award of punitive damages.

. . . Typical was Bruce Sanford, a Washington-based First Amendment
lawyer, who told the Associated Press that the Food Lion jury was "punishing
the messenger, plain and simple." Sandra Baron, executive director of the
Libel Defense Resource Center, told the *New York Times* that such lawsuits
could lead reporters to "exercise caution, perhaps undue caution" when pursuing investigative stories. It would be unfortunate, she later told AJR, "if, as
a result of the cost of litigation, good stories are not done."

. . . The prime time magazines must compete for ratings with entertainment shows, so they are under enormous pressure to tell clear, simple stories,
with victims and villains, preferably illustrated with eye-catching video. It's
rare that the networks portray a good person or company as bad; more often,
the desire to entertain and simplify can overwhelm nuance and balance.

. . . By now, even if you didn't see the program, you've surely heard about
the 1992 ABC "PrimeTime" broadcast that accused Food Lion of selling rot-
ting meat, fish dipped in bleach to disguise its putrid smell, cheese nibbled on
by rats, even produce removed from fly-infested dumpsters.

You've probably also heard about the way *ABC News* producers Lynne
Dale and Susan Barnett lied and induced others to lie to get hired at Food Lion

supermarkets in North and South Carolina. Dale, in particular, laid it on thick, writing on her job application, "I love meat wrapping. I have heard Food Lion is a great company. I would like to make a career with the company." She even persuaded her dentist to give her a false reference. This enabled Food Lion lawyer Andrew Copenhaver to tell the jury: "Can anyone really trust ABC? . . . Lying is part of the very fabric of 'PrimeTime Live.' "

You may also have heard that Food Lion, despite its claims that the program was false and unfair, didn't sue for libel—a point made repeatedly by ABC. "They didn't attack the story because they knew it was true," Arledge says. Instead, the supermarket chain sued for fraud, trespass and breach of fiduciary duty—meaning that the ABC producers, once hired, owed their loyalty to Food Lion. These newsgathering issues, and not the program itself, were the focus of the trial and verdict.

Most news accounts of the Food Lion trial, however, haven't gone beyond the issue of hidden cameras to examine other problems with ABC's reporting and editing. Documents show, for example, that the ABC producers applied for work at Food Lion as soon as their story was approved—in apparent violation of the network's own guidelines, which say hidden cameras should be used only after other means of getting the story have been tried. In the Food Lion case, ABC could have checked state or federal health inspection reports to learn about Food Lion's food safety record. Or the producers could have purchased food at Food Lion and had it tested at a laboratory for contamination, the most effective way of proving that the public's health was at risk. Neither was done or even considered, court documents show.

In effect, ABC opted to shoot first and ask questions later. What's more, the ABC producers worked closely for months with the United Food and Commercial Workers Union, which has waged a bitter campaign against non-union Food Lion. The union proposed the story to ABC; provided disgruntled workers to testify about alleged food-handling problems; arranged for Dale and Barnett to observe the operations of a deli and meat market so they could pass themselves off as experienced workers; and obtained false job references for the producers and for an ABC photographer from friendly supermarket owners. Of course, reporters seek information all the time from foes of companies they are investigating, and legitimate news stories often result. The difference here is that the union was intimately involved in the newsgathering process.

Finally, and most troubling, is the fact that ABC did not present to viewers evidence that would have undercut its indictment of Food Lion. Start with state health reports: In 1992 in Virginia, for example, Food Lion ranked third in food sanitation practices among eight major supermarket chains, according to the *Richmond Times-Dispatch*. Then ponder a commonsense argument—that Food Lion, then the nation's fastest growing supermarket chain, would have to have the world's dumbest customers to sell so much tainted food. Most important, consider the outtakes from the undercover tapes, which Food Lion lawyers obtained after a long, hard-fought battle with ABC. Transcripts of the tapes submitted to the court, which include more than 50 hours of unaired material, show that some of the broadcast material was taken out of context.

There's a moment in the show, for example, when a Food Lion worker sniffs a tray of rice pudding and agrees that it doesn't smell good. While the implication is that the pudding is for sale, Food Lion contends that outtakes show the tray was in a work area, awaiting disposal, after being removed from the sales counter. And there's no doubt that unaired footage shows Dale and Barnett trying to coax Food Lion workers into discussing rotten food and not always getting the answers they wanted. One Food Lion worker says, "Man, I could feed the dorm at [college] where I live with all the food I throw away." Another worker—who at one point is shown complaining about a spoiled chicken marinade—later says the store manager told her to dump food anytime she thought it was no good and that she does so.

No comment favorable to Food Lion was shown by ABC. Robert Lissit, a Syracuse University journalism professor and former network television producer who was hired as an expert witness by Food Lion, charges, " 'Prime-Time' was guilty of flagrant violations of journalistic ethics by deceptively editing its hidden-camera footage."

David Westin, president of ABC and its former corporate counsel, who has followed the Food Lion case carefully, concedes that the producers could have checked public inspection reports and that the program could have been more carefully balanced. But he says of the editing, "We never made a claim that every piece of meat was mishandled. So the fact that there were instances where things were done properly—or even a lot of times—was really not the point."

As for the suggestion that ABC could have submitted Food Lion products to laboratory tests, network executives say that Food Lion surely would have disputed the results. Only visual images could prove their case, they say. That *ABC News* worked with the union isn't unusual, Westin says, since reporters frequently seek information from people with vested interests and then test it against other evidence. ABC, he adds, has 70 employees confirming on-the-record accounts of poor sanitation. (Food Lion disputes this.) And, Westin says, ABC "bent over backwards" to get Food Lion's side of the story as the broadcast neared, even submitting to the chain a detailed summary of the charges to be aired.

"Their position was that they would not talk to us until we agreed not to use any undercover footage," he says. By the time of the program, *ABC News* and Food Lion, which had sued to try to block the broadcast, were bitter antagonists.

Westin, who is known for his fairness and integrity, remains convinced that ABC's Food Lion story was truthful and accurate. Perhaps it was, but the fact that the story was built on a foundation of deception that was bound to be challenged means that "PrimeTime" could and should have worked harder to be scrupulously fair.

DISCUSSION QUESTIONS

1. What do you think about the methods used by *ABC News* on the Food Lion story—hidden cameras, fake personnel backgrounds, and working closely with the union?
2. Is a hidden camera a valuable investigative tool in television or simply an underhanded production method that has become commonplace?
3. If you were on the jury for the Food Lion case, how would you have voted and why?

Information Age Ethics: Privacy Ground Rules for Navigating in Cyberspace

Carl Hausman

∎

T he delicate balance between the public's presumed right to know versus the individual's right to privacy has historically had a rather elastic fulcrum. Recent advances in communication and information technology, though, have led many to wonder if the mechanism is hopelessly out of kilter, and what our ethical responsibilities are if we wish to repair it.

Of particular interest is what we often informally call "re-massaged" information—data collected for one purpose but used for another. In many cases, this information is taken from public records and documents, but when it is mixed with other information it is sometimes viewed as intrusive and a violation of privacy. Communication technology, it would appear, is a finely honed tool and is double-edged. To cite one (admittedly drastic) example, note that a couple of years ago these events were occurring more or less simultaneously:

1. In Detroit, reporters for various news organizations were tracing the strands of a major web of organized crime by recording license plate numbers on autos parked outside a reputed mobster's home. (Serrin, personal communication, February 12, 1994)
2. In Los Angeles, a disturbed young man who doted on an actress spotted her at the wheel of her auto, hired a private investigator to run her plate number through a data base, and learned that her address was in the Fairfax neighborhood of Los Angeles. The obsessed fan shot actress Rebecca Schaeffer to death as she opened her front door. (Thorpe, 1992, p. 112)

These two cases had startlingly different results, but both are rooted in what many observers feel is the premier emerging issue for the 20th and 21st centuries: Control of information in cyberspace—that ethereal zone where computers connect and propel data along the information highway. Within this zone, information is mixed and matched and resold to other users—users who frequently view our private lives as public commodities.

Motor vehicle data, for example, are typically sold (by the state, usually for about $5 per name) not only to the general public but also to marketing and investigative firms. What you may have assumed was one of a number of private transactions involved in everyday citizenship actually unleashes a datastorm of information, including your home address, your height and weight, medical restrictions on your license, and in many cases your Social Security number.

Control of motor vehicle information is an excellent example of debate on the parameters of privacy because it clearly illustrates a fundamental dilemma of re-massaged information and is exemplary of how we often play catch-up with laws and ethics after the technology has overtaken us. This example is revisited after some relevant historical ground is covered.

THE COMPUTER AND "THE RIGHT TO BE LET ALONE"

The struggle for control of computerized data is precisely the type of situation that typically forces us to re-evaluate privacy issues. What we might call "the philosophy of privacy" has never been determined by an all-inclusive attempt to overhaul privacy policy from top to bottom, but often by technology-induced skirmishes fought over the small frustrations and injustices we face in everyday life.

For example, the well-known phrase *the right to be let alone* (Warren & Brandeis, 1890), which was made famous in an article that is often regarded by legal scholars (Prosser, 1980) and philosophers (Schoeman, 1984) as the first truly sustained and explicit discussion of the legal and ethical dimensions of privacy, dealt with just such a technology-based intrusion. Warren and Brandeis's article was in response to reporters crashing a party at Mr. Warren's house. Intruding on a person's home was a serious breach of etiquette in 1890 because private parties were considered just that—private. In fact, people of a certain social standing at the turn of the century felt violated just by seeing their names in print.

The fact that a newspaper would even consider sending reporters to cover a party at a lawyer's home was a direct outgrowth of an unanticipated effect of technology. The refinement of rotary presses had made newspapers inexpensive and made it possible to produce a lot of them with great speed. As a result, there was a lot of space to fill and journalists rushed to fill it. But with what did they fill it?

Warren and Brandeis (1890) put it this way: "Gossip is no longer the resource of the idle and vicious, but has become a trade, which is pursued with industry as well as effrontery."

177

In fairness, this was an isolated case in which the press pushed too hard and Justice Brandeis retaliated with a bit too much artillery, but the point is that Brandeis realized that new rules needed to be drawn up because an evolving technology (the mass-circulation newspaper) had changed the game.

1994 "RIGHT TO BE LET ALONE": WHAT PRECEDENT?

What is of particular interest in the discussion of ethics in the information age is that if you extend the "game" metaphor it becomes apparent that the study of privacy—if we assume it began in earnest with Warren and Brandeis in 1890—is younger than the game of baseball. More than 100 years later, the rules are much less clear than most other games. There is a conspicuous paucity of political, philosophical, and historical precedent on which to base the discussion, a point Warren and Brandeis themselves noted.

Essentially, when I cite "a paucity of precedent," I refer to these three contentions, which are listed and then briefly discussed:

1. Unlike many other clearly delineated rights, privacy is not guaranteed by the United States' fundamental legal and philosophical documents; it is essentially absent from the Constitution.

2. Privacy is not dealt with to any great degree in the literature of philosophy either. Although one can find volumes of discussion on theories of obligation, for example, the privacy shelf is virtually bare.

3. To further complicate matters, when privacy is discussed it is often debated in the context of its value versus other rights, especially the public's right to know. But this right is equally nebulous.

The U.S. Constitution and the Bill of Rights were wrought in simpler times—times when privacy was simply not an issue of particular import. The documents do not directly address privacy. Article One of the Bill of Rights indirectly deals with the privacy of one's own thoughts (free religion, speech, and assembly); Article Four glances on privacy when it guarantees the right to be "secure in our persons"; and Article Five allows us some limitations on the secrets we are not bound to disclose. However, privacy as such is never explicitly discussed and the word *privacy* does not appear in the document.

The purely philosophical heritage of privacy, for all intents and purposes, barely exists. An excellent illustration was provided when Lisa Newton (1989) of the applied ethics program at Fairfield University was writing a study guide for the Columbia University seminar, "The Politics of Privacy." She reported that

> the concept of "privacy" has no history in the literature of philosophy. . . .
> For its philosophical foundations, we look to the literature of human dignity and the literature of privacy property; odd as the term may seem,
> one's property in one's own dignity may be the best cognate of privacy.
> (pp. 244–245)

When the dignity argument is brought full circle in the contention that privacy must be sacrificed at the altar of the public's right to know, we invoke a dimly defined right. That particular right entered the popular lexicon after World War II, popularized in part by Kent Cooper, then general manager of the Associated Press. This view, as paraphrased by Conrad Fink (1988), maintained that

> while the First Amendment gives the press the *right* to freely print the news, the people's right to know gives the press the *duty* to print it. Thus developed the idea of a press serving as surrogate of the people and demanding access to news, as well as freedom to print it, on behalf of the people. (p. 11)

Right-to-know arguments carry considerable weight when dealing with public affairs and tax dollars, but as the issue becomes further removed from public affairs (perhaps a poor choice of words, given the context of tabloid journalism), the basically unresolved right-to-know argument becomes a bit more shaky.

In *Secrets*, Bok (1982) argues that such a right is clearly far from self-evident.

> Taken by itself, the notion that the public has a "right to know" is as quixotic from an epistemological as from a moral point of view, and the idea of the public's "right to know the truth" even more so. It would be hard to find a more fitting analogue to Jeremy Bentham's characterization of talk about natural and imprescriptible rights as "rhetorical nonsense— nonsense upon stilts." How can one lay claims to a right to know the truth when even partial knowledge is out of reach concerning most human affairs, and when bias and rationalization and denial skew and limit knowledge still further?
>
> So patently inadequate is the rationale of the public's right to know as a justification for reporters to probe and expose, that although some still intone it ritualistically at the slightest provocation, most now refer to it with a tired irony. (p. 254)

Note that none of the concepts is inherently flawed. There certainly may be some Constitutional right to privacy, and certain rights have been extrapolated from the document, although primarily in abortion and forced-sterilization rulings. We may have to stretch, but we can find some guidance, ethically and philosophically, about privacy in the body of philosophy (as Bok did in citing Bentham, even though he obviously was not thinking of privacy in his discussion of stilted nonsense). It is also logical to assume that the public has a right to know something even if we cannot precisely define who that public is and what that information comprises. Our problem is not with lack of insight but rather with lack of experience in applying our wisdom to developing technological dilemmas.

Politics, Philosophy, Right to Know, and the Computer

Lack of experience comes full circle when we fast-forward to the present and return to examination of the role of the computer in media and information technology. One might argue that we are certainly far more technologically advanced than in Warren and Brandeis's day, and ought not be astonished by the fact that computers can alter information in intrusive ways. How is it that we could be blindsided by this familiar technology the way that media took Warren and Brandeis by surprise at the turn of the previous century?

The answer is, in part, that the computer of 1994 makes a 15-year-old unit seem like a mental pygmy. The advance in computer technology has been astonishingly rapid. Although a case can be made (and will be) that we should be more adept at gaining foresight from hindsight, it is important to remember that few observers of a decade ago would have predicted that in 1994 an $800 computer available at the local Sears outlet would dwarf the then-available industrial mainframe—but that is indeed the case.

It is also the case that the computer has unleashed a data storm that is washing away the traditional lines between public and private information. To return to the discussion of motor vehicle data, we can see that there are few, if any, fundamental legal/philosophical precedents, and few clearly defined rights. We are forced, then, to plow some new ground, including reevaluating traditional concepts of public information, in order to deal with the issue.

Motor Vehicle Data: An Illustrative Case

There are files on about 125 million registered automobiles and 150 million licensed drivers in the United States. The information in these data banks not only tells whomever sifts through it your home address, age, height, weight, and so forth, but also provides an indicator of your economic condition and consumer taste—namely, the type and model year of the car you own.

I testified before the House Subcommittee on Civil and Constitutional Rights in favor of a bill that would restrict, in most cases, access of the press, direct marketers, and the general public to motor vehicle data unless the providers of that data signed a waiver allowing such use. (A subsequent version of H.R. 3365 and a companion bill were recently approved by a conference committee and included in the Omnibus Crime Bill, which at the time of this writing was awaiting Congressional action.)

My argument for entertaining the concept of restricting information was derived from the contentions stated earlier because (a) the precedents are not clear and (b) the supposed rights claimed by both sides are far from clear-cut. We therefore have some latitude—and, in my personal view, a responsibility—to change the rules of the game and act proactively in order to keep laws and ethics abreast of the bounding technology that has brought about an ecological change in information ethics. I use the word *ecological* in its literal meaning and paraphrase what Neil Postman (1992) wrote about media ecology: "Europe fifty years after the printing press was not old Europe plus the printing press—it was a different Europe" (p. 18).

The evolution of the computer has brought about such a fundamental ecological change in the nature of information. Information with a computer is part of a different world than would otherwise exist if there were no computer. In short, the information assumes other characteristics.

HOW INFORMATION CHANGES ITS FUNCTION

For example, a driver's license is no longer just a document allowing you to drive a car. Computer-connected departments of motor vehicles, under the direction of state legislatures, have begun to use drivers' licenses as instruments of social control and information sharing. In Wisconsin, a court can suspend a driver's license for nonpayment of any fine, and that includes library fines. Kentucky has a law that allows for suspension of a student's license if that student cuts class or is failing classes. Massachusetts has a law that prohibits renewal of a Massachusetts license if any other state lists a revokable offense against the license holder, but Massachusetts would not get into specifics of what should qualify as a revokable offense. (If it is on the record, it is your problem and you must clear it up with whatever state issued the ruling; Garfinkel, 1994, pp. 87, 88.) Maine has begun collecting overdue child support via the threat of suspending licenses ("Maine Lifts," 1994, p. 58).

Such interconnection will be further facilitated if and when new licenses that resemble credit cards are implemented: the American Association of Motor Vehicle Administrators is developing new software to integrate traditional driver data on a magnetic strip, and to electronically store and match digitized pictures of drivers (Garfinkel, 1994, p. 127).

So what is the problem in taking the consequentialist view that because good is accomplished by using the driver's license for purposes other than originally intended, what is the harm? One answer, of course, is that remassaged information can be put to uses that are ethically questionable. The now-classic (but still, it is hoped, hypothetical) example is the newspaper story on "The Fattest People in Every State." As noted by Elliot Jaspin, systems editor of Cox Newspapers in Washington, DC and a specialist in using computer data bases for journalistic fact gathering, motor vehicle records

> give every person's height and weight. You could conceivably match those proportions and come up with "The 10 Fattest People in Ohio." Getting the information is no problem—it's public. And producing the list with a computer is no problem, either. But should a newspaper do it? I think not.

It's a terrible use of technology and resources . . . and the story has no compelling public interest. (personal communication, May 11, 1994)

As a sidelight, note that computer mixed-and-matched information, which obviously includes much more than motor vehicle data, is so prevalent that you probably encounter cases where you are a computer-generated commodity and do not even recognize it. If, for example, you have subscribed to a magazine, donated to a charity, filled out a change-of-address card at the post office, registered an automobile, or even called a company for product information, your name and any other information about you may have become a saleable item.

Some firms use a type of caller-ID to capture your telephone number when you call in and put you on a list for future solicitations (*Kiplinger's Personal Finance Magazine*, 1992, p. 44). People who move spend a lot of money in the first few weeks after they relocate, which accounts for all the "welcome to the neighborhood" mail you received after the post office printed out your name on a list available to marketers. Magazines, charities, and other special-interest groups keep, share, and sell mailing lists of people who share common interests.

RESTRICTING RE-MASSAGED INFORMATION: IS IT ETHICAL?

But all this does not answer the primary question: Is it ethical to restrict public information that is being re-massaged? In some cases, I would argue yes.

First, I again invoke the three points made earlier. In the absence of clear Constitutional or philosophical precedent, we are reasonably free to start with a clean slate. This does not mean that lack of literature and documentation on the subject gives us free rein to pass laws helter-skelter; it simply assumes that because technology typically outpaces debate on the social impact of technology it is reasonable to ratchet up the effort to create and implement some new guidelines. (I have no specific guidelines to offer here. Again, my only argument is restricting some uses of public information is not, per se, unethical.)

We also, in my opinion, need not reflexively bow to the public's right to know because that right did not, as some would have us believe, come from the Constitution nor did it come from Moses. That right was invoked by opponents of the bill, who claimed that this public information has traditionally been unfettered. *Right-to-know* and *tradition* are powerful words, and indeed cannot be dismissed lightly. But they do not carry the argument simply by their force. Right to know, as we have seen, is not surgically precise. And tradition and technology do not always mesh constructively. For example, it was traditional not to have speed limits on the interstate highway system when the first section was built. That would be a difficult tradition to honor today.

QUESTIONING THE MEANING OF *PUBLIC*

Public itself is also a difficult word to use with precision, because it can connote the notion of "available to anyone." But I contend a clean verbal slate allows a redefinition of this word, and the first step is to admit that there is plenty of public (generated by our government with our money) information that we restrict because it makes sense to do so. Tax returns and student records at public schools come to mind.

The fact that something is created with public funds does not automatically mean it is a public commodity; we do draw lines. For example, a trial, a lesson in social studies at a public school, and an operation at a public hospital all fit the category of things created with public money. Trials have been public from the beginning of this republic; yet, we have hedged a bit at the notion of new technology—television—intruding into the process. But in most cases, we have recognized the fundamental public nature of a trial and made provisions for television cameras.

But what of a camera broadcasting from a classroom? No, that does not seem appropriate, because the interaction of students and teachers was never something truly designed to be public. And the presumed sanctity of a public hospital's examining or operating room makes the notion of public coverage seem absurd, except under particular circumstances where everyone has offered informed consent.

In truth, this example was offered not so much as a refutation of the concept of *public*. What I intended to illustrate is that we have an instinctive reluctance to take information that was designed for one purpose and make it widely available for another purpose. We know that a social studies class is not the same thing as a public event, and it is not meant to be broadcast or reported verbatim. There is no logical connection between the public funding and public use of the proceedings. Although the teacher is certainly accountable to the public in some manner, it would be a tortured argument indeed to insist on complete access, up to and including access to students' grades.

As useful and beneficial to the public good as it may be, on occasion, to locate someone's home address by running his or her license plate number, it is difficult to see how there is a logical connection between the fact that the government extracted the information and the public's presumed right to have it.

The fact is that you are forced to divulge this information in order to drive a car, which for many people is essential for making a living and even for their personal safety if they live in a remote area. Try as I might, I cannot construct a rational argument based on the premise that, "because I have to drive a car, people have a right to my home address."

Having said that, I recognize that whenever access to any sort of information is withdrawn, it is a matter of concern. But technologies change the ground rules. Even the most adamant Constitutional original-intent argument, for example, must take into account that the right to bear arms has to be restricted in some sense because the Founding Fathers never could have envisioned machine guns, flame throwers, grenade launchers, and nerve gas.

IMPLICATIONS FOR THE FUTURE

This particular bill to restrict access to DMV data was viewed, in part, as a test of press freedom. But, in that context, if the bill is viewed as a press freedom issue, we must realize that there are all sorts of restrictions on press access to information, and admit that some are reasonable. Almost every journalist, including myself, realizes that there are some data that simply have to be off limits. So we are all advocates of restricting information. It is just a question of what information.

Obviously, we also know the computer is doing something to the nature of information and privacy. In 1890, soon-to-be Justice Brandeis knew that the technology of the newspaper industry was doing something to the nature of privacy.

Yet, it is difficult to maintain that we have done a stellar job in anticipating privacy problems in those 100-odd years. Issues such as media technology and wartime censorship, presidential illnesses, or the ability to monitor a worker electronically always seem to catch us by surprise. On occasion we move proactively, such as the House bill to restrict motor vehicle data, but it must be noted that the Schaeffer murder was an important incident to which the drafters of the bill reacted.

At this point, though, we know that the computer is changing information ethics; my point is that although we are not fortunetellers, we do have some vantage point and should be able to say, as Neil Postman (cited in Friedrich, 1993) did, that

> we have to be more aware, as best we can, of the possible consequences of new technologies, so we can prepare our culture for those technologies. If, for instance, we knew in 1902 what we know now about the automobile . . . there were plenty of things we could have done to prepare ourselves for that technology. And in 1946, no one really thought about, or made any preparations for, television—at least here in America. We are going through the same mindless, stupid process with the computer now. The computer is here, people are not even considering some of the negative consequences of computer technology.

DISCUSSION QUESTIONS
1. Should privacy be protected in cyberspace? Why, or why not?
2. How can an individual or the government protect personal privacy?
3. What concerns do you have about keeping your personal records protected from the public view?

CHAPTER 13

THE TITANS

Brent Schlender, *What Bill Gates Really Wants*
Geraldine Fabrikant, *Murdoch Bets Heavily on a Global Vision*
Geraldine Fabrikant, *Talking Money with Ted Turner*

T he media have always had their titans. At the turn of the century, William Randolph Hearst of the *New York Journal* and Joseph Pulitzer of the *New York World* battled for readers and personal importance. When famed artist Frederick Remington was hired to produce drawings of the Spanish-American War in Cuba, he cabled Hearst to say nothing was happening. "You provide the pictures," Hearst reportedly cabled back. "I'll provide the war."

In this era, there are three media magnates who stand out. Bill Gates was a computer nerd who built Microsoft into a huge computer software company. He is now the richest man and perhaps the most important media mogul in America. He has turned his attention to news, creating MSNBC, the Microsoft Network, and *Sidewalk*. Rupert Murdoch started his media conglomerate in Australia and now has operations throughout the world in the form of newspapers, magazines, satellites, and the Internet. He and Cable News Network founder Ted Turner are such enemies that when Murdoch's network televised the 1996 World Series, it did not show a close-up shot of Turner sitting in the front row, despite the fact that Turner owns one of the teams that played, the Atlanta Braves. Turner, who created CNN, has sold his media operations to Time Warner and now serves as vice chairman of that conglomerate. "I like something with the word 'vice' in it," he says.

Individually, these men are far more powerful than William Randolph

Hearst and Joseph Pulitzer could ever have dreamed possible. But is big necessarily bad? The three readings in this chapter are profiles of these media moguls. Clearly, each has his own agenda and interests in mind. Although these selections provide only a glimpse into the world of these three powerful individuals, you can probably judge for yourself from them whether they have your interests at heart as well.

WHAT BILL GATES
REALLY WANTS

Brent Schlender

■

I t's November 1987, and Bill Gates is vacationing in Brazil with a friend. As usual, his hiatus from the hurly-burly of running Microsoft has a definite theme. No, not learning the samba nor going on an ecotour of the Amazon. This time, the goal is to learn everything they can about biotechnology. Packed among the bathing suits and bottles of sunscreen are chunky tomes with titles like *The Molecular Biology of the Gene.* His companion, venture capitalist and former software entrepreneur Ann Winblad, is just happy that, if they have to hit the books, at least it's in an exotic locale. Says she: "You see, to Bill, life is school. There's always something more to learn."

Who is Bill Gates? He is, of course, many different things to different people. To his family he's still the precocious kid with big ideas. To his friends he's a pesky debating partner. To Microsoft's employees he's the franchise. To high-tech entrepreneurs he's the ultimate role model. To Microsoft investors he's the sugar daddy. To Macintosh aficionados he's a lucky creep. To Robin Leach he's a video segment. And to competitors he is Attila the Hun.

By now the Bill Gates bio is pretty well known. He is the scion of a wealthy and prominent Seattle family—his father, William H. Gates II, is a big-shot corporate lawyer, and his mother, Mary, was a national United Way official, a bank director, and a regent of the University of Washington. As a youth, Bill attended Seattle's exclusive Lakeside School, where he first hooked up with a computer as well as with Paul Allen, the buddy with whom he would later found Microsoft. By eighth grade he and Allen, a tenth-grader, had started their first company—Traf-O-Data—which made a rudimentary computerized device to count automobile traffic at busy intersections.

Gates later attended Harvard College for a couple of unsatisfying years; toward the end he was joined in Cambridge by an unemployed Allen. It was

187

exactly 20 years ago that Allen, while strolling through Harvard Square, spotted the January 1975 issue of *Popular Electronics* that featured on its cover a photo of the very first personal computer—the MITS Altair 8800. It was the accompanying article that prompted Gates to drop out and start Microsoft with Allen. The rest, as they say, is history.

A couple of more chapters were added in 1994. On New Year's Day, Gates married Melinda French, 30 years old, a business manager at Microsoft. Then, last summer, Gates' mother passed away. Gates and his family were deeply shaken, and friends say bouncing back has been perhaps the toughest challenge Bill has ever faced.

We all know, too, about Gates' wealth and the house he's building, rumored to be costing $50 million. But what is he like? He is, like many brilliant people, a bundle of contradictions. He can be acerbic, condescending, and even rude—around Microsoft, he's notorious for chastising subordinates who, in his eyes, haven't done their homework—yet he can also be a sentimental, almost sappy guy; he likes Frank Sinatra's music, Cary Grant's movies, and *The Bridges of Madison County*. While he loves movies and music from the Forties and Fifties, Gates is surprisingly oblivious to the popular culture of today; he had to consult a friend to find out who Sting was when the rock star called to ask to meet him. (Gates concluded afterward that Sting was "a really smart guy.") He's all-curious yet will go to great lengths to avoid being distracted; as a billionaire bachelor he refused to buy a television set for fear of getting hooked on trashy programs. A friend finally gave him one, but the tuner had been disabled so he could watch only videos.

Brilliant as he is, his grades were never that great. In junior high and high school, he was what guidance counselors would call an "underachiever," acing subjects he liked, such as math and science, but almost deliberately getting bad grades in others. Even at Harvard, Gates had trouble concentrating on subjects that didn't catch his fancy.

But Gates doesn't have many gaps in his knowledge, probably because he has always loved to read. In fact it is the one passion that matches his fascination for computers. As a kid his reading covered the gamut—encyclopedias, history books, science texts, magazines, and novels. But usually with a purpose. In junior high he went through a Napoleon phase, reading everything he could about the French conqueror.

Gates is, if anything, an even more avid reader today, and a more diligent student. . . . Before buying da Vinci's codex, he read all he could find about the multitalented inventor, including a translation of the book itself. These days Gates probably reads biographies more than anything else. Says he: "I am always fascinated by the question of whether the most talented people end up in critical positions—in politics, business, academia, or the military. It's amazing the way some people develop during their lives."

If he has time, Gates reads an occasional book about financial theory or politics. It's not all dry nonfiction, though. Recently Gates plowed through

E. Annie Proulx's *The Shipping News.* He loved Ernest J. Gaines' *A Lesson before Dying*, but was disappointed by the sequel to *The Bridges of Madison County.*

What does he look for in his "serious" reading? Gates seems obsessed with learning the mechanics of complex processes, systems, and organizations—biotechnology, evolution, the brain, and DNA are recent interests. Says Gates: "I read the most about scientists. The purity of their thinking and how they are measured makes them very attractive to me." And yes, he reads lots of books about business: "I think Alfred Sloan's *My Years with General Motors* is probably the best book to read if you want to read only one book about business. The issues he dealt with in organizing and measuring, in keeping [other executives] happy, dealing with risk, understanding model years and the effect of used vehicles, and modeling his competition all in a very rational, positive way is inspiring."

In short, Gates has not only a sharp mind but a brain crammed with, as he would put it, "a lot of stuff." When confronted with a business problem, his understanding of intricate systems, markets, and organizations makes him a much quicker study than many business leaders, and often he can foresee consequences that others miss. It's as if he were playing 3-D chess while everyone else was playing the plain old 2-D variety.

DISCUSSION QUESTIONS

1. What is your personal reaction to Bill Gates? What word would you use to describe your attitude toward him—respect, envy, dislike, or something else? Why?
2. What contributions do you think Bill Gates has made to the world? Why?
3. If you could speak with Bill Gates, what would you ask or say? Why?

MURDOCH BETS HEAVILY ON A GLOBAL VISION

Geraldine Fabrikant

.

I t was vintage Rupert Murdoch. On Thursday evening, July 18, Mr. Murdoch, the Australian-born chairman of the News Corporation, and the American entrepreneur Ronald O. Perelman lingered after dinner on the outdoor deck of the investment banker Herbert Allen's home in Sun Valley, Idaho.

Mr. Perelman had wanted to sell his company, New World Communications with its 10 television stations, to Mr. Murdoch for months, but the two had haggled over price. Now Mr. Perelman was playing hardball, threatening a deal to shut out the News Corporation. "He had me over a barrel," Mr. Murdoch conceded.

And so, dismissing the concerns of some of his own executives, on the following Sunday night, Mr. Murdoch, back at his ranch in Carmel, Calif., called Mr. Perelman on Long Island. By Monday, they had a deal.

Critics said Mr. Murdoch was paying a steep price, $3.4 billion, for stations that already carried his Fox Network. But the deal would make Mr. Murdoch the biggest owner of television stations in terms of viewership, reaching 40 percent of the United States, and a true contender with the major networks.

And so, as he often has, Mr. Murdoch—known as an opportunist willing to act quickly, ignore naysayers and spend heavily to enhance his strategy— paid a premium of roughly $300 million, analysts said, well aware that it would hurt his stock.

Nor was that Mr. Murdoch's only purchase that week. It was also announced that a consortium of companies including the News Corporation won a $1.3 billion bidding war for Metro Goldwyn Mayer Inc.

The summer shopping spree capped 12 months of aggressive investing in which Mr. Murdoch had already bet $1.8 billion on new businesses, including a United States satellite-television business and a rival news service to Turner Broadcasting System's Cable News Network.

Certainly no one underestimates the graying 65-year-old billionaire, who created the Fox Network against all odds that the public wanted another broadcast service and—nearly bankrupting the News Corporation six years ago—began a satellite-TV service in Britain. But despite the razzle-dazzle of his deal, some on Wall Street are worried.

"No one knows what the returns of all these new investments will be," Jessica Reif, who follows the News Corporation for Merrill Lynch & Company, said.

Nevertheless—and coldly confident—Mr. Murdoch is at it again: reshaping his flagship company beyond its well-worn core publishing businesses, often making big bets in little-understood markets. The goal: to own every major form of programming—news, sports, films and children's shows—and beam them via satellite or TV stations to homes in the United States, Europe, Asia and South America.

"We want to put our programming everywhere and distribute everybody's product around the world," Mr. Murdoch said in a recent interview, as he sat slouched in a white armchair at his New York headquarters, his eyes darting to seven televisions. The office has none of the oversize bowls of fruit or shiny plaques favored by other media moguls. But the man whose family holds 30 percent of the News Corporation dominates his space, as well as the conversation, by brooking few interruptions, dismissing questions and speaking so softly he can be difficult to hear.

"We've got to move to entrench ourselves the best we can, as fast as we can," he said.

Today, in many ways, Mr. Murdoch is well positioned to do so. The News Corporation has slashed debt from $12 billion to $5.2 billion and increased its cash flow to comfortably meet interest payments. The company has converted short-term debt to long-term obligations—due beyond the year 2000—alleviating pressure for quick payoffs.

Mr. Murdoch's style is well suited to an era of rapidly changing technologies and multicountry alliances. Because he controls 30 percent of the News Corporation, he can move fast and—as the shark his critics sometimes call him—dip into deep pockets and grab opportunities.

"Rupert is not so much about money as he is about power," one investment banker who knows him well said. "A lot of poeple doing deals are very focused on cash flows, returns on investment and how much they can put into their own pockets. Rupert thinks more about how the deal will expand his position around the world than he does about crossing the t's and dotting the i's on the financials."

Indeed, Mr. Murdoch seems relatively unfettered by concerns about public opinion, or the News Corporation's stock price.

"Rupert worried about the effect of New World on his stock, but he believes that as the largest stockholder of News Corporation, if he is willing to wait, others should be, too," a second investment banker familiar with his style said.

And more than most rivals, Mr. Murdoch also has what some see as an icy willingness to use his media operations as handmaidens to his business ends. For instance, he caused widespread unease when his *TV Guide* promoted a troubled TV show on his Fox Network and when he took the BBC off his Asian satellite to satisfy the Chinese.

Regardless of criticism, Mr. Murdoch's global strategy has set the agenda for competitors. "Rupert wants to rule the world, and he seems to be doing it," Viacom's chairman, Sumner M. Redstone, has said. Mr. Redstone apparently used Mr. Murdoch as a model when he flew to Germany recently to negotiate a film distribution deal.

But Wall Street is not enamored.

The News Corporation's financial performance, hampered by newsprint costs, weak performance at the Fox Network and operating losses at its Asian satellite business, has been disappointing this year. Ms. Reif of Merrill Lynch expects a 6 percent drop in cash flow, to $1.33 billion, for fiscal 1996, which ended June 30, despite a 8.5 jump in sales to $9.7 billion.

Several analysts agreed that next year, buoyed by 20th Century Fox's "Independence Day," the News Corporation's cash flow could rise 20 percent. Beyond that, weighing the impact of new start-ups is a forecasting nightmare. One result: The stock has hovered at about $22 a share for the last year. Wall Street is "suspicious of how much Rupert will spend and how he accounts for it," John Tinker, who follows media for Montgomery Securities, said. "There is no doubt he'll get it right. The question is when."

Moreover, opaque accounting for the Australian-based global company makes analysis tough. For example, Australian policy lets companies wait a year before writing off some costs of new businesses and "delays the impact on the income statement by a significant amount," Ms. Reif said. "Other companies don't do it as aggressively and few have so many new businesses or such a magnitude of spending."

And though it is a boon to investors that the News Corporation, through complex worldwide maneuvering, pays taxes of about 7 percent, low even for Australia, analysts say its accounting is confusing at best. "If you can't analyze the present, how can you forecast the future?" one analyst asked.

For example, a company official acknowledged that Mr. Murdoch pays almost no taxes on his United States businesses, though they account for 70 percent of operating profit. One tax-efficient ploy: In 1985, the News Corporation acquired Ziff-Davis travel publications for $350 million. However, the purchase was made by a News Corporation division based in the Netherlands Antilles, a tax haven with virtually no income taxes. That subsidiary also held *New York, Seventeen, Soap Opera Digest* and other magazines.

A big percentage of publishing profits—close to an estimated $100 million in 1989—was siphoned off to the Netherlands Antilles company in the form of a royalty, thus reducing United States taxable income. Meanwhile, in 1986, after paying $1.8 billion for United States TV stations, the company began writing off most of that purchase price against profits, further reducing taxable income. And, when the Netherlands Antilles company sold the Ziff-Davis magazines for a $325 million profit, it avoided most United States capital gains taxes by keeping much of the profit offshore. Mr. Murdoch's view: "If you can move assets around like that, isn't that one of the advantages of being global?"

Australian companies get another boon that makes financial comparisons difficult. Even though they can write off the cost of acquisitions for tax purposes, they do not have to write off those costs in the financial data that investors see, as is required in the United States. The result: The News Corporation's reported profits are less penalized by Mr. Murdoch's buying sprees than they would be for a comparable American company.

. . . Today, Mr. Murdoch is also making more prudent financial deals than he once did. Unlike the days of B Sky B, or British Sky Broadcasting, when the News Corporation raised all the money itself, Mr. Murdoch now has a partner, MCI Communications, which has agreed to put up as much as $2 billion in a deal widely viewed as a coup for Mr. Murdoch, who got equity without giving up voting control.

He and MCI invested in direct broadcast satellites in the United States. But they are late arrivals. "You can say that I was slow to jump into D.B.S. in this country," Mr. Murdoch conceded. "Looking back, it was the worst mistake ever," he said, adding that initially he feared cable companies would not sell programming to rivals like direct broadcast satellites. Nevertheless, if A Sky B, or American Sky Broadcasting, works, it would help the News Corporation spread programming costs by assuring a presence not only in Asia, Europe and South America, but in the affluent United States market.

Until now, Mr. Murdoch has oddly avoided TV news. And some News Corporation investors are skittish about a planned 24-hour news service that must fight the entrenched Cable News Network and the new MSNBC, the joint venture between Microsoft and General Electric's NBC, which recently went on the air to good reviews.

"Betting against Rupert has often proven wrong, but he is coming in very late against Ted Turner and NBC," worried Gordon Crawford, senior vice president at Capital Guardian, whose funds own 9 percent of the News Corporation. "There is a question as to whether the demand is there."

Mr. Murdoch, though, believes he must move into news now and relishes competing with Ted Turner. "We are a news organization," he said. "To be a meaningful broadcaster, you have to have news. We will do one, and it will be much better than CNN."

"I watch CNN on TV, but it doesn't have much news," he added. "I have a love-hate relationship with CNN. I watch it when I get on my exercise machine in the morning. There are long commercial breaks and it's quite repetitive."

There are some who think pushing the conservative angle is in some measure a marketing ploy, that at heart Mr. Murdoch believes news is simply entertainment, an analysis Mr. Murdoch denied.

"News is a commodity that is of no more importance to Rupert Murdoch than a TV sitcom," said Alex S. Jones, host of the radio show "On the Media," referring to Mr. Murdoch's raunchy British tabloid, the *Sun*. "He crafts news for the audience, but in fact his sense of what the audience wants is skewed to sensation and a lowering, not an elevation, of standards."

Mr. Murdoch makes no excuses. "Look, the first thing you have to do in a public company is to survive, and I don't make any apology for a paper or a magazine," he said.

DISCUSSION QUESTIONS

1. Watch a Fox Network news program, if possible, or visit the Fox Web site. What, if any, differences do you see between the news on Fox and that on the other network or local stations?
2. Although Murdoch, who was Australian, is now an American citizen, there was concern about his influence in the United States before he received citizenship. Was that concern justified?
3. Should news seek to reach a large audience by providing information that attracts people with a variety of interests, or seek to reach a small audience or niche market of intellectuals? What are the implications of reaching one audience versus the other?

TALKING MONEY
WITH TED TURNER

Geraldine Fabrikant

■

Forget his company's $7.5 billion merger with Time Warner Inc. Forget his war of words with Rupert Murdoch over cable news in New York City. Forget even his Atlanta Braves' flameout in the World Series.

Ted Turner, the blunt-talking entrepreneur whose marriage to Jane Fonda and penchant for controversy have made him one of the nation's most talked-about business people, is carving out a new empire that obsesses him almost as much as his cable-TV business did while he built it up over 30 years. Mr. Turner, who turned 58 this month, is pouring a big chunk of his $2.7 billion fortune into that most ancient of all investments, land, and he is populating it with that mythic American beast, the buffalo.

Only this time, for a change, he is pursuing his dream out of the limelight.

Starting from scratch nine years ago, Mr. Turner has amassed nearly 1.3 million acres of ranch land, roughly enough to fill the state of Delaware, on eight ranches in Montana, New Mexico and Nebraska. Already one of America's top 20 landowners, Mr. Turner shows no sign of slowing his acquisition frenzy. He is now negotiating the purchase of his first ranch outside the United States, a 9,000-acre spread in Argentina.

A self-described environmentalist, Mr. Turner vows he will never develop his ranch land. Instead, he is giving it the nation's biggest herd of buffalo, as American bison are commonly known—about 12,000 so far. While he won't be making anywhere near the money he would if he laid down roads and sold off plots, the land gives him the physical freedom he seems to crave and the excitement of creating a business he seems to need.

On a recent Sunday, maneuvering his Land Rover over the muddy roads of the Flying D, his 107,000-acre ranch near Bozeman, chomping tobacco and greeting the occasional hunter he allows to pay $9,500 for five days of shooting on the property, Mr. Turner, dressed in boots, jeans and a knit sweater, fairly shouted over the din of the motor: "I joke that this is my backup life. In case I don't like being vice chairman of Time Warner, I can always come here."

As Time Warner's largest shareholder, with 11 percent of its stock, Mr. Turner says he has adapted to his new corporate role. "So far, I like it fine," he said. "Most entrepreneurs don't last very long in big companies. But I'm not normal. Like my psychiatrist said: 'We are all different. We are all like snowflakes.' "

. . . Like most entrepreneurs, Mr. Turner wants to be in control. But while other billionaires collect networks or palatial homes or jet planes, he says: "I'm a collector of land. I have eight ranches and three plantations. If you have an olive, you want an olive tree. You want a little more. You want the whole tree. Then you want a little this and then a little that."

Total control means Mr. Turner never has to make compromises. "You know, sometimes you have to compromise in television," he said. "I've had to do stuff and put on programs or films that I didn't agree with and was not sympathetic to," and then he added, unable to resist a jab at his arch rival, "though they were never as violent as some of Rupert Murdoch's shows."

"But out here, I don't have to."

Turner Broadcasting owns several movie divisions, including New Line Cinema, as well as the Cartoon Network that competes with the Fox Children's Television Network, a venture of Mr. Murdoch.

The Flying D is Mr. Turner's flagship ranch and perhaps his favorite. He brought Ms. Fonda here the first weekend they went away together. ("I called her every day after that, but I didn't see her for a month," he recalled. "I was traveling. That was probably a mistake. She fell in love for a while with a younger guy.")

Since they married five years ago, the couple have built a log-cabin hideaway on a man-made lake with panoramic mountain views, and they have furnished it with oversized white-wool sofas, carved wooden chairs with bear-claw handles and animal-skin rugs. The stuffed heads of elk and other wild game shot by Mr. Turner and his children adorn the walls. Ms. Fonda's two Oscars and other awards from her acting career are displayed in a cabinet. The bookcases contain titles like "The Last Rain Forest" and "California Style." The coffee table holds arrowheads and other Native American relics from Mr. Turner's ranches, as well as two thick leather-bound books embossed with the words "Home Sweet Homes" that contain Ms. Fonda's photographs of their properties.

It was around the dining room table here that Mr. Turner and Time Warner's chairman, Gerald M. Levin, hammered out their merger agreement in the summer of 1995. And Mr. Levin was just one of a parade of guests, including former President Jimmy Carter, who have come to the Flying D.

. . . Mr. Turner, who likes to say he got into cable when "cable wasn't cool," similarly boasts about his early entry into the bison business. "It was like CNN," his company's news network, he said. "It was an adventure."

Why bison? "They are lower in cholesterol," Mr. Turner said. Also, "they are healthier and can survive the difficult seasons without as much hay or care." Maybe, though, it was more than the animals' nutritional value or low maintenance that captured Mr. Turner's attention. After selling off the cattle that came with the Flying D, he tore down the miles of fence that had broken up the ranch into pastures and let the buffalo roam free as they had for centuries.

WHO will inherit all this? Mr. Glover said that the vast holdings would go into a trust for Mr. Turner's three sons and two daughters and then be transferred to the Ted Turner Foundation upon the children's deaths.

Mr. Turner has been giving away some of his money lately, including $150 million to his foundation. He has also pledged $25 million to each of three schools, including his sons' alma mater, the Citadel, the South Carolina military college that ended its 153-year all-male admissions policy this year after the Supreme Court ruled it unconstitutional.

And what did his independently minded wife think of his support for a bastion of male exclusiveness? "Jane and I talked about it," he said. "Jane went to Emma Willard," an all-girls high school in Troy, N.Y. "When we were first going out, we had these discussions about women being equal. I told her I didn't think they were equal, I thought they were different. Finally we settled on their being 'roughly equivalent.' "

"Look, I gave the money," he added. "It is in the school's hands. I gave it with no strings attached. They used some of it to settle a legal battle to keep women out of the Citadel."

Mr. Turner had previously sold Turner Broadcasting stock to make his Western land purchases. But he has no immediate plans to sell Time Warner stock to finance future land deals, he said, because he doesn't want to reduce his position as the company's largest shareholder. Indeed, his reluctance to part with any of his 64.2 million Time Warner shares recently prompted him to shelve a plan to put an additional $350 million into his foundation.

The problem is that Time Warner's dividend yield is currently less than 1 percent, while American tax law requires foundations to give away 5 percent of the value of their assets each year—meaning Mr. Turner's foundation would have to sell some of its Time Warner holdings to make up the difference.

"You never know," he said. "Edgar Bronfman of Seagram made a run at the company a couple of years ago. No one person controls it. You never know what can happen.

"It's not like there are a bunch of classes of stock. One vote can swing it. It's like an election. You don't know what the future holds." Anyone at Time Warner who expected Mr. Turner to ride off into the sunset, live off his $23 million in annual dividends and take up buffalo breeding as a full-time career is bound to be disappointed, it appears.

Does this mean Mr. Turner's frantic land-acquisition drive is over? For a man who once declared, "If I want to save the West, I'll have to buy it," that seems unlikely.

But how much more of the West can he buy without unloading chunks of Time Warner stock? "Well," he says, "you can do that slower."

DISCUSSION QUESTIONS
1. Watch a news program on CNN. How is it different from a network news program?
2. What impact has CNN had on television news?
3. What do you think Ted Turner meant when he said: "Most entrepreneurs don't last very long in big companies. But I'm not normal. Like my psychiatrist said: 'We are all different. We are all like snowflakes' "?

CHAPTER 14

THE FUTURE

Christopher Harper, *The Future of News*
Ellen Hume, *How New Technologies Are Changing the News*
Katherine Fulton, *A Tour of Our Uncertain Future*

T he American public is losing confidence in the media, particularly in the traditional media of newspapers and television. Fewer people are reading newspapers than ever before, and television news shows have seen huge numbers of viewers flee from the TV set to the computer terminal. For the first time in recent years, music labels are seeing weakening sales, and movies are either blockbusters or duds. Nearly one in four American households has a computer, and one in ten Americans has an Internet connection at home, with the number growing dramatically every month.

What do these changes mean? What will the future look like? Will it be like *Star Trek* or *The Jetsons*? In *Being Digital*, MIT media guru Nicholas Negroponte describes a paperless world in which people will curl up in bed with a liquid-display crystal tablet that displays what used to be called a book. In contrast, Clifford Stoll, the author of *Silicon Snake Oil*, isn't convinced that the digital world will be significantly better than today. In fact, he thinks it just might be worse.

The first reading in this chapter looks at the current state of the media and gives some suggestions on what can be done to convince more people to trust the media. The writers of the last two selections look at the "uncertain future," specifically how society will receive news and information.

Ellen Hume is a long-time journalist who wrote this chapter's second reading for the Annenberg Foundation, and Katherine Fulton ponders the future, including her own, in the third reading, written for the *Columbia Journalism Review*.

THE FUTURE OF NEWS

Christopher Harper

■

W hen a senior executive took over as one network's head of standards and practices, one of his missions was to make certain that every member of the news division knew the rules.

So he convened a series of meetings about ethics and libel, and issued new policy guidelines for the news division. At one seminar for news magazine personnel, he told the group—mainly junior staff members who had never met him—what he would do if anyone violated the standards he set. "I'm just looking for someone to crucify," he told the audience.

At another session on the growing legal challenges faced at the network, he remarked that the purpose of the meeting was simple: to make certain the news division faced fewer libel suits. "We've been sued by rich and poor, prominent and unknown," he said. "Some of the worst scumbags have sued and gotten very far."

Even though the executive said that legal challenges were simply a cost of doing business, the message was clear. It cost money to win lawsuits, let alone lose them. It was better to stay out of the courtroom than win. "We want to help you put on the strongest piece possible," he added, "that is defensible."

Without any embarrassment whatsoever, he maintained that he stood by the motto of his craft: "Our mission is to comfort the afflicted and afflict the comfortable."

Is it? I guess as long as you don't offend anyone or, God forbid, get sued. As I reached today's topic: "The Future of the Newspaper," I decided that the future of newspapers is dependent on the future of the news. And, today, that future does not appear good. The three major networks have caved into major corporate interests—ABC to Philip Morris; CBS to Brown and Williamson and NBC to General Motors. Major newspapers print terrorist screeds; others send some of their best people packing. Is it surprising that *American Journalism Review* titled a recent article about newsrooms: "The Thrill is Gone"?

Some of the reasons for our problems are obvious. Some are not. Some are tied to money; some are not. But we do have trouble, and we must do something about it.

News has almost always been a business. In the past decade, however, news has become big business. And media corporations are some of the biggest businesses around. Disney and Capital Cities/ABC. General Electric and NBC. Westinghouse and CBS. Gannett Co., the nation's largest newspaper publisher, runs 142 newspapers with a combined circulation of 6.4 million. Gannett owns 15 television stations, a security alarm system and serves 450,000 cable television viewers. The Tribune Company publishes the *Chicago Tribune*, produces "Geraldo" and owns the Chicago Cubs baseball team. Cox Enterprises, publisher of the *Atlanta Constitution* and the *Dayton Daily News*, also happens to be one of the leading companies in the wireless telephone business. And Cox owns cattle and flower ranches, farming operations and the biggest used-car auction company in the world. The New York Times Company owns television and radio stations, the *Boston Globe* and other newspapers. Hearst owns television stations, the *San Francisco Examiner, Esquire* and has a livestock division. Rupert Murdoch's News Corporation is among the biggest of them all with Fox, the *New York Post, TV Guide* and newspapers spanning the globe in Britain, Tasmania, Fiji and Queensland, Australia. Time Warner is so big it can't figure out how to make much money except by buying CNN.

Back in 1983, Ben Bagdikian wrote *The Media Monopoly*, a much-noted book that studied the implications of the expansion of worldwide media companies. In the early 1980s, he said, just 46 companies in the world controlled most of the global business in daily newspapers, magazines, television, books and motion pictures. By the time the third edition of Bagdikian's book was published in 1990 that number was cut in half to 23. Today, I am certain the number is even smaller. Here are some examples of what's going on.

The *Los Angeles Times*

With a nod to the marketing success of such products as Cheerios and Hamburger Helper, the chief executive of the Times-Mirror Company, Mark H. Willes, makes it clear that he intends to apply the same business standards to journalism as he had as a key manager at cereal giant General Mills.

Within six weeks after taking over the Times-Mirror, Willes closed down the New York edition of the newspaper, *Newsday*. Wall Street cheered and the stock price went up.

Murray Kempton wrote in his last column for *New York Newsday* that "there cannot be much health left in a social order where corporations can clamorously proclaim a failure on Friday with entire assurance that therefore their stock will go up on Monday." But Willes was hired to get the stock price up. And he did it.

The *Miami Herald*

At the *Miami Herald*, the newspaper's publisher said the paper was now going to "focus its newsroom resources on nine subject areas that readers have told us are especially important and useful."

The *Miami Herald*'s Top Nine list: local government, education, sports, environment, consumer news, Florida news, health and medicine, Latin America and crime.

The presidential race didn't make the cut. "I think the net effect of this is a lot of head scratching in the newsroom," says Tom Fiedler, the *Herald*'s chief political writer.

"If anyone has an idea on what to do with the Bosnia story, I welcome it," Executive Editor Douglas Clifton wrote in the memo. "I'm embarrassed to say I long ago stopped reading this story of enormous human tragedy and significant global consequence."

There are many other examples, not many of them good. That's not to say that big media are inherently bad. Studies do show, however, that big media companies don't make things better for the public unless you happen to be an investor.

Our second problem. Our relationship with our readers and viewers. The public has never really liked us, and that's not necessarily problematic. As trust in most institutions has plummeted, journalism has lost favor too. According to the Yankelovich Monitor, 55 percent of citizens had "a great deal of confidence" in news reports on television in 1988, but by 1994 that number had dropped to 29 percent. Concurrently, confidence in newspapers dropped from 51 to 24 percent, and confidence in magazines fell from 38 to 14 percent.

Not only have journalists failed to maintain their credibility with the average citizen, but 71 percent of the people polled by the Times-Mirror Center in 1994 said they believe the press interferes with society's ability to solve its problems.

Here are two examples of why the public may be right. The *New York Times* Week in Review section led with this article: "The Red Menace Is Gone. But Here's Islam" and the ominous and dramatic photograph of Ayatollah Khomeini's eyes.

Look at the last paragraph of the story. John Esposito of Georgetown, the author of *The Islamic Threat: Myth or Reality*, says: "There are religious extremist leaders and organizations, but there is no global Islamic threat." That certainly is not the impression I get from the headline and the photograph.

Another example. *Breaking the News: How the Media Undermine American*

Democracy by James Fallows, the Washington Editor of the *Atlantic Monthly*. The book is Fallows' analysis of what's wrong with the media. Within 20 pages, however, I found the following:

1. A reference to Jane Curtis of *Saturday Night Live*. It was Jane Curtin.
2. A reference to Peter Lisagor of the *Chicago Sun-Times*. Unfortunately for all of us both Peter Lisagor and his newspaper, the *Chicago Daily News*, are dead.
3. A reference to Capital Cities/ABC paying the legal bills of $3 million to Philip Morris to drop its libel case. The sum was at least $15 million.

Each of these errors would result in failure in my beginning reporting classes. If Fallows can't get some basic facts right, how many other errors does he make?

What's even more important, I believe, however, is that we have lost our moral compass. Professor Jay Rosen of New York University refers to this problem as the loss of our spirituality—that we know what we oppose, but it is difficult for many of us to describe what we support. We no longer want to comfort the afflicted, and afflict the comfortable. We are comfortable, too, and have lost touch with our readers in some cases. In Washington, it once was important to be on the enemies list of the White House. Now it's critical to be on the guest list.

Many journalist/speakers make more in one night than many Americans make it in a year. Cokie Roberts and Sam Donaldson, both of ABC, have had to admit that they received money from organizations investigated by their own news organization. In Donaldson's case, the instances occurred on his show, "Prime Time Live." Can journalists be bought? I can demonstrate no quid pro quo, but the appearance of impropriety does the craft little good in the eyes of the public.

Yet, when Clarence Page, a columnist for the *Chicago Tribune*, was asked about the money he made from speaking engagements, he said: "I did not take a vow of poverty when I became a journalist."

Perhaps that's part of the problem. While cloaked in the First Amendment protections, we have chided politicians for making money, but we are free to do so because we journalists are private citizens.

CONCLUSIONS

So what do we do? It strikes me that journalism programs throughout the United States must be in the forefront of trying to change what is happening to our craft. We must speak boldly and loudly about the state of our craft. Otherwise, who else is there? Disney, GE, Gannett, Knight-Ridder?

First and foremost, we must teach our students the basic tenets of journalism—how to write clearly, concisely, correctly and completely.

Second, we must investigate those matters that the mega-media fail to do.

A while ago, a commission analyzing the media found that the advertising-based commercial character of the media, and the attendant quest for maximum audience, left them prone to yielding to the demands of private interests and public pressure groups. The concentration of ownership had effectively removed competition while increasing profits, to the point where the proprietors of the media were now in the upper-income brackets and tended to reflect the views of the privileged classes.

The report continued that the mass media upon which a great majority of people depended emphasized the exceptional rather than the representative, the sensational rather than the significant. "The result is not a continued story of the life of a people but a series of vignettes, made to seem more significant than they really are."

Sound familiar? Robert Hutchins, then the president of the University of Chicago, finished his report in 1947. The media attacked the report as either desiring Communist or fascist control of the press. Similar analyses have been made by Edward R. Murrow in his address to the Radio and Television News Directors Association, and the Kerner Commission. In 1988, Richard Harwood of the *Washington Post* wrote: ". . . the ethics and standards of journalism are a morass of contradictions and hypocrisies. We rend each day moral judgment on the rest of humankind, but insist on divine rights of immunity for ourselves. . . . We—newspapers and other media enterprises— have acquired considerable wealth, influence and perhaps real power in this century. We are ripe for reexamination."

There is certainly a role for public journalism in involving citizens with their newspapers and television stations.

But here are some other ideas—some of them old but put into new forms:

- A National News Council should start anew with federal tax requirements that profit-oriented news corporations pay a fee for each subscriber or viewer. The goal of this organization would be to serve as a watchdog on the press with continuing reports on what the media does well and what it does poorly and also the problems it faces.
- All major news awards such as the Pulitzer, Polk, DuPont, Investigative Reporters and Editors should require all entrants to provide federal income tax schedules concerning outside speaking income. If the schedules are not provided, or the entrant earned more than $10,000 in such speaking engagements, the entrant will be disqualified from the competition.
- The sale of television licenses will be taxed at a capital gains rate of 75 percent, so that the treasury can earn money from the resale of licenses of the public airwaves.
- The sale of all future broadcast bands will be done at auction with a 10 per cent set-aside for not-for-profit corporations.

It is time we stopped wrapping ourselves in the First Amendment. We are the only craft protected by an amendment to the Constitution, and we are making a mockery of it.

Wichita Eagle Editor David Merritt has said:

> Rather than accurately diagnosing the problem and devising a useful remedy, journalists set out in frantic pursuit of the departing audiences. Concerned about our weakening commercial franchise, we ignore our truer and far more valuable franchise: the essential nexus between democracy and journalism, the vital connecting with community, and our role in promoting useful discourse rather than merely echoing dissent.

If we don't take these problems seriously and seek solutions soon, we do not have to worry about the future of newspapers because there will be little future for the news.

Discussion Questions

1. Is the concentration of media ownership a problem? Why, or why not?
2. Do you think journalists should face specific sanctions if they make mistakes? Should journalists be licensed as in other professions?
3. In your opinion, should journalists be allowed to make speeches to business groups for money?

How New
Technologies
Are Changing
the News

Ellen Hume

∎

The old media deliver the old politics: the insider's game, presented on high, from the elite to the masses. The new technologies break the journalist's monopoly, making some of the new news an unmediated collaboration between the sources and the audience.

As we have seen, citizens can program their computers to retrieve their own "news," assembled easily from original sources far more diverse than the journalist's official Rolodex. Newly empowered, they also can second-guess what professional journalists produce.

According to technology marketing analyst Nicholas Donatiello, people are eager to control which communications come into their homes and when. They also want to be "more selective about what segments they want to watch of the news. . . ."

They will want a quick, efficient way to obtain precisely what they are looking for, whether it's a trustworthy overview of the world's events, a copy of Julia Child's lemon mousse recipe, or a conversation with a fellow basset hound breeder. As media analyst Denise Caruso explains it, "The message of this new medium is 'I want what I want and nothing more.' " Journalists, if they're smart, will offer continual information guidance that obviates the need for such robots. To do this, they may not have to be as entertaining or as ideological as Rush's reports, but they will have to be more accurate, more relevant, and more attuned to their audiences than most are today.

The new technologies offer journalists not only the potential perils of competition and scrutiny but also the potential benefits of an expanded role: connecting citizens to information and to each other. To succeed, journalists cannot connect simply for the sake of connecting; they will have to deliver something of additional value to the customer.

Interactivity is only one of the dramatic technologies now changing the news. Journalism, already instant and global, can be released by digital technology from many time and space constraints, offering unlimited opportunities for both consumers and providers. Surveys indicate that this time-shifting and indexing, always available to some degree with print and now available for television and radio, is attractive to consumers. It also is a great boon to journalists because it opens up a new market for recycling material that currently appears once and then vanishes into the air. Stories in the new digital media are archived so they can be accessed when consumers actually want to learn about these subjects; material omitted from the original story also can be packaged and sold.

Major news archives have been available for years in library clip files, on microfilm, and in databases like LEXIS/NEXIS. But now they will be easy and inexpensive for the public to access from their homes, at a moment's notice, especially if journalists package and resell them to accompany current news.

The incentive is to reuse everything because the news hole has expanded beyond the current news staff's capacity to fill it.

Thus, time, which is now one of the journalist's greatest foes, will lose its power to define the news story. If deadlines are fixed as they are now by arbitrary distribution deadlines, they can force a rush to judgment that erodes the trustworthiness of the news product. . . .

More significantly, the hot "scoop" loses its commercial value, in this environment. Scoops are prized by reporters, who rate each other on who gets the news first. However, the value of the time-sensitive scoop is lost in the constant news marketplace, except in financial and some other specialty markets. Even though more and more news stations "burn their brand" into each video frame to mark their scoops, the news consumer rarely remembers who had a news item first as she surfs through scores of channels. Furthermore, if the news truly is a major break-through, it will be picked up in nanoseconds and carried by hundreds of other news sources.

Instant scoops on Los Angeles local television stations about evidence that was being developed for the O. J. Simpson trial generally backfired; there were too many, too often to identify with a particular purveyor, and they usually were incorrect. In the multichannel environment, why would a customer deliberately look for a newscast that rushed to judgment and proved incorrect?

On the other hand, a news organization will need something exclusive to offer if it is to occupy a distinct niche in the multichannel environment. A news channel with a trusted anchor will have an advantage in the new marketplace, and a different kind of exclusive scoop—a research or analysis piece that has been developed by the news organization alone—will sharpen the purveyor's competitive edge.

In the digital world, journalism is liberated not just from time but from space constraints. The reporter's dream has come true: now there is a bottomless news hole, thanks to new technologies and the Internet. Online news customers become archaeologists; they can start at the surface with the headline, digest, or summary of the news, and then click on words or pictures to enter layer upon layer of longer stories, related features, analysis pieces, and sound and video clips. Finally, they will reach original documents and discussion groups on an issue.

Thanks to satellites and the Internet, the communications media can defy not only space and time but place. Cable viewers in Washington, D.C., now can see the latest newscasts from Moscow, New York, and Tokyo, in addition to other traditional American media, including CNN.

Previous communications technologies made the news more global. Now the new media also make it more local. Improved access to the rest of the world's news raises the value of local journalism sent directly from the original location where the news occurs. It can sell itself to new markets because it has a unique product that no one else can produce. Remember when all 64 channels were carrying O. J. Simpson's white Bronco live as it sped along the Los Angeles Freeway? Most networks were carrying pictures provided by the same few local television stations in Los Angeles.

The foreign correspondents and international "parachute journalists" who go from crisis to crisis for CBS and the *Washington Post* are less valuable in this new media marketplace. Unless they offer a framework and context that add value to the raw footage, more foreign bureaus will close as customers seek to get their news live and fresh from the locals on the scene, the wire services, and international specialists like CNN and the BBC.

Customized news also becomes local in a different way—rooted locally to a new geography of "virtual," rather than physical communities. Ironically, as we reach everyone in the world at once through CNN and the Internet, we respond by retreating to small virtual communities of specific interest. We turn inward to smaller groups because, as political writer E. J. Dionne observes, the global community is "too big to put [our] arms around." Thus, the expensive, high-powered network news loses its aura as something special; instead, it sits on the bench, next to local news, CNN, Fox News, entertainment news, sports news, and weather news. How will a consumer decide which to pick? A channel surfer will probably land on the news with the hottest production values or the most dazzling story of that millisecond. Or viewers may stop for a while because they see the story being delivered by someone they like and trust.

DISCUSSION QUESTIONS
1. What is more important to you—information that is delivered quickly or information that is accurate?
2. Do you think that information provided quickly *and* accurately may not be possible in today's world? Why, or why not?
3. What do you think about the idea of "parachute journalists"?

A TOUR OF OUR
UNCERTAIN FUTURE

Katherine Fulton

∎

C an technology help solve some of journalism's problems?

Yes, although it's easier to see how things fall apart than how they might reassemble. The problem is defining the problems.

Neil Postman of New York University turns the question around in a way I find helpful: What is the problem to which the profession of journalism is the solution? (And what will you need to be like in twenty years to solve whatever problem you think journalism solves?)

The power of this formulation is that it forces journalists to think about the needs of their customers rather than the needs of journalists or the limits of current news manufacturing and distribution processes.

Why, after all, do people need journalists?

Postman argues that journalists haven't adapted to the world they've helped create. In the nineteenth century, he says, the problem journalism solved was the scarcity of information; in the late twentieth century the problem has become information glut. The problem isn't getting more diverse forms of information quicker. "The problem," says Postman, "is how to decide what is significant, relevant information, how to get rid of unwanted information."

Too much of what journalists do adds to the clutter. Much of the new media does the same. The information glut, meanwhile, masks a corresponding scarcity—high-quality reporting and interpretation that helps people make sense of their world.

"I think the scoop of the future will be the best interpretation, the best written account, the most descriptive account, but most of all the one that explains to you why you need to know it and what it means," said the veteran broadcaster Daniel Schorr as he watched the on-line world unfold before him at the Annenberg Washington Program last winter.

This, of course, is what much great journalism has always done. The difference is that journalists now have powerful new tools for dealing with the bias against understanding so prevalent in modern media.

Hypertext—which allows you to move easily among files and computers by pointing and clicking—really does connect people easily with information, ideas, and other people. Consider reading the latest story on Bosnia and linking to a timeline and a map to remind yourself what it means. Or imagine reading a book review, linking to the first chapter of the book, and ordering it on-line if you like. . . .

Nora Paul of the Poynter Institute envisions a whole new genre, which she calls annotative journalism. Here, if, say, the president gave a speech, you might link to what he said before on the subject and to the counter-arguments of the critics. The innovative on-line magazine *Feed*, the Net's answer to *Harper's*, illustrates a version of this: somebody writes an opinion and then several people offer counter-arguments to specific points, via links that the reader can hit or not. Experiments in creating information webs challenge the often well-guarded borders of today's journalistic products. Sometimes, another journalist, or a university, or a nonprofit organization, will provide the best link—or a viewpoint that doesn't make it through today's mainstream media filter.

What's happened so far is probably quite tame compared to what's coming. And again, you have to look beyond pure journalistic efforts to see the potential. The Discovery Channel Online, when last I checked, touted its "Originally Produced Interactive Stories with Film, Music, Photography and Illustration." The channel invites viewers to join its expeditions by sending in questions on-line, and it features viewers' own adventures.

Reinventing America, an on-line game sponsored by the Markle Foundation, is a twenty-six-week experiment in voter education, in which players will study issues and set hypothetical federal spending levels. *Word*, a stylish and somewhat hard-to-define magazine available only on-line, is a striking example of how a new generation of graphic designers will play with the ways users take in information and ideas.

These experiments begin to hint at the really radical thing about new technologies: they enable people to have more control over what they want to know and when they want to know it. Already on the Internet, very different sorts of information providers are scrambling to create services to help you choose a city to live in, buy a house, or purchase a car. You can get help deciding whom to vote for, using the service *Mother Jones* magazine has created, "The Coin-Operated Congress." The much-touted personal newspaper, which allows people to adjust for their own combinations of news, opinion, and features, is already offered by a college student (CRAYON), a major new entrepreneurial effort (Individual, Inc.), and the *San Jose Mercury News* (Newshound). And if you miss a special NPR report, you can now listen to it on your own schedule.

As people get used to asking for what they need, whole new businesses will be created to serve them. "The future belongs to neither the conduit or content players, but to those who control the filtering, searching, and sense-making tools we will rely on to navigate through the expanses of cyberspace," writes Paul Saffo, of the Institute for the Future, a non-profit think tank based in Menlo Park, California. Some of these tools may include software "agents" that explore on-line networks for us, alerting us that our favorite band will be playing nearby next month or that the airlines have just announced a sale. Other new businesses are already competing to become the next generation's Internet version of *TV Guide*, as capital flows into on-line indexing and searching systems such as Yahoo and Magellan.

Eventually money may also flow to information brokers who will charge to find the information you need. If I'm diagnosed with breast cancer, I'd be willing to pay a fee to receive the best recent news reports, the Web-site references, and the addresses of mailing lists and newsgroups where patients offer each other support and information.

The great on-line opportunity is finding ways to inform people more deeply—and save them time. The question is whether people will turn to journalists or to someone else in ten or twenty years, when they need a better information filter. Journalists, who have already lost so much authority and standing in the culture, are going to have to re-earn their right to both.

DISCUSSION QUESTIONS

1. In your opinion, will journalists and editors be more important, less important, or of about the same importance in the next ten years?
2. Describe how you think a journalist's job will change over the next ten years.
3. How do you think the reader's or viewer's role will change over the next ten years?

ACKNOWLEDGMENTS

Joel Brinkley. "Who Will Build Your Next Television?" *The New York Times*, March 28, 1997. Copyright © 1997 The New York Times Co. Reprinted by permission.

Tim Clark. "Web Advertising." *CNET: The Computer Network*, October 4, 1996. Copyright © 1995–97 CNET, Inc. All rights reserved. Reprinted with permission from CNET, Inc.

Joseph Deitch. "Portrait of A Book Reviewer: Christopher Lehmann-Haupt." First published in the *Wilson Library Bulletin*, December 1987, pp. 61–63. Reprinted by permission.

Edwin Diamond and Gregg Geller. "Campaigns, Elections, and 'Public Journalism': Civic-Mindedness or Mindless Cheerleading?" Reprinted by permission.

Edwin Diamond and Gregg Geller. "Idiots with Email: The Dangers of Internet Journalism." By permission of the authors.

DM News. "Wholehearted Commitment: Profile of An Editor." May 22, 1995, p. 6. Copyright © 1995 DM News. Reprinted by permission.

Geraldine Fabrikant. "Murdoch Bets Heavily on a Global Vision." *The New York Times*, July 29, 1996, Section D, p. 1. Copyright © 1996 The New York Times Company. Reprinted by permission.

Geraldine Fabrikant. "Talking Money with Ted Turner." *The New York Times*, November 24, 1996, Section 3, p. 1. Copyright © 1996 The New York Times Company. Reprinted by permission.

William Falk. "Louder and Louder: A Look at How Talk Radio Has Elbowed Its Way into Media Prominence." *Newsday*, May 29, 1996, p. B4. Copyright © 1996 Newsday, Inc. All rights reserved. Reprinted by permission.

Suzanne Fields. "Propaganda in the Guise of Truth: Oliver Stone's Movies Give Young Americans a Distorted View of History." *The Atlanta Constitution*, January 4, 1996, p. 14A. Copyright © 1996 Suzanne Fields. All rights reserved. Reprinted by permission of The Los Angeles Times Syndicate.

Monica Fountain. "Tucker Battles against Lyrics of Gangsta Rap." *Chicago Tribune*, November 10, 1996. Copyright © 1996 Monica Fountain. Reprinted by permission of the author.

Kathleen Fulton. "A Tour of Our Uncertain Future." Reprinted from *Columbia Journalism Review*, March/April 1996. Copyright © 1996 by Columbia Journalism Review. By permission of Columbia Journalism Review and the author.

Marc Gunther. "The Lion's Share." *American Journalism Review*, March 1997. Reprinted by permission of American Journalism Review and NewsLink Associates.

Katie Hafner and Jennifer Tanaka. "This Web's for You." *Newsweek*, April 1, 1996, p. 74. Copyright © 1995 Newsweek, Inc. All rights reserved. Reprinted by permission.

LynNell Hancock. "Computer Gap: The Haves and the Have-Nots." *Newsweek*, February 27, 1995, pp. 50–53. Copyright © 1995 Newsweek, Inc. All rights reserved. Reprinted by permission.

Amy Harmon. "Bigots on the Net." *Los Angeles Times*, December 14, 1994, p. A1. Copyright © 1994 Los Angeles Times Syndicate. All rights reserved. Reprinted by permission.

Christopher Harper. "Digital Journalism: Doing It All." From *American Journalism Review* (December 1996). Reprinted by permission of American Journalism Review.

Christopher Harper. "The Dark Side of the Internet." First published in *Editor & Publisher*, October 1996. Reprinted by permission of the author.

Christopher Harper. "The Future of News." Reprinted by permission of the author.

Carl Hausman. "The Medium versus the Message." First published in the *Journal Of Mass Media Ethics*, September 3, 1994, pp. 135–144. Copyright © 1994 by Carl Hausman. Reprinted by permission of Lawrence Erlbaum Associates, Inc.

Andrew Heyward. "What We Are Doing Wrong." Excerpt from the Edward R. Murrow Awards Address presented by Andrew Heyward, President, CBS News, at the Radio & Television News Directors Assoc., Oct. 9, 1996. Los Angeles. © 1996 Andrew Heyward. Reprinted by permission.

Ellen Hume. "How New Technologies Are Changing the News." *Tabloids, Talk Radio, and the Future of News: Technology's Impact on Journalism.* Copyright © 1995 by The Annenberg Washington Program in Communications Policy Studies of Northwestern University. Reprinted by permission.

Lisa Lockwood. "What Will You Read in 2006?" *Women's Wear Daily,* May 24, 1996, p. 10. Copyright © 1996 Fairchild Publications/WWD. Reprinted by permission.

L.A. Lorek. "E-Zines: The Once Fanciful Electronic Magazines Are Making Their Way into the Internet." Published in the *Sun-Sentinel,* August 18, 1996. Reprinted with permission from the Sun-Sentinel, Fort Lauderdale, Florida.

Julie McHenry. "Take Your PR out of Box: Clients Are Demanding Creative Thinking." Published in *Marketing Computers,* November 1996, p. 61. Reprinted by permission of BPI Communications, Inc.

D.T. Max. "The End of the Book?" First published in *The Atlantic Monthly,* September 1994, pp. 61–71. Copyright © 1994 by D.T. Max. Reprinted by permission of the author.

W. Russell Newman. "The Media Habit." Excerpt from pages 89–97 of *The Future of Mass Audience* by W. Russell Newman. Reprinted by permission of Cambridge University Press.

David Noack. "Gathering News Online." Excerpt from *Editor & Publisher,* September 21, 1996. Reprinted by permission of the author.

O'Dwyer's PR Services Report. "Internet Boom to Revamp Way PR Pros Deal with Reporters." Published November 1996, p. 1. Copyright © 1996 J.R. O'Dwyer, Co., New York. Reprinted by permission of Jack O'Dwyer, President.

John Pareles. "Talkin' 'Bout Two Generations—at Odds." *The New York Times,* May 5, 1996. Copyright © 1996 The New York Times Company. Reprinted by permission.

Phil Patton. "Who Owns the Blues?" *The New York Times,* November 26, 1995, Section 2, p. 1. Copyright © 1995 The New York Times Company. Reprinted by permission.

Jimmie Reeves and Richard Campbell. "Coloring the Crack Crisis." Carole Rich. "The Thrill is Alive." *American Journalism Review,* January/February 1997. Reprinted by permission of American Journalism Review.

Elaine Rivera. "Spike Lee Speaks His Mind." *Newsday,* November 10, 1992, p. 52. Copyright © 1992 Newsday, Inc. All rights reserved. Reprinted by permission.

Mike Rose. "Reading My Way Out of South L.A." Excerpt from pages 18–22 in *Lives on the Boundary: The Struggles and Achievements of America's Underprepared* by Mike Rose. Copyright © 1989 by Mike Rose. Reprinted with the permission of The Free Press, a Division of Simon & Schuster.

Jay Rosen. "Public Journalism: A Case for Public Scholarship." Published in *Change* magazine, vol. 27, no. 3, May 1995, p. 34. Published by Heldref Publications, 1319 Eighteenth St., N.W., Washington, D.C. 20036-1802. Reprinted with permission of the Helen Dwight Reid Educational Foundation.

Leslie Savan. "2-OH-OH-OH: The Millennial-Ad Challenge." Originally published in *The Village Voice,* February 18, 1997, p. 28. Copyright © 1997 by Leslie Savan. Used with permission of the author.

Brent Schlender. "What Bill Gates Really Wants." *Fortune* magazine, January 15, 1995. Copyright © 1995 Time, Inc. All rights reserved. Reprinted by permission.

Robert Steyer. "Firms Advised to Respond Quickly in Time of Crisis." *St. Louis Post-Dispatch,* February 21, 1993, p. 1E. Copyright © 1993 St. Louis Post-Dispatch. Reprinted with permission of the St. Louis Post-Dispatch.

Gloria Steinem. "Hollywood Cleans Up Hustler." *The New York Times,* January 7, 1997. Copyright © 1997 The New York Times Company, Inc. Reprinted by permission.

Richard B. Woodward. "Books are Dead! Long Live Books! How an Outdated Piece of Hardware Just Keeps on Going and Going and . . ." Originally published in *The Village Voice,* March 5, 1996, p. 26. Copyright © 1996 by Richard B. Woodward. Reprinted by permission of the author.

Malcolm X. "A Homemade Education." Excerpt from pages 171–179 in *The Autobiography of Malcolm X* by Malcolm X, with the assistance of Alex Haley. Copyright © 1964 by Alex Haley and Malcolm X. Copyright © 1965 by Alex Haley and Betty Shabazz. Reprinted by permission of Random House, Inc. and Hutchinson & Co. (U.K.)

214

INDEX

advertising
  behavioral effects, 17–18
  costs for various media, 130
  and millennium, 124–27
  recall and commercials, 18
  See also Web advertising
African Americans, magazine for
    women, 119–21
Agrippa, 91
Allen, Paul, 187–88
Allure, 114
alternative rock, 53–54
Altschiller, David, 113–14
American Renaissance, 33
Amodeo, John, 114
Arnell, Peter, 114
Atlantic Monthly, 112
attorneys, Web site for, 103

baby boomers, music preferences, 50–54
Bacon, Francis, 90
Bagdikian, Ben, 202
Barnays, Edward, 133–34
Barnett, Susan, 172
Baron, Sandra, 172
Barry, Marion, 164–65
behavior, media effects, 17–18
Being Digital (Negroponte), 30
Bennett, W. Lance, 149
Benton, Randi, 79–80

Bergevin, Paul, 139
bigotry, hate groups on Internet,
    32–35
Bill of Rights, on privacy, 178
blues, 55–59
  resurgence in popularity, 55–57
  traditionalist perspective, 57–59
Bodette, John, 155–56
boilerplate copy, journalism, 153
book reviewer, workings of Lehmann-
    Haupt, 92–98
books
  on CD-ROM, 82, 85–88
  celebrity autobiographies, 78–79
  death of books concept, 75–76, 78–79,
    81–91
  drop in number published, 86
  fiction on Internet, 84
  high point in book buying, 76–77
  hours per day reading, 15
  hypertext novel, 91
  limitations of, 83–84
  print versus new media versions,
    78–79, 87, 89–91
  reference books, 87–88
  very-rare-books collection, 90
Boorstin, Daniel J., 150, 152
brainstorming, for PR ideas, 137
Brinkley, Joel, 36, 45
BznetUSA, 103

215